The RAINBOW AGE of TELEVISION

The

RAINBOW AGE
of TELEVISION

*An
Opinionated History
of Queer TV*

SHAYNA MACI WARNER

ABRAMS PRESS, NEW YORK

ABRAMS The Art of Books
195 Broadway, New York, NY 10007
abramsbooks.com

Dedicated to
SUSAN, SCOTT, SARAI, NYX, ISABELLA, BRYCE.
THANK YOU FOR LOVING ME.
THANK YOU FOR BEING THERE.

Also dedicated to
GREY'S ANATOMY.
YOU KNOW WHAT YOU DID.

Contents

Introduction

ON OWING EVERYTHING TO
(AND WANTING MORE FROM) QUEER TV

My first loves were television and women.

If we were to meet in person, this would probably be one of the first fun facts you learn about me: a little more than a decade ago, right before I came out as bisexual, I only knew I loved television and that for some reason I was still obsessed with my pretty middle school teachers. I could rewind even further to my first Television Woman love, Piper Halliwell (played by nineties icon and landmark lesbian kiss recipient Holly Marie Combs[1]) on the WB's sister-witch epic *Charmed* (1998– 2006). Perhaps I knew that there was more than just admiration at play, but at the time, I simply didn't have the language to describe what stirred within me when Piper vanquished monsters using her bare hands and pure strength of will.

I would be able to specifically point you to season 4, episode 12, "Lost and Bound," as my favorite episode, but I probably would not willingly share with you that it's because Piper finds a young, ostracized boy in need of help and serves him chocolate chip cookies while soothing his worries about hurting people because of his inherent, uncontrollable predilection for starting spontaneous fires. She reassures him he's special, just like her, only she has learned to control her urges and channel them into a talent. In light of her approval, he is loved by a group of similarly feared outsiders; all he needed was a mentor to show him he wasn't evil at his core. Lest I center my journey solely on the metaphor of belonging, I must also mention that Piper's ultra-2000s fashion of the episode featured a squeaky pair of leather pants.

Maybe Piper Halliwell is the first witch I can fully pinpoint as the reason I am like this (in love with older women in leather), but it wasn't until Dr. Calliope Torres (Sara Ramirez) fell in lust with Dr. Erica Hahn (Brooke Smith) on a certain groundbreaking, never-ending medical soap that, as Dr. Hahn might say, the big green blobs on trees became leaves. That's right. *Grey's Anatomy* (2005–) made me gay.

Yes, this is a simplification and fodder for anyone who would like to yoink this book from the hands of impressionable, naturally straight children (as if they needed another weak excuse), but from the moment Dr. Torres so magnificently displayed the signs of confusion, disbelief, then confirmation that *girls could kiss boys* and *girls*, I saw my own long-present dear friendships and adulation sharpen. Ramirez, who most recently played an utterly divisive fuckboy on the *Sex and the City* (1998–2004) reboot, *And Just Like That . . .* (2021–), is now publicly out as queer and nonbinary, but Callie Torres was a beacon far before that.

Brilliant, temperamental, driven, and vulnerable by turns, Dr. Torres felt like a real person struggling to claim her identity not as her parents or partners outlined it, but as her own. She was a fully developed, multifaceted bisexual person, albeit one who made terrible decisions and worked in a hospital where everything that could go wrong did. It's a tough job to stay in the good graces of a highly invested soap fandom as a relatable, beloved character, especially in the throes of every imaginable melodramatic turn only a maniac like a *Grey's* writer could fathom. (For instance, becoming pregnant with the child of a platonic best friend and said child being conceived directly before her ex-girlfriend returned from Malawi to plead for her hand in marriage and delivered amid musical hallucinations sprung from a traumatic car crash.) In large part thanks to Ramirez's expressiveness and distinct ability to convey hunger and heartache, Dr. Torres more than pulled it off. Amid long-familiar HomoTV 101 themes like gay panic, family estrangement, and reconciling religious upbringing and sexuality, Dr. Torres somehow remained charismatic and distinct throughout a ten-year run, before Ramirez chose to depart the series in 2016.

I've written about Dr. Torres, and Sara Ramirez, before, and one of my most embarrassing moments was admitting to Ramirez that I wrote a GLAAD-published article celebrating their unknowing contributions to my and many others' affirmations of our own identities. I was in love with many before them, and I have had an equally difficult time looking any of the actors or creators of my favorite characters directly in the eyes (but I am willing to try). The enormity of such a gift as recognition is overwhelming. Queerness* is the best thing to ever happen to me, so it's no surprise that I, and many others, would feel a personal attachment to the people who made our lives nameable.

Seeing that one aspect of myself on television was life-changing, and that's the primary reason I wanted to write *The Rainbow Age of Television*. The number of LGBTQIA2S+ characters on television has exploded since my mom first asked if Santana (Naya Rivera) and Brittany's (Heather Morris) sweetly twisted relationship on gay TV monarch Ryan Murphy's second high school satire, *Glee* (2009–2015), made me gay (close, but no stethoscope). So has the outspokenness and fervency with which viewers claim characters as their own. It's gotten to a point that I'm more likely to have heard about the supposed flaws or perfections in a queer character's design and read an essay-length tweet thread dissecting their fan base than I am to have actually seen the show being referenced. One thing is certain: in these turbulent twenties, we have no shortage of queer (primarily cisgender lesbian or gay but increasingly gender-nonconforming) characters. In attempting to write

---

* For the purposes of this book, I'll be using "queerness," "queer," and "gay" as umbrella terms, specifying further with individual examples of gay, bisexual, lesbian, trans, nonbinary, intersex, asexual, and two-spirit characters and themes (among others).

this book, I've had to face the happy and stressful truth that I will never be able to account for, or even become acquainted with, everyone's favorite character. However, the quality, nuance, and dimensionality of many roles in this overflow of queer characters can often still feel shallow. Or, far worse, boring.

For the purposes of this book, I define the Rainbow Age as in its infancy with *Will & Grace*'s (1998–2006) success, picking up speed with queer cable series circa 2000, and fully integrated into the American television landscape by 2013 until its seeming peak in 2023. While there has been a chronological explosion and expansion of representation by numbers alone, I want to talk about the quality, longevity, and meaning of queer representation in an age no longer solely accountable to Nielsen ratings, the historical measurement of audience viewership, but continually jeopardized by a fervent culture of conservatism and arbitrary algorithms. I want to explore how depictions of queers have evolved alongside the medium as out queer people have increasingly become not only a target audience but also a growing behind-the-scenes population. Driving this examination is an exhausting question: Does queer representation still mean the world to queer people and to me? Or is "representation" only a buzzword used to dissuade us from demanding more from our most widely distributed cultural products, even as what we lay a fierce claim to continually shrinks and slips through our fingers?

The First of Many Notes on Representation

When I first started crafting this project, I was sincerely driven by the concept of representation. I didn't recognize it as what it is: an ideological tool, a marketing ploy, a way to fundraise for organizations that make money off the image of young and eager queers. I simply knew that women on television, and the people playing them, had made it possible for me to feel joy in my own image and name. The more I talked to other queers about it, the more I realized that so many felt similarly to me. For many of us, our first gay friends were not the elders or activists who paved the way. Rather, they were the beautiful faces that beamed into our living rooms or out from hastily ripped and uploaded YouTube compilations with titles like "The OC Lesbian Storyline Part 6."

As Stephen Tropiano, professor, television scholar, and author of the essential text *The Prime Time Closet*, relays, after television began to compete with the pervasiveness of film, it became the first contact that visualized to so many of my generation of queers (and several generations before) who we could be.[2] That also meant it perpetuated that we could be cast aside, murdered, converted to heterosexuality, or disappeared into the ether of an abruptly pulled contract, but that's not all that far-fetched given Western historical precedents Traumatizing as those frequent storylines were, the important parts still seemed to be in the very concepts of existence and reflection. When a queer character stayed on for more than a guest arc and engaged in only a few harmful stereotypes, it was a victory for all—even if the character looked, acted, and felt nothing like us. Right?

At this point in my life, I've struggled with writing about queer representation. I was twenty-one years old when GLAAD awarded me a small grant and the much more impactful "Media Advocate" title that eventually garnered this book contract. At the time of writing (rewriting) this introduction, I have a much more cynical bent toward the business of entertainment and a recurring flare of shame that accompanies a fascination with something as viciously monetized as "representation." Most days, I wonder: Does any of this matter?

Yes. And no. And yes. And it depends on who you ask. Queer representation on television is still important to this particular bitter, media-obsessed dyke because television is what I first grasped onto to experience a queer life. Even if I'm grieving the naive part of me that thought perfect representation would save us, I still love watching! Be it network or cable or streaming or a network's streaming offshoot on a badly glitching app, television is still wildly important because of its function to sell us so many things: an escape, a belief, a sense of belonging, a collective history.

Beautiful, sparkling, increasingly poorly lit television is designed to make us receptive to a product. Or an idea or a feeling that will make a product more enticing. Historically regarded as one of the lowest, most barbaric forms of populist entertainment by the Hollywood big-screen elite (that is, before television began stealing their moviegoing viewer base), television nevertheless has shaped our culture. At its most basic and original form, it was meant to communicate directly to the American populace—those with purchasing power.

From the earliest days of scripted television, when it was just finding its footing in the transition from radio, the medium was meant to evoke friendly images of people "we" (read: white or aspirationally white suburbanites) might know, buying things "we" might need. As an illustrative early example, Mama Hansen (Peggy Wood), the titular warm, compassionate German-immigrant matriarch from the nostalgic 1949–1957 television show *Mama*, would care for her family as her viewers presumedly cared for theirs. And she'd use warm, compassionate Maxwell House coffee and nutritious, family-friendly Post cereal to do so.

From the 1970s' advent of direct advertising to today's use of direct data mining, advertisers have become hyperalert to the far more socially, economically, and ethnically diverse makeup of American society, and white Western European, two-parent, two-point-five-children households are no longer the only group whose eyeballs are worthy of competition. It may seem like stating the obvious, but the deviants have some purchasing power, too. But can capitalism bend that much-evoked moral arc of the universe forward?

New portrayals of LGBTQIA2S+ identities have become so publicly correlated with progressive politics and inclusive television that it might feel better to willfully pass over the fact that queer characters are inextricably tied up with financial dealings. We may feel so excited about finally seeing series regular queer and trans characters on television that we don't care to investigate further than their screenwriters and actors and take brazen PR at its word. A series as groundbreaking as

Pose (2018–2021), Steven Canals's 1980s-set ensemble drama, notable not only for its glittering origin stories of New York City's ballroom culture but also for its investment in trans workers above and below the line, was rightly hailed for its rarely explored, historical tragi-celebration of the lives of queer and trans people of color. However, as historian, filmmaker, and butch icon Jenni Olson reflects, while in praise of the show, the series would not have been picked up if not for the involvement of the already mega-successful, cisgender white producers Ryan Murphy and Brad Falchuk.

As Olson explains, while the show is driven by Black trans people—not just characters, but actors, writers, directors, and choreographers—it is also constrained by people who stand to make the most profit . . . and take the fewest risks. "Like everyone else," Olson notes, the Black trans creatives behind the authenticity of the show "are also having to cope with the powers that be [saying], 'You can't say that,' or, 'Oh, that's too much for TV.' They are being compensated, but they are also creating a product. [*Pose*'s network] FX is not doing this just out of the goodness of their hearts. They're not a nonprofit being."[3]

Speaking from my own disillusionment, it can feel dismissive to boil down additions of our favorite characters to monetary stakes, data collection opportunities, and corporate pinkwashing,* but it is also refreshing to acknowledge that the viewer doesn't owe networks anything. If we don't like what we see, there's no obligation to keep watching or cling to any single network or show as the promised revolutionary.

———————

It is worth noting that television can be and regularly is used as a political weapon and a means of mass literacy in all different subjects, two overlapping uses that are also diametrically opposed in a

---

* "Pinkwashing" is a by now common way to refer to corporations (and nations) slapping rainbow flags on their logos and products as a way of attracting LGBTQIA2S+ consumers and allies while ignoring (or washing over) their much larger societal malfeasance, including harm done to queer people. Because no real change is made, pinkwashing can be undone easily when the political tide turns.

congressional hearing. The perpetrators of these perpetually escalating culture wars recognize the ability of television to cater to, inform, and affirm audiences outside a formal education—and they know just how dangerous for them that can be if messaging strays from state regulation of bodies and brains. The debatable effectiveness of said messages is closely intertwined with the reason anyone might sit down to watch a show in the first place: quality storytelling that comes from somewhere other than your own tired brain.

Some viewers return to television week after week—or four-episode drop after two-episode soft rollout—for the deep, personal connections they've developed with their fictional counterparts over a long-form series, connections that may not be otherwise available, especially as a young person living under the guardianship and rules of a household they don't control. Some come for the storylines that provide brand-new information on the lives of others—or lives that could be theirs. Some come for titillating depictions of the most censored, shadowy, and moralized aspects of human existence: sex, money, and power. Some come for just the smallest evidence that they are not alone. And some just want to watch somebody else's house burn down for once. Like you, I have been all of these "some" ones.

Storytelling, like any good superpower, turns good, evil, and/or propagandistic according to the ways in which someone uses it. When done right, television is an enthralling enough medium of storytelling that it just might change a person's entire conception of themselves and their relationship to the world, or at least fulfill a specific craving and make life slightly more bearable for thirty minutes. When done wrong, it somehow still manages to get six seasons and a spin-off because enough people are talking about how offensively wrong it's been done. As a nonscientist, I have no real jurisdiction to say that it isn't also rotting our brains and increasing the strength of our glasses prescriptions, but there is no denying that television and digital media have immense access and opportunity when it comes to knowledge production and persuasion. As Tropiano so concisely says, television is important because it's casually enmeshed in the very fabric of American culture.[4] Everywhere we are, so, too, is television.

Over the course of coming out in a post-*Glee*, now post-*Roe* world, I've come to realize that everything that goes into the dissemination of knowledge about queer people through the middlemen of sponsors, executives, producers, streamers, and the camera itself is a factor in "good representation." Nobody can dissuade me from my strongly held belief that it only took watching a melodramatic bisexual storyline to begin my very first explicit deviation from fourteen years of compulsory heterosexuality—but how do we look at that individual comfort and enlightenment in a world where *most* networks have caught on to needing at least one queer character on their show to check a box and call that catering to a monolithic "community"?

How do we look at queer representation when we know that increased visibility, when not coupled with an expansion of human rights, can lead to increased visibility of queers not as human beings but as targets?[5] Do we have a responsibility to know our history in television, too, even as rapidly conglomerating streamers and copyright laws make our historical media presence harder and harder to access? Has anything changed now that queer showrunners have the reins to their own series but many of those series don't last past two seasons? Can't we just enjoy things in this rapid environmental decline?

Maybe you're not reading this book because this author has some very panicked questions about "life? *Itself?!*" Maybe you would prefer to breeze through a celebratory guidebook of some of the best of the best of LGBTQIA2S+ storylines and characters on television. Maybe you would enjoy interviews with critics, showrunners, activists, and audience members who have found their lives shaped by landmark programs. Maybe you'd just like to know if *Top Chef* (2006–) is the gayest series of all time. To that I say, you're in luck! As I grapple with straddling the precarity of loving something and needing to criticize it, I've gone out and attempted to answer my Big Gay Questions by enlisting people I've admired, watched, and read for years, many of whom also happen to love and be deeply indebted to television. My hope is that this book isn't simply a series of unanswerable questions, but a thoughtful look at a specifically televisual evolution: what's come, what's gone, what seems to frustratingly or delightfully stay the same, and what glorious gay TV is yet to arrive.

Chapter 1

FOR THE VERY FIRST TIME

What's so important about a first time anyway?

In our lives, we often attribute incalculable meaning to our firsts. First kiss, first crush, first taste of betrayal, and first heartbreak are all monumental events that signify something irreplaceable in the formation of our personalities. There's a cultural nostalgia that shrouds a first, even if individual memories are sour or perhaps altogether unremarkable.

From flipping through lacquered pictures of Lucille Ball, Mary Tyler Moore, and Carol Burnett on *CBS: The First Fifty Years* or *NBC: The First Fifty Years*, you can easily tell that there's also a monumental, monetary, and sometimes exaggerated importance attached to the firsts of television and to chronological firsts of visual and demographic representation. Unlike our sentimental, personal memories, however, these historical milestones can be hotly debated in a public forum, even as they hold the same significance to some as that first swelling of love or the heartbreak of recognition with little hope of follow-through.

Establishing firsts in television is tricky on a number of levels—down to the contestation of its inventor.[*] When TV first migrated from the radio waves, it was structured in much the same way as its purely aural counterpart. Broadcast came to you live throughout the 1930s and '40s and was intended to be consumed ephemerally. Once a program was

---

[*]   Like the invention of cinema before it, several different inventors have been credited with unknowing, simultaneous creation—Vladimir K. Zworykin and Philo Taylor Farnsworth are often cited as having been in a bitter battle for the patent.

over, it was really over. It wasn't until the 1950s that studios began recording their broadcasts on videotape, and then only with the intention of rebroadcasting a show once or twice, not preserving it. Recording and editing an episode on tape was expensive, and before the longevity of any program or the cash cow of syndication was even remotely considered, a show's budget sometimes called for erasing and recycling their tapes to fleetingly capture the next episode.

Though we have incredible resources in academic and nonprofit institutions dedicated to preserving television's history, such as Chicago's Museum of Broadcast Communications; individual amateur heroes such as the fascinating broadcast news archivist Marion Stokes;* and much-maligned Internet Archive worker bees dedicated to uploading favorite classic episodes alongside the most esoteric moments of television one could dream up, there are still gaps in our television history that will never be fully restored.

This astounding loss affects immediately recognizable shows whose permanence one might take entirely for granted; for instance, the BBC exterminating their original *Doctor Who* tapes before they knew to ship overseas for hungry foreign audiences is unthinkable to a legion of Whovians, but ninety-seven episodes are still unrecovered.† In a more specific instance of US-centric representation on television, several of the episodes from movie star, musician, and major civil rights activist Harry Belafonte's week of guest-hosting Johnny Carson's *The Tonight Show* in 1968 are completely lost to retaping, and only audio and memories remain.‡ Guests included Dr. Martin Luther King Jr., Dionne

---

* For more on Stokes's personal archive of recorded television news footage spanning thirty-five years, as well as her singular personality, please watch Matt Wolf's *Recorder: The Marion Stokes Project* (2019).

† *Wiped!:* Doctor Who's *Missing Episodes* by Richard Molesworth is full of juicy technical details on this phenomenon.

‡ *The Sit-In: Harry Belafonte Hosts* The Tonight Show (2021) is a marvel of archival treasure hunting that gives an entirely new dimension to the starkly white history of late-night talk shows.

Warwick, Paul Newman, Buffy Sainte-Marie, and Petula Clark—an earthshaking lineup. Just imagine the absence of episodes and series that don't have the same rabid support or widely accepted cultural significance!

Similarly, there have been hundreds of series that were canceled after their first few weeks that never made a blip in television history documentation, much less preservation.* Because of this loss of firsthand source material, it's difficult to say with certainty the very first time any particular action, type of person, or plot appears on television—especially when it comes to queer identity. We can acknowledge something as among the earliest in its portrayals, but in terms of hard-and-fast representational study, media archeology—by way of local listings and discussion in queer newsletters, for instance, or oral histories from those who remember watching the shows on their local stations—can support but not fully confirm everything that has ever traveled by cathode tube.

In the digital age, when so many independent platforms and long-established networks can place much of their libraries on display for any subscriber to view, it may seem like this access issue is solved for any future firsts. However, digital preservation faces a lack of investment and a threat of collapse, and streaming presents its own problems. Rights issues, network conglomerations, and lack of transparency ensure that some shows will be pulled from platforms, sometimes without warning to audiences or creators, while some older shows will be kept in the vault indefinitely. If you can't watch a show, did it ever exist? With a good VPN and great determination, much more is possible, but you'd better be really dedicated to playing detective.

All this is to say we should take any casually marketed "first" claims for themes, plots, or characters with a grain of salt. Such assertions are difficult to disprove or prove, even with the better archival practices of the

---

*   Even the most impressive encyclopedia on the subject, *The Complete Directory to Prime Time Network and Cable TV Shows, 1946–Present*, was last updated in 2009, can't capture every syndicated program or series not made accessible to at least half of American households, and was admittedly overwhelmed by the "flood" of cable shows.

seventies, due to the sheer volume of televisual muck one would have to watch to make those rock-solid claims. That being said, though there may be some gay treasures that go undiscovered indefinitely, by now we have built a fairly solid understanding of the more significant early mentions and appearances of LGBT existence on television. What follows is a survey of some of the acknowledged first LGBT characters to appear on television, including early queer-coded characters, while the following chapter dives into a still-expanding field: the first appearances of QIA2S+ characters.

LGT (or Are They?)

As Stephen Tropiano covers thoroughly in the "Diagnosis: Homosexual" chapter of *The Prime Time Closet*, many of the earliest discussions of homosexuality were held in investigative or medical contexts in the 1950s. These discussions came on the coattails of Dr. Alfred Kinsey's 1948 and 1952 scientific studies that held homosexuality and fluidity to be far more common than the wider American society, as well as the American medical profession that defined homosexuality as an illness until 1973, assumed.

While homosexuality was being prodded at as a source of worry and blunt fascination in local news and talk programs as early as 1954, one of the earliest fictional depictions of coded male homosexuality glittered to life in sketch comedy. Television innovator and comedian Ernie Kovacs's lisping, outrageously bespectacled poet laureate character of Percy Dovetonsils is among the crème de la crème of stereotypical por-trayals of an effeminate, limp-wristed, and overwitted gay man in the history of television.* Before *Will & Grace*'s gay man's gay man Jack

---

* As Steven Capsuto details in *Alternate Channels: Queer Images on 20th-Century TV*, an even earlier portrayal of a barely coded gay character is swishy, costume-designer sidekick Clarence Tiffingtuffer (played for TV by Franklin Pangborn) in the adaptation of the popular 1930s radio soap *Myrt and Marge*. However, the 1949 pilot reportedly aired only once and was then scrapped, never quite solidifying his character's transition from radio to TV in any sort of public memory. The TV show being a casualty of lost tape syndrome, only the audio of the original radio show remains. The only preceding coded "character" to join Kovacs in public popularity was "Gorgeous George," the prancing, perpetual loser wrestling persona of professional wrestler George Raymond Wagner.

McFarland (Sean Hayes), *Sex and the City*'s "fifth lady" Stanford Blatch (Willie Garson), and even two years before *The Liberace Show* (1952–1969), Dovetonsils was the zebra print–outfitted mold from which only camp and effervescence sprung.

First emerging in 1950 on Kovacs's early-morning public broadcast variety hour *Three to Get Ready* before moving to late night with *The Ernie Kovacs Show* in 1952, Dovetonsils was never explicitly named as homosexual, but it would be an uncomfortable stretch to attach him to any other orientation. Delighted by his own witticisms and silly, gentle poetry, Dovetonsils was one of the more earnest and pleasant of Kovacs's characters, described by Kovacs himself as "a beautiful soul who hasn't quite made it over the line into this rude, virile world."[1] The crew on Kovacs's show certainly seemed to think the same thing, occasionally playing pranks on the segment.

To today's audience, Dovetonsils's possibly Truman Capote–inspired coding might be tame, but from 1950 through 1956, he was something of an outlier on television in his popularity. In some segments, Kovacs ad-libs slightly more risqué dialogue, admiring the looks of his cameramen, or makes coy reference to his offscreen "friend" Bruce,* but because Kovacs skirts naming his feather-worded friend as gay, it's never anything that could be accused of moral corruption or indecency. If he had, he would have been faced with the decision to either explicitly condemn Dovetonsils's behavior as undesirable or take him off the air altogether.†

Most historians wouldn't consider Dovetonsils as a positive queer representation for a few reasons—his overblown stereotype, his never expressly stating or consummating his queerness, and his playing into

---

* While the origin of "Bruce" as a fey name is contested, Kovacs kicked off the televisual tradition of using it as a barely disguised allusion, drawing it out into a lisp. Shows like *The Tonight Show with Johnny Carson* and *The Simpsons* would follow.

† The Code of Practices for Television Broadcasters, also known as the Television Code, explicitly condemned any endorsement of sexual "abnormalities" in its network-adopted set of ethical standards. The code would remain in use from 1952 to 1983.

what gay TV expert Steven Capsuto calls the widespread fifties stereotype of the "giddy incompetents"[2]—but he was also a much more consistent and kindly written television presence than many of the homosexuals who came shortly after. He's also an engaging, dynamic personality who participated in many of the experimental visual gags that Kovacs pioneered, and one Kovacs reportedly wanted to develop further before his life and work were cut short.

Though a joke himself, Dovetonsils's levity was mostly out of reach for his 1960s and '70s lesbian-coded counterparts. Queer women beat gay men to representation in network dramatic programs, among the first being an episode of the medical melodrama *The Eleventh Hour* (1962–1964) and a police procedural, *The Asphalt Jungle* (1961).

Both shows' lesbians of the week are mentally unstable, sexually repressed, and prone to dangerous dramatics. In *The Asphalt Jungle*'s 1961 "The Sniper" episode, a mystery assassin is murdering young women while they're out with their boyfriends, and it's up to Deputy Matthew Gower (Jack Warden) to catch the killer before he strikes again. The killer turns out to be local diner owner Miss Brandt (Virginia Christine), who slips into a blood rage whenever she witnesses these sweet, angelic young white women dipping their toes into sin. One such young woman who narrowly escapes the same fate is Susan (Natalie Trundy), a favored waitress and near-surrogate daughter at Miss Brandt's diner. Though Miss Brandt is never labeled explicitly as a lesbian, her more than platonic affection and overbearing steering of Susan clearly plays into a Freudian lesbian mommy dynamic. It's an early predecessor of *Law & Order: Special Victims Unit*'s (1999–) abusive maternal terrorists whose sexual control toward young men or women stems from repression of their own unnatural urges,* as well as an inverse of the

---

*   "Totem" is a particularly berserk 2011 episode of *Law & Order: SVU* that combines the most psychosexual aspects of both *The Eleventh Hour* and *The Asphalt Jungle* for a truly unhinged episode fakeout that still leads to killer lesbians with mommy issues.

decades-spanning lesbian burial trope, in which queer women die or disappear directly after consummating their lust.*

In *The Eleventh Hour*'s "What Did She Mean by Good Luck?," similar mommy issues emerge, this time for an anxious young actress with undiagnosed PTSD who has instead been diagnosed with "lesbian tendencies" by the series' resident psychiatrist protagonist, though she eventually beats those allegations. Caught between the firm woman director she feels inappropriate affection toward and a domineering stage mother, Hallie's (Kathryn Hays) nerves get the best of her, and she displaces her mother's physical assault of her onto the hands of her director. When it is revealed that Hallie's mother abused her when suspecting her daughter of being too physically and emotionally affectionate toward a favorite drama teacher, all is sorted. She didn't have an inappropriate lesbian affection toward her director after all! That pesky lesbianism actually resolved as soon as she found the root of her trauma!

In American narrative series, transfeminine-coded characters made very early appearances as spectacles who were just as unstable as their lesbian counterparts; for example, in the form of a cross-dressing killer nurse in "An Unlocked Window," a 1965 prime-time episode of the anthology series *The Alfred Hitchcock Hour*. And who could forget the amnesiac "professional female impersonator" whose memories of his murders were wiped as soon as he stepped out of drag in "Mask of Death," a 1974 episode of the Michael Douglas–starring series *The Streets of San Francisco*? However, some of the earliest narrative examples of small-screen transfeminine antics are arguably found in a much fuzzier package.†

---

* The dead lesbians phenomenon is so intertwined with broadcast that the very first lesbian-coded character in a radio program, imported from the 1951 British program *The Black Museum*, died by strangulation.

† Cisgender gay characters, especially those who weren't designed to be sympathetic, overlap with trans-coded characters, mostly because of an automatic correlation of "unnatural" or "nontraditional" gender presentation with effeminate gay men.

Enter stage left: a brilliant, deeply aggravating, and child-beloved bunny with a tendency to outwit any wabbit hunter or generally annoying anthropomorphic creature that crossed his path. Bugs Bunny is virtually inseparable from American iconography, and from the very beginning of his reign of terror and laughs in *Looney Tunes* and *Merrie Melodies*, officially debuting as the Bugs we know and love in 1940 with *A Wild Hare*, he's been an avid fan of hyperfeminine drag. When Bugs and the gang made their way to television in 1960 with *The Bugs Bunny Show*, so did Bugs's endless supply of dresses, makeup, and breathy, high-pitched voices. Although Bugs often uses his feminine wiles to ensnare, and often smooch, an easily duped foe, his alternate personas aren't all used as an escape. Sometimes he's in drag just because he wants to be.

When *The Bugs Bunny Show* moved from prime time to its long-running spot on Saturday mornings in 1962, Bugs's drag became a staple of kids' Saturday-morning cartoon ritual. Of course, one could easily offer that Bugs is simply a character that does drag rather than a trans character. But, as filmmaker and trans historian Susan Stryker and filmmaker Lilly Wachowski (*The Matrix*, *Bound*) relay in the 2020 documentary *Disclosure: Trans Lives on Screen*, Bugs resonated as one of the very few instances of trans femininity, in which the bearer of the bunny ears wasn't the butt of the joke.*

Not without the wry knowledge that she is indeed discussing a cartoon rabbit, Wachowski says, "There was something about Bugs Bunny that activated, in my trans imagination, this idea of transformation."[3] Stryker similarly references this transformation, as well as the fact that Bugs as a woman "was desirable and was powerful." Whether Bugs Bunny is strictly trans, gender fluid, or merely a fast-talking rabbit who does drag is actually the least important factor in this discussion—it's

---

*   While nonexhaustive, *Disclosure: Trans Lives on Screen* is a source of some excellent interviews with many trans creatives who have been on the behind-the-scenes side of bringing trans characters to the small screen.

that Bugs is a character who, through transformation, is an accessible symbol of transfeminine possibility.

This wascally wabbit provides a simple way to explain the satisfaction and historical worth of queer-coded characters. Even before it was possible to get a canonical trans character onscreen, it was possible to present a character—especially a harmless bunny—with exciting visual qualities of transness and none of the verbal, more easily censored language, and let queers fill in the rest.

Nonbinary, agender, genderqueer, and other gender-nonconforming characters would have a difficult time landing on US small screens for decades. A particularly eyebrow-raising example of television's conservatism around gender nonconformity—and an early, fantastical version of a metaphorically intersex or nonbinary character—emerges in the saga of Japan's 1967 *Princess Knight* anime. The charming, clearly tame kid's cartoon from famed Mushi Studio (*Kimba the White Lion*, *Astro Boy*) head Osamu Tezuka featured the adventures of Sapphire, a royal princess born with the blue heart of a boy as well as the pink heart of a girl, who often masqueraded as a prince to ward off the kingdom's enemies. Though hugely popular and influential in Japan, when it was shown to NBC Enterprises executives for potential broadcast in the United States, the cross-dressing and ambiguity were too evocative of a "sex switch" storyline.*

Sensing the gold mine NBC was missing out on, independent animator Joe Oriolo (*Felix the Cat*) purchased the rights to the series and sold a compiled, dubbed film of *Princess Knight*'s first three episodes, retitled as *Choppy and the Princess*. The boyish girl, with her silk cape, Tinker Bell–esque companion, and multi-thumping hearts were syndicated and licensed to independent US television stations in the 1970s, bounding across some home sets in a shortened film and limited

---

* According to Fred Ladd, coauthor of *Astro Boy and Anime Come to the Americas: An Insider's View of the Birth of a Pop Culture Phenomenon*, he was the only man in the NBC exec room who could get past the princess both dressing, riding horseback, and fighting like a boy *and* having the secret desire to wear dresses and kiss boys.

run. Unfortunately, the full, unedited series wouldn't make it to the United States until 2013.

Transmasculine characters would live in this coded, though still sometimes censored, space of visual but unacknowledged queerness for decades, most often in the form of the genre-hopping, gender-flipping young tomboy—albeit rarely with the lore of doubly gendered organs. Young girls who wanted to wear pants instead of skirts, couldn't care less about their hair, and wanted to learn to run, fight, and shoot guns across the hills of Westerns (*Annie Oakley*, *The Adventures of Brisco County, Jr.*) or on school playgrounds (*Peanuts*, *Recess*, *The Facts of Life*) have been popular, if not explicitly gay, representations of gender nonconformity since the 1950s. Of course, a tomboy can be interpreted as a representation of a butch, queer, budding trans or a cishet character going through a phase. Without verbal confirmation one way or another, a tomboy is open to be claimed by anyone. In this case, as in many others, the queerness is in the eye of the beholder.

LGBT (For Sure This Time)

Narrative programs continued to broadcast this unspoken queerness to inquiring audiences who looked closely enough for several decades before any characters were actually named outright as anything other than cisgender and straight. When openly gay, lesbian, and transfeminine characters did make their first appearances in series, they popped up on medical serials or police procedurals in short arcs that were sympathetic but mostly condescending toward the conditions of queerness that had been foisted upon a poor sap. In medical programs, queerness was still an illness, something that may not be able to be remedied but nonetheless was considered undesirable to a healthy, presumedly straight person. In police procedurals, being queer was a potential death sentence.

The very first episode of narrative US network television to feature an expressly named gay character was "Shakedown," the 1967 pilot episode of ABC's police procedural *N.Y.P.D.* (1967–1969).* The episode charted a blackmail ring that targeted closeted men, using faux-gay hookups to seduce and then threaten to out them to everyone they knew. The episode is notable both for a clumsy but earnest attempt to form solidarity between a Black police officer (Robert Hooks) and a white gay blackmail victim (Matthew Broderick's father, James Broderick), as well as its featuring of three gay characters: Gaffer, Broderick's reluctantly cooperating victim; Spad, an out-and-proud gay businessman played by John Harkins; and the main victim of the blackmail ring, who ends his life when his fear and shame overcome him.†

Another early episode to play along the lines of this gay-but-not-okay overtone was "Undercurrent," a 1970 episode of CBS's mod hospital series *Medical Center* (1969–1976). Usually a vehicle for handsome, white, blue-eyed doctors Dr. Paul Lochner (James Daly) and Dr. Joe Gannon (Chad Everett) to squabble between themselves and fight for the rights of their patients, "Undercurrent" was an episode in which another doctor's professional and personal lives were on the line right next to his patient. In a storyline of indignities and prejudice, Dr. Gannon must fight for the more effective research of a colleague he believes is being smeared with untrue rumors about his sexuality—that is, until his handsome, straight-passing colleague comes out to him under duress of the situation.

Though *Medical Center* was also among the early shows to feature an intentionally named lesbian character, it was just narrowly edged out as first by the minor character of Meg Dayton (Kristina Holland) in the courtroom drama *Owen Marshall, Counselor at Law* (1971–1974). In the September 1972 episode "Words of Summer," Meg is a young

---

*   Steven Capsuto, author of *Alternate Channels*, argues that the first expressly gay or bisexual character to appear on television is Russell (Carleton Carpenter), a flamboyant fashion photographer who appears as a minor part in the difficult-to-find 1954 special broadcast of the musical *Lady in the Dark*.

†   As recently as the 2022 episode "Tommy Baker's Hardest Fight," *Law & Order: SVU* continues to produce episodes that concern gay blackmail plots, albeit those in which queer men are revealed to be both the murderers *and* the blackmailers. Progress!

lesbian taking the stand to defend her straight friend who has been falsely accused of being a child molester.[4] Meg's time in the episode is brief, as she's only there to provide her testimony and support for the accused, but she's notable as a figure who stands firm in her identity and describes herself as having been a queer youth. This was a demographic entirely absent from television until that point, unless it was a young boy or girl terrified of their *potential* queerness. Up till then (and even within the same episode, when the accuser recants), all was resolved by the end of the episode, when the young'un realizes their innocent feelings are totally natural and totally temporary.

Just a month later, TV's first romantic queer women's couple would flounce onto ABC's medical drama *The Bold Ones: The New Doctors* (1969–1973), in a storyline less educationally minded than *Medical Center*'s, more central to the narrative than *Owen Marshall*'s, and far more fraught with Freudian tension. Though imperfect, there's an argument to be made that the episode's open ending actually gives us one of the first representations not just of two queer women in a relationship, but of a bisexual character.

In the convoluted "A Very Strange Triangle," the wisecracking, chauvinistic young Dr. Cohen (Robert Walden) doggedly pursues Valerie (Donna Mills), an old flame who just happens to be a new nurse at the hospital. Unfortunately for him, the virginally beautiful, somewhat overwhelmed Valerie is in a relationship with an aspiring clinical psychologist, Eleanor (Hildy Brooks). Although the two appear to have a stable and loving relationship, as the episode progresses, it seems that Valerie is uncertain of her identity, especially with Dr. Cohen back in the picture. Not only that, but Dr. Cohen butts heads with Eleanor, accusing her of controlling Valerie against her natural inclinations.

Ultimately, Valerie agrees with Dr. Cohen—but only to the extent that Eleanor is too overbearing for their relationship to continue.[*] In a

---

[*]   The morally questionable influence of a lesbian character on a straight character can be found sprinkled across recent series, from *The L Word* to *The O.C.*, *The Bisexual*, and *Euphoria*, for just a

controversial move, she sleeps with Dr. Cohen, not to leave Eleanor for him but to prove to herself what she knew all along: she has to be her own person. Dr. Cohen is a misogynistic piece of work, and Eleanor somehow Svengalifies after a touching introduction, but it is satisfying to watch Valerie focus on her own identity while leaving them both in the dust. It may seem like an incredibly regressive decision to have Valerie use the advice of her male psychoanalyst and the power of sexual liberation to help her make a decision, but such storylines of experimentation continue today, with the additional understanding that bisexuality and fluidity are not sidesteps, but true options.* It is also the first television episode to include a time-honored stereotype: that a bisexual person's favorite pastime is cheating because they just can't decide.

Though she goes through one hell of a trial, Valerie fares far better than many of the next documented bisexual characters on television, who were, more than any real characters, the subjects of investigation. The off-kilter, eerie, and absurdist syndicated soap spoof *Mary Hartman, Mary Hartman* (1976–1977) hosted a recurring bisexual character, Annie "Tippytoes" Wylie (Gloria DeHaven), from 1976 to 1977, who did little more than instigate affairs and serve as a foil for the overly paranoid and bicurious Mary (Louise Lesser). On the prime-time front, in the mystery-crime and ill-fated unofficial *Columbo* spin-off *Kate Loves a Mystery*† (1979–1980), the titular Kate (Kate Mulgrew, better known by her future turns in *Star Trek: Voyager* and *Orange Is the*

---

few examples, but it would be an omission not to at least mention "Flowers of Evil," a 1974 episode of *Police Woman* that showcases the evil lesbian temptress in full force.

* Flashing forward thirty years in prime-time medical drama history, the longest-running and first regular bisexual character on television, Callie Torres, experiments with her own sexuality in much the same way. This time, her male lover is her best friend, and her identity is contested not by him but by her newly out lesbian romantic interest, who has just had her entire world rocked by their hookup.

† First titled *Mrs. Columbo*, then repeatedly changed in order to find a never-reached target audience.

New Black, among others) is a case-cracking news reporter who keeps the police on their toes. In the 1979 episode "Feelings Can Be Murder," the victim of the week is a married woman, Claire (Shannon Wilcox), murdered in cold blood by an unknown assailant. In attempting to find the murderer, Kate also uncovers Claire's romantic relationship with another married woman, Elaine (Kathleen Lloyd). Although Elaine is at first reluctant to admit anything other than a casual friendliness formed through their being in the same alternative therapy support group (hosted in a fabulous conversation pit), she eventually reveals the truth.

Just a few years after the television establishment of queer women as sexually depraved murderers, Kate regards Elaine and Claire's relationship only as a piece of the puzzle rather than the shocking, immoral impetus for the crime. As Kate candidly explains to Elaine, "I'm trying to help solve a murder. I am not remotely interested in exposing anybody's private life."[5] Unfortunately, Kate's lack of biphobia doesn't exactly help Claire or Elaine with their material circumstances—Claire is dead, and the fearful Elaine loves her husband and family and has no desire to bring that conversation to them. However, the episode is a perfect segue to discussing the difficulty of data when it comes to bisexual people onscreen.

Neither Claire nor Elaine states their orientation in this episode; only Elaine describes their relationship, naming the physical component of their relationship as something of an afterthought. Elaine tells Kate she "just wanted to please Claire," and she genuinely loves her husband and children. It's a layered statement that can be read in so many different ways: that Elaine was taken advantage of by Claire; that Elaine was so infatuated with Claire that a new sexual identity wasn't as important as their individual relationship; that Elaine is bisexual and potentially polyamorous. In any case, because Elaine doesn't outright say she is a lesbian, bisexual, or straight (unlikely), it's very much left up to the viewer's determination.

———————

As Riese Bernard, cofounder of the LGBTQ+ women- and trans-focused news site *Autostraddle*, reflects in one of her many crucial analyses of the state of queer television, "The most difficult part of analyzing LGBTQ+ data of any kind is deciding how to define any of the terms in that acronym—terms that are always evolving and mean different things to different people."[6] When it comes to bisexual, trans, and nonbinary identity, potential umbrella terms that overlap visually with myriad other identities, there can be more nuance and fluidity than a singular quantitative lens can accommodate. If we were to rely on a character stating their identifier in dialogue, we would have to discount the majority of bisexual characters on television, who use language like "sexually fluid," "I don't do labels," or a simple shrug when confronted by a confused onlooker. Similarly, many storylines include women like Elaine or Claire, who have been or still are in relationships with men before their encounters with women.

"Women who date women," a metric that GLAAD uses to categorize lesbian characters, doesn't really account for the characters, especially in earlier media, who don't use specific language at all. That doesn't, however, mean that these characters are coded. They may not be expressly labeled one way or another, but as in life offscreen, individual sexuality is complex and may not be accounted for by a strict categorization anyway. Perhaps the most concise thought on the matter is from Bernard writing on the strict separation of nonbinary and trans characters onscreen, a category that, like bisexuality and lesbian identity, overlaps far more than television writing accommodates: "Relying on characters with notoriously limited screen time and cis writers/creators to label their characters feels . . . tricky."[7] In early one-off episodes, where the queers of the week barely have the screen time to utter their last words before being killed or otherwise interrupted by their husbands, immutable labels feel especially unnecessary.

For uncoded, unambiguous representation of a transfeminine character, *Medical Center* finally takes the ribbon, though Norman Lear's sitcom hit *All in the Family* (1971–1979) would debut its own jolly "transvestite" character, Beverly La Salle (drag queen Lori Shannon), less than a month later, and Lear's *The Jeffersons* (1975–1985) would air one of the most widely recognized, and overwhelmingly positive, portrayals of an early, Black trans woman character in Edith "Edie" Stokes (cis actress Veronica Redd) two years later.

Medical Center's two-episode seventh-season opener, "The Fourth Sex: Part I" and "The Fourth Sex: Part II," in 1975 has a sitcom connection as well, in that its guest star of the week is none other than America's Dad: Robert Reed of *The Brady Bunch*. Reed plays Dr. Pat Caddison, an old colleague of Dr. Gannon's who returns to the hospital after two years in South Africa to ask Gannon for his help in "sexual reassignment." Gannon, at first astounded, eventually relents and puts his support behind Caddison, who faces a treacherous uphill battle of poor health, an oblivious estranged wife and son, and the hospital's medical board at first refusing to treat Caddison, leading to a failed suicide attempt.

The concept of gender transition is played for its highest drama, with music cues that emphasize the horror experienced by Caddison's circle rather than Caddison's own experience. Caddison's wife, Heather (Salome Jens), is especially histrionic, reacting to her husband's news by sobbing, refusing to believe Pat, and dashing up the stairs. Caddison's adult son, Steve (Gary Frank), is even more overwrought, threatening suicide or alcoholism as a direct result of the loss of his father. Heather's sister, also a doctor at the hospital and Gannon's love interest, is somehow allowed in on the board's discussion to argue against the operation, largely due to her own transphobia and the pain she sees her sister going through. Caddison's own pain in being refused medical treatment is, of course, completely ignored by all but Dr. Gannon. The "think of your family!" storyline is unfortunately still resonant, especially in the increasing right-wing politicization of trans identity as either a disingenuous invasion of cis women's spaces or as a fanciful new trend reserved only for impressionable young people.

Despite the melodrama and accusations from so many around Caddison, the two-part episode resolves in Caddison, post–successful surgery, briefly reuniting with her wife and reconciling on a tender final note. In shadowy silhouette, the two exchange a casual conversation about Heather's new job and life with their son and wish each other happiness as they go their separate ways. There's no subtlety to the role, and the episode is clearly made for a straight, cisgender public whose only experience with trans identity may have been utter fascination with Christine Jorgensen. It checks almost every "what not to do" box when it comes to trans representation, including the preproduction sin of casting a cisgender male actor in a transfeminine role and the automatic association of sexual orientation with gender.[8] Still, it's valuable for Reed's performance and for the decades-long trends it would set with regard to introducing ideas about the supposed dangers of medical transition.[†]

Unlike transfeminine characters, it is incredibly difficult to find evidence of expressly transmasculine people and characters on television before the 1980s, and even between the eighties and nineties they're few and far between. However, some of the earliest characters show up in the most critically acclaimed and popular series of the time: *St. Elsewhere* (1982–1988) and *The Golden Girls* (1985–1992).

Best remembered for its improbable, all-timer series finale and for kick-starting Denzel Washington's acting career, pioneering medical ensemble drama *St. Elsewhere* in its 1983 episode "Family History" presented a trans double whammy. Continuing the storyline of the previous

***

[*]   It's important to note the solid argument behind this—that casting men in trans women's roles leads to the false and dangerous association of trans women with deceit, dishonesty, and costuming over real personhood—also applies to casting cis women as trans men. Actor and writer Jen Richards, whose advocacy around casting capable trans actors to play trans roles has been integral to more mainstream understanding, has also made a nuanced argument for the neutrality of cis women playing trans women.

[†]   Reed won an Emmy for his arc, which could also make this among the first in the decades-long trend of awarding cis actors for their bravery in playing trans characters.

episode, in which hospital patriarch Dr. Mark Craig (Emmy winner William Daniels) is shocked by an old college friend's appearance at St. Eligius for a "sex-change operation," Craig tries to convince Bob Overland (Andy Romano) that she's making a terrible mistake. Bob, of course, will not be swayed, and unlike early transfeminine surgery-focused episodes like the one from *Medical Center*, the hospital is on Bob's, not Craig's, side.[9]

Helping Bob through surgery—and ultimately making Craig see the error of his ways—is Bob's lover and sex therapist, Alan Kentley (Joe Lambie), who also happens to be a trans man. A tall, handsome, sandy-haired man with a concise, straightforward demeanor and a dog in the fight, Al is a serious romantic character. All he wants is for Craig to recognize how much his approval means to Bob, who has lost every-thing—career, friends, and family—in the pursuit of transition. In his short appearance on the episode, we're treated to an unexpected number of firsts: a confident, intelligent transmasculine character who is clearly successful in his field; a trans character who has no need to capitulate to or impress a cis man in a position of authority; and, perhaps the most unintentionally groundbreaking of all, a love story between two trans characters.

Like *Medical Center*, *St. Elsewhere* employs many of what we would regard as missteps when telling a trans story today. The focus is primar-ily on surgery, a cisgender character's feelings are centered over a trans character's point of view, and both trans roles are played by cisgender actors. When viewed today, Alan Kentley is still a remarkable character who, in telling Craig to snap out of it and center his old friend in a mile-stone of a moment, challenges some of those by now tired ideas within the episode itself. Having a trans woman and trans man on the same episode of television is still thought of today as new and exciting. Trans friendships, much less romantic relationships, are so rarely depicted that you'd be hard-pressed to find a meaningful story arc in the forty-year gap between *St. Elsewhere*'s first attempt and, say, the brief date between Micah (Leo Sheng) and Claudia (Isis King) in the second season of *The L Word: Generation Q* (2019–2023) in 2021.*

Airing four years after Al and Bob's story, geriatric sitcom and gay darling *The Golden Girls*' 1987 episode "Strange Bedfellows" also included a transmasculine character, this time as the sole focus of the episode, though the funny-cringeworthy-exhausting way the show attempts to navigate his identity is a lot shakier. The setup is that Gil Kessler (cis actor John Schuck) is the driest, "wimpiest" politician to ever grace a Florida city council race; he's in fact *so* boring that he supports the local paparazzi's false claims that he and proud slut Blanche (Rue McClanahan) slept together, if only for the public interest it finally stirs. Of course, his conscience (and Blanche) gets the better of him, so he decides to come clean—and then some. In a press conference punch line, he reveals that his claim to Blanche's bed was false and that her integrity has inspired him to reveal his past as "part-time stenographer and mild-mannered housewife Anna Maria Bonaduce."[10] Later, charming dolt Rose (Betty White) is fixated on Gil's anatomy, asking all sorts of penis-specific questions that Dorothy (Bea Arthur) brushes away, as she always does, out of an annoyance for Rose's stupidity, but there's genuine confusion: the writers are questioning how Gil's penis could be real, too.

"Strange Bedfellows" is a much-better-remembered episode than "Family History" and is sometimes proposed as the very first time a transmasculine character appeared anywhere on television, and even so, it's not often remembered as the most pressing gay "message" episode of *The Golden Girls*. At a time when gay men and (sometimes) lesbians were appearing on television with some regularity, trans men

---

*   An exception lies, as it usually does, in a *Star Trek* offshoot, *Star Trek: Discovery* (2017–2024). Much like its previous incarnations, *Discovery* uses its sci-fi conventions to do away with binary gender, this time combining an old (*Deep Space Nine*), politely parasitic and genderfluid alien species, the Trill, with nonbinary human characters and trans actors. In 2020, *Discovery* introduced trans Trill Gray (Ian Alexander) and nonbinary human Aria (Blu del Barrio), who have a sweet queer relationship complicated by the fact that Gray is actually deceased. Or is he?

wouldn't make many more appearances until the 2000s, so it's especially easy to feel as though these two episodes were mere blips. Transmasculine roles would take after the fascination with anatomy and failure of masculinity that *The Golden Girls* juggled, though, so it's difficult not to see it as the chosen, rather than accidental, predecessor. Handsome, self-assured, protective trans men wouldn't make their way back from the annals of *St. Elsewhere* for quite some time.

Chapter 2

QIA2S+: FIRSTS AND FAR TO BOLDLY GO

Much has been written about LGBT characters on television, but what of the "rest" of the alphabet—identities that *have* been represented in one way, shape, or form over the years, but, for the most part, find their explicit depictions starting much later? Perhaps for that reason, these are the identities that are most likely to be used as a hook when trumpeting a revolutionary step on queer television and, in some cases, have yet to find a satisfying or lasting presence on our screens.

The final alphabetical "first" to emerge in a medical context was significantly later than any of its screen-preceding LGBT counterparts. This first had very little screen time and no intelligible lines whatsoever. Arriving halfway through the 1996 *Chicago Hope* (1994–2000) episode "The Parent Rap," the unnamed baby Broussard is one of the earliest intersex characters on American television and is used mostly as a plot device to discuss—you guessed it—parenting. In one of the episode's several parent-based subplots, Dr. John Sutton (Jamey Sheridan) is tasked with convincing new parents Bob and Gail Broussard (Paul McCrane and Cynthia Lynch) to keep their baby after he delivers the news that their child has indeterminate sex traits.

In a time when a wider public was just being made aware of what and how common intersexuality is (according to interACT, an estimated one in two thousand babies are born with genital differences that a doctor may suggest unnecessary surgery to "correct," and that doesn't even account for variations in chromosomes or internal organs), the story arc is mostly a nail-on-the-head explainer.[1] However, it skips right over what intersex activists were rallying behind: that babies or minors who develop sex organ differences do not in fact need any surgical intervention, and waiting for any individual to have autonomy over their body is far more valuable than assigning a "normal life" without consent.

Dr. Sutton is portrayed as heroic for convincing the couple to assign their child female genitalia through surgical intervention. The Broussards are depicted as ignorant, desperate Southern traditionalists for their first intention to give the baby up for adoption, but the possibility of allowing the child to grow up as an intersex individual is never even mentioned. The episode closes with another member of the hospital staff, Dr. Aaron Shutt (Adam Arkin), giving a bitter, off-the-cuff send-off at his own father's funeral service, calling him "the most selfish man I've ever met," much to the discomfort of the gathered mourners.[2] In this honest but venomous eulogy, one can almost prophesize baby Broussard's childhood in the care of two guardians who are so reluctant to keep their child even with surgical intervention to make them into a "normal" girl.

Many intersex characters who came after baby Broussard would often be used as the butt of a joke (*Friends*, *Will & Grace*, *The New Normal*) or a medical mystery and springboard for a more esoteric theme (*Grey's Anatomy*, *Masters of Sex*). One slightly more complex, non-medical-drama example of an early intersex storyline is in the character of Amy Andrews (Jessica Campbell), the feisty, band geek girlfriend of Ken Miller (Seth Rogen) on Paul Feig's short-lived cult high school dramedy *Freaks and Geeks* (1999–2000). Although Amy and Ken date from the twelfth episode ("Garage Door") to the end of the series, Amy appears in only two of those seven episodes. In her second appearance ("The Little Things"), Ken is obviously infatuated with her—that is, until they get to know each other a little better and Amy entrusts him with her intersex identity. This information, along with a healthy side of xenophobia from his buddies, plunges Ken into an existential spiral of confusing his attraction toward Amy for homosexuality. In typically misguided teenage fashion, he betrays her trust before profusely apologizing and deciding that her condition shouldn't have any effect on their relationship.

Ken and Amy's reconciliation is sweet if frustrating, as she's still positioned with an otherness that Ken has to overcome in order to love, but the more interesting point of the arc is how Amy sees herself. She first tells Ken that she's relieved her parents decided to remove her "boy parts," because being a girl is how she sees herself. But further in the episode, when Ken is majorly fumbling his reaction, Amy admits that there's always going to be a part of her that feels like a boy. In *Freaks and Geeks*, that statement is explored only as far as it affects Ken's view of his sexuality, where, if pushed just the slightest bit further, it could have been an invitation not to shut intersex people into one strict box for the comfort of everyone around them. Thankfully, the last few years have brought a handful of fully realized intersex characters to the small screen (teen rom-com *Faking It* [2014–2016] being a particularly interesting example), but they're still disproportionately few and far between.

The first character on US television to state their identity as nonbinary strode onto screens in 2016. On the ruthless Showtime drama *Billions* (2016–2023), actor Asia Kate Dillon would find their own offscreen identity through portraying brilliant, aloof hedge fund intern and eventual CEO Taylor Mason, who introduced themself by "they," "their," and "them" pronouns in their second appearance.[3] However, the historically shifting language as well as individual variation around nonbinary, genderqueer, agender, and other fluid gender identities simultaneously confuses and unlocks a wealth of characters that might not be officially described as nonbinary.

Some might point to the body-hopping Trill of *Star Trek: The Next Generation* (1987–1994) and *Star Trek: Deep Space Nine* (1993–1999) as clear metaphors for utopian possibilities of gender fluidity, and there are pre-*Billions* characters whose gender flouting is even more concrete. As previously discussed in Chapter 1, a chopped version of *Princess Knight* made its way to the small screen in the form of a TV movie as early as 1973, but that wasn't the only kid-geared cartoon to use gender fluidity as a means of adventure. One of the first US-originating series to include a young character who is expressly not a girl or a boy is the far-out Saturday-morning ABC fare *Lloyd in Space* (2001–2004), from *Recess* creators Joe Ansolabehere and Paul Germain.

In season 3's "Neither Boy nor Girl" (whoa!), Lloyd and the gang welcome a new kid, Zoit, to the Intrepidville Space Station. An adorable purple potato of a creature, Zoit (brought to life by veteran voice actor and frequent fictional gender swapper Pamela Adlon)* belongs to a species of alien that is genderless before their thirteenth birthday. In the episode, the feuding "girls," led by Valley girl alien Brittany, and "boys" (as much as anyone can call a disembodied brain with glasses a boy, or blue-finned, two-headed butch/femme alien twins a girl) haggle over Zoit for their own purposes. Each group wants an extra vote to tip the scales in their prepubescent war of the sexes, with urgent matters such as which group's favorite intergalactic band is best. When they turn to Zoit to settle the debate, each group is met with a surprise—Zoit gives such a measured answer, equivocating for both and neither musical act, that they start to question themselves. Is Zoit a boy, as the boys assumed, or a girl, as the girls assumed?

After both groups fail to root out Zoit's gender through sneaky means, Zoit cheerfully tells them that their species in fact choose their genders by their thirteenth birthday. So now it's not a race to figure out *what* Zoit is, but *how* the groups can secretly influence them to pick their side by Zoit's birthday that Monday. Zoit loves the newfound attention and invitation to both "boys" and "girls" activities; that is, until they find out that

---

*   As a teen, Adlon, then credited as Pamela Segall, starred in *Willy/Milly*, a 1985 young adult fantasy about a girl who longs to be a boy—and wakes up one day with the equipment to match their wish! Adlon's own series, *Better Things*, includes a central character's inconclusive, ever-evolving journey through gender that doesn't ever limit them to one type of queerness. *Better Things* is discussed more in Chapter 4.

their warm welcome is based only on an ulterior bet. Realizing that their pushiness has put real friendship with Zoit in jeopardy, both groups then make a hard left, encouraging Zoit to choose their opponent's gender. Of course, this just leads to a similar obstinacy, and Zoit is up to their little purple antennae with both sides attempting to make their decision for them, finally (adorably) exploding with, "There you go again! Pushing me and pulling me, back and forth. 'Be a boy, be a girl.' Well, I've had it!"[4] Zoit emphasizes that while they love each group, the decision is up to them. Anyway, it shouldn't matter which they choose—they're still going to be the same Zoit.

The episode is more focused on exposing the silliness of "boys versus girls" than it is on explaining nonbinary identity as we would perceive it today, and it ends on a note automatically aligning gender and sexual orientation. However, much of the language used is similar to portrayals we see today, especially concerning a character coming out but remaining "the same person" their friends and family know and love. Zoit's species is of a dreaded utopian queer future: one in which an individual can live their lives as themselves before choosing their own gender. By the end of the episode, Zoit takes that one step further by deciding their gender is a private matter. They're painfully aware of how people (and aliens) interact with them based on whatever gender they're perceived as, and even though there's an implication that Zoit has chosen . . . something, any gendered expectations will have to wait. Maybe Zoit will remain totally genderless! As with many pioneers, Zoit appears in only one episode of *Lloyd in Space*, so we'll never know.

Sci-fi/fantasy, and space in particular, is a genre that frequently plays with expectations of gender and sexuality outside a traditional medical or pathologized context. The vast, futuristic reaches of the unknown have no real rules, and finding out which beings populate the final frontier is at least half the fun of the genre. It only makes sense that a genre famous for boldly going where no straight has gone before would seek to push the boundaries of what earthbound denizens find normative. In that realm, space was arguably the first place for ace as well—at least, in a way slightly more concrete than coding.

Star Trek fans have long related to the easily perceived queerness of its characters—after all, audience obsessions with the relationship between promiscuous, charming human Starfleet captain Kirk (William Shatner) and his allegedly emotionless number one part-human–part-Vulcan Spock (Leonard Nimoy) in the original series spawned pre-internet fandom culture as we now know it.[5] Though show creator and grandfather of television sci-fi Gene Roddenberry has denied the homosexuality that Trekkies read into the show, instead preferring to focus on breaking other taboos onscreen, this hasn't stopped anyone from claiming characters for their own.

In addition to reading Spock as gay for Kirk, some have seen his near-total aversion to women (unless, of course, he's intoxicated by space pollen or another hallucinatory flower) as a form of sex-repulsed, asexual representation. Even in the throes of pon farr, an every-seven-years hijacking of a Vulcan's body that forces them to choose a sexual partner or die, Spock expresses a great sadness that he has not been able to avoid his "biological" urge to choose a wife.

Spock's sexual orientation is still debated, what with *Star Trek: Discovery* introducing more depth to many of his relationships beyond Kirk. The first character to have his asexuality plainly spelled out in the franchise, however, is the lovable, obtuse-for-being-so-damn-smart anthropomorphic supercomputer Data (Brent Spiner) of *Star Trek: The Next Generation*. Like Spock, Data is distinguished from his human and alien crew members by an inability to fully experience human emotion and sentiment in the same way that they do. Similarly to Spock, Data becomes all too human throughout the series, forming deep friendships and relationships with his crew.

Data's asexuality is also debated, sometimes based on his fondness for Lieutenant Geordi La Forge (LeVar Burton), but mostly because of his intimacy with one crew member in particular: Tasha Yar (Denise Crosby). In the second episode of the series, and what many propose to be the real start to *TNG*'s excitement, the crew is hit once again by the somehow ever-present sex pollen ("The Naked Now"). As Captain Picard (Patrick Stewart) and his usually industrious crew try to stop it from destroying inhibitions and flinging them all through the air lock, Data and Tasha fall prey to its wiles. More specifically, Tasha asks if Data has the capabilities to please her, and a confused but ever-truthful Data assures her that he functions quite normally. He's programmed to accomplish a "broad variety of pleasuring," no less.[6] The pneumatic doors of a bedchamber shutter, and off they go to an unpictured round of horny human/slightly intoxicated motherboard relations.

Though the concept often confuses those unfamiliar with the term, asexuality does not automatically mean sex is off the table. Like many of the labels discussed in this chapter, the mileage of a term varies based entirely on the person who claims it, and the umbrella of asexuality splits into many different facets of muted attraction, repulsion, and neutrality toward sex. In short, many asexual people do indeed have sex, and Data, though never conceived as an asexual character in the GLAAD-defined sense, is simply one of them. He never confirms an attraction to Tasha, merely a closeness with her, as he states to Captain Picard when being cross-examined to determine his own sentience ("The Measure of a Man"). Five episodes prior to his cross-examination, Data could not state it any more clearly: "Sexual attraction in this context is not part of my programming."[7]

Data's asexuality continues to be juxtaposed with his hornier crew members' libidos throughout *The Next Generation*, sometimes written in parallel to his learning about other key aspects of humanity (for example, a sense of humor in "The Outrageous Okona"). Even so, some object to readings of him, as well as Spock, as ace because it falls in line with an unfair branding of asexuality as alien or corresponding with a lack of human emotion.[8] As author and YouTuber Rowan Ellis argues in her video "The Problem with Asexual Representation," these onscreen robot and alien representations play off an old stereotype that asexuality is cold and unfeeling.

For Spock, this is certainly true—as a rule, he's disinterested in anything categorized as passionate. Data, however, aspires to the emotions and context of neurotypical humanity, but he does not attempt to change the orientation of his programming; he doesn't need to. As Ellis points out, Data's tendency to kiss or have sex with those who express interest in him is, in a way, a highly relatable depiction of asexual and/or aromantic people choosing to engage in sex and romance with the people they care about, deriving pleasure from doing something for their partners' and friends' benefits. The *TNG* writers' room version of asexuality may be somewhat unintentional and uninterested in the realism of such an orientation, but theirs is still one of the very first sustained examples of a type of repeatedly affirmed asexuality on the small screen.

Unfortunately, the first certifiably human representation of asexuality on television knows less about the orientation than Data and is no more interested in fair or accurate depictions. Craig Kilborn's sketch character Sebastian, the Asexual Icon debuted on *The Late Late Show* (1995–2023) in 2003 to much laughter from a studio audience and no expectation that the object of hilarity was a real person. Reminiscent of Ernie Kovacs's days as Percy Dovetonsils, Kilborn dons ill-fitting spectacles, wears a striped scarf, and sometimes twirls a rose as he recites scoffing one-liners like, "The closest I get to making love is fondling a first edition of Dickens," and, "When I listen to David Bowie's *Space Oddity*, I think: *If* I had nipples, they would be hard right now. That's a pretty big if." After each laugh, a disembodied voice repeats in a stage whisper, "Asexual icon."[9] It's pretty clear: the writers don't take asexuality seriously, and you shouldn't either. What I wouldn't give for an unattended air lock.

Our final "first" is one in which US programming is seriously lagging behind, both in quantity and quality. Unfortunately, a dearth of two-spirit representations isn't much of a surprise, what with Hollywood's violent allergy to portraying, with any accuracy, the first inhabitants of the so-called United States. As with other colonial attempts to forcibly separate Indigenous people from their cultural specificity, including a long history of gender nonconformity, early Hollywood played a huge part in completely misrepresenting indigeneity. When they did appear, Native characters were often played by white actors in redface, pushed to disposable backdrop, and slotted into one-dimensional stereotypes.[*] While independent Indigenous filmmaking really began gathering speed in the nineties, and Canadian and New Zealander television started introducing shows with Indigenous leads in front of and behind the camera in the 2000s, American television has only just started to turn the corner on Native-led series that likely have the best chance of expanding two-spirit representation on television.[†]

Discussions with two-spirit individuals can be viewed as early as 1991 on local cable access, and the first representation to hit national television was PBS's *Independent Lens* (1999–) broadcast of the 2009 documentary film *Two Spirits*. No fictional storyline since has even approached the nuance with which real people in these programs speak about the complexity of queer Indigenous identity.[10] It's not exactly a surprise that American television would have a difficult time reckoning with an identity so suppressed by US imperialism. The first fictional two-spirit character to ever appear on a US series, which happens to be

---

[*]   The 2009 documentary *Reel Injun*, directed by Neil Diamond, Catherine Bainbridge, and Jeremiah Hayes, is a great primer of Indigenous representation on US screens.

[†]   Especially notable is New Zealand's first Fa'afafine series regular—flamboyant school principal and "close personal friend of Lucy Lawless," Brother Ken—on the raucous, hugely popular animated series *bro'Town* (2004–2009). In a series that mostly derives its sense of humor from stereotypes, Brother Ken is not what some might call positive representation, but he is a kind, encouraging presence in the lives of the misfit kids he supervises.

an American Canadian co-production, is Sam Blackcrow in Starz's dark fantasy adventure series *American Gods* (2017–2021). Sam, played by queer Kanien'kéha Mohawk actor, filmmaker, and activist Devery Jacobs, appears in two episodes ("Muninn" in 2019 and "Conscience of the King" in 2021) as a young, contemporary shepherd for protagonist Shadow Moon (Ricky Whittle) as he climbs away from yet another harrowing near-death plunge into the war between New and Old Gods.

A curious, charismatic Jacobs makes the most out of Sam's first appearance, which essentially uses them as a mouthpiece for some brief Indigenous lore in a dense, circular episode about sacrifice. As they prevent Shadow from scamming a gas station attendant and then ferry him to his next destination by way of their dirty, beat-up truck, most of their dialogue is about their identity.[11]

Split across several scenes, they speak about their struggles as a "two-spirited" person, including a brief mention of the father who never accepted them for their mixed parentage and the (presumably white) mother who raised them by the law of one God and good book alone.* They couldn't find peace in either world, but rather found their home in "the stories of [their] ancestors," including that of "the Crow Nation warrior named Finds Them and Kills Them."[12] The script smashes together several pieces of tribe-specific information, flattening the real Crow warrior Osh-Tisch/Finds Them and Kills Them into a much later Pan-Indian interpretation of a third gender rather than one of the last of the traditional Crow Nation baté.

Notably, Sam and Shadow both use "he" pronouns for a figure often referred to in oral histories by "she" pronouns. It's a puzzling change when considering Osh-Tisch's role as one of the baté forced into masculine-designated dress and labor by US government agents. In a series that heavily mythologizes queerness and brings to sardonic,

---

* The inclusion of racial bias coming from their "full-blood Cherokee" father's side and religious prejudice coming from their mother's side is a muddled one-liner that raises more questions than are answerable. If anything, the script seems to be shoving every possible otherness onto Sam without taking the time to fully realize, even in subtext, their cultural background.

fantastical life figures from so many different cultures, Sam and Finds Them and Kills Them's inclusions are welcome but strangely and disappointingly generic. Traditional pre-colonial roles for gender-variant Indigenous people varied widely across nations, with some designated as healers or performing valuable ceremonial roles, but they were and continue to be real people, not just the stuff of legend.

HBO's singular season of *Lovecraft Country* (2020) attempts a two-spirit storyline similarly steeped in mythos, but unfortunately it falls even shorter, and is far more inaccurate, than that of *American Gods'*. While violence and death are par for the *Lovecraft* course as its protagonists stumble into the monsters that populate Jim Crow era America, the dehumanizing, *Crying Game*-reminiscent, genitalia-focused introduction and brutal murder of Arawak two-spirit character Yahima (cisgender actress Monique Candelaria) was disappointing to fans and critics alike. However, in an unusual addition to the typical story of clumsy "early" TV portrayals that either discard or blatantly misrepresent LGBTQIA2S+ people, *Lovecraft Country* showrunner Misha Green responded to audience disappointment by apologizing for Yahima's storyline shortly after it aired.[13] As welcome as this kind of acknowledgment may have been, *Lovecraft Country* was canceled the next year, killing any potential efforts at reviving Yahima or telling a better two-spirit story alongside it.

More than a decade after *Two Spirits*, it's astounding that no other explicitly two-spirit characters have made it past two episodes on any US television series. However, the ever so slight uptick in Native-led series by way of Graham Roland's thriller *Dark Winds* (2022–), Sterlin Harjo and Taika Waititi's excellent dramedy *Reservation Dogs* (2021–2023), and Sierra Teller Ornela's bureaucratic sitcom *Rutherford Falls* (2021–2022) began to lay the groundwork not just for one-off episodes with two-spirit characters but for an Indigenous worldbuilding in which gender-variant and queer Indigenous characters need little introduction. While *Rutherford Falls* and *Reservation Dogs* have now unfortunately reached their end, in its three seasons, *Reservation Dogs* built a code for implicit queerness in a Native television world, no doubt driven by queer and two-spirit talent in front of and behind the camera.

I've done my best to chronicle obvious and more or less easily interpretable "first" mentions, hints, and usually brief appearances of LGBTQIA2S+ characters from shows that can be hypothetically watched if you have access to the internet, your local library, the Internet Archive, and your friends' passwords for half a dozen streaming services. As for finding and recognizing these firsts, it took several months to comb through television history and media theory books, *TV Guide* listings, retired fan blogs on the Wayback Machine, *Autostraddle*'s thoroughly researched lists of lesbian and trans television characters, and sometimes just watching episodes of landmark series because I had a hunch that what I was searching for just hadn't been written about extensively yet. And all this to write what I consider to be an extremely limited survey of these firsts! Beyond *Alternate Channels*, which is an incredible resource that does not extend into twenty-first-century television, there is no means to easily cross-check the veracity of these timelines—but why would networks take the time to dredge up an entire queer history?

Knowing, from the process of writing this chapter, that it is incredibly difficult and sometimes jaw-droppingly dull to put together a timeline of firsts, I have very little hope that someone trying to sell a television show would have all that much interest in fact-checking queer firsts. And besides, if you can always disingenuously tack on "one of the first" or "one of the first openly ___" as a prefix and pretty much cover your ass, why would you put in all that fact-checking time anyway?

Let's say we weren't fact-checking at all. As you can easily glean from nearly every first in this chapter, many explicit early depictions of characters with marginalized identities really aren't all that good. As Stephen Tropiano acknowledges, if we reflect on the fifties, sixties, and even the early seventies, we can see these television firsts as societal "attitudes about 'homosexuality,' as it was referred to. It helps us connect the dots, to see that it isn't just that these shows were on and a wall came down. There's a connection between a lot of the social myths and misinformation that were perpetuated at the time about gay men and lesbians really early on, and television actually contributed to that."[14]

In that vein, the most significant aspect to firsts today isn't whether a contemporary introduction of a rarely depicted character can, with 100 percent honesty and accuracy, back up their claim to being the first character of their kind. Contemporary firsts can still use the same basic building blocks to sympathetically belittle, condescend, dispose of, or straight up misunderstand the identities with which they claim to break new ground.

Of course, none of this is necessarily important to a network or streaming service, which views queer audiences as an easily won and kept target demographic. Inaccurate claims and offensive depictions don't matter unless they're challenged. On the journalist and critic side, minimal enough research could probably disprove most self-inflating claims made on press tours, but unfortunately, as easy as it would be to turn away any of these firsts as marketing points, they're rarely contested. Sometimes, it seems that laying a claim to a narrow "first" or "only" is the only way to get a queer show any press—unless it's June and major publications are finally interested in roundups about new queer shows or iconic gay characters.

As with any aspect of using queer identity to market a show, the hope from an audience member is that a show will do something with its allegedly groundbreaking queer characters, not just trot them out and leave them to breathe shallowly. We can now move to a place of understanding that there are decades of bad queer representation behind us, and the almost point-system-based promotion of a series by its mere inclusion of a nonintegral, underdeveloped character does not have to guarantee any measure of dedication from a queer audience. Especially when the corporate-political tide can easily turn, and it becomes more convenient to once again dispose of queerness altogether, a "first" in the 2020s isn't just archaic; it's insulting.

Queer & A: Lilly Wachowski

Credits: *Bound, The Matrix, Speed Racer, Cloud Atlas, Sense8, Work in Progress*

When I began to write this chapter, filmmaker Lilly Wachowski's commentary on the delightful trans possibility of Bugs Bunny was something that stuck out in my mind as a purely joyful highlight of early queer and trans representation—especially when there's little else that's decipherable. Wachowski's own genre-smashing and -defining films are full of implicit and explicit queerness, and her move to television brought two exuberantly queer series to our screens.

In 2015, Wachowski, her sister Lana Wachowski, and J. Michael Straczynski brought the humanistic, globetrotting sci-fi series *Sense8* (2015–2018) to Netflix. Bright, sophisticated, and endlessly imaginative, the series revolved around an empathically linked cluster of eight wildly different people suddenly thrust into a web of conspiracy, telepathy, and, of course, gorgeously shot psychic orgies. Among *Sense8*'s many joyful innovations was a character, and a relationship, that was rare for US narrative series: Nomi Marks (Jamie Clayton), a sharp trans blogger and hacker in a loving relationship with another woman, Amanita "Neets" Caplan (Freema Agyeman).

After the unexpected cancellation of *Sense8*, Wachowski's next project was something completely different. She became an executive producer and director on Showtime's searingly funny *Work in Progress* (2019–2021), improv duo Abby McEnany and Tim Mason's zany, gallows-humor, semi-autobiographical character study of a forty-five-year-old fat, OCD-diagnosed butch at the end of her rope.

I was lucky enough to ask Lilly about her personal journey through queer television as a viewer and maker, and what she hopes to impart on up-and-coming queer media makers. This is an edited excerpt of our conversation.

SHAYNA MACI WARNER: Do you remember the earliest coded characters, or characters you could project onto, on television?

LILLY WACHOWSKI: On television, all the characters that I can think of are mean; there's so many characters that are just villains. When I returned to this headspace, when I think about trans feminized characters particularly, the list goes from Norman Bates in *Psycho* and Michael Caine in *Dressed to Kill,* or the Three Stooges dressing up in drag or any type of broad comedy, like *The Honeymooners.* It's endless as I start going through the library in my brain. I think I even spoke to Susan Stryker about it before, a couple of years ago. She had been over for dinner and mentioned it, and then it clicked in my brain that I had a similar experience. There's something about [Bugs Bunny] that exists in pure imagination that allowed me to access the idea of transformation easier than, say, a character like the Billy Crystal character on *Soap.*

As I started to get older, I would find the character from *The World According to Garp* played by [John Lithgow]. Then there was a period where I was starting to find older films, like the Hammer films with the lesbian vampires and all that sort of titillation. Then after that, Ken Russell and *The Lair of the White Worm.* [The main character is] not explicitly lesbian, but there's a lot of queer baiting in that film. That's why I always like to return to Bugs Bunny or those kinds of things, because I was meeting the creator in this halfway space where I can imagine something and the creator is also imagining it and we're meeting halfway, as opposed to an actor who was a cis person playing a trans person. There was always something that I could tell wasn't doing it for me. I couldn't suspend my disbelief. I would always go, "Oh, that's Billy Crystal."

I came out much later in life, in my forties. So, you're talking about me growing up in the eighties, and there's just nothing. Then I get to around sixteen, seventeen, and I start finding trans people, trans women particularly, in porn, and there was something about that experience I found deeply affecting. Because I could begin to think about my own body in the way that there's potential for me. The idea that in porn, this person is being loved in this way, being desired. That was sort of a profound moment for me. I can look back on how I looked at media and consumed media, and that had more of a profound effect for me than anything. Like even Bugs Bunny, I had to retroactively dig through my personal history and go, "Oh, yeah, you know what, I do think Bugs Bunny was the character." And I can't even remember the name of that particular episode, where Bugs Bunny is Brunhilde ["What's Opera, Doc?"].

SMW: So seeing trans women in porn was more accessible?

LW: Yeah, for sure. There were even some true crime magazines that we were buying back in the day, and they were always very titillating. But as you got into the back of the true crime magazines, there would be these advertisements and drawings of female-bodied characters with penises, and I was just fascinated by that. About when I was in high school, I found this comic book called *Black Kiss* by Howard Chaykin. It's got a trans woman as the villain, of course, but because it was drawn so explicitly it really activated my imagination. It's a completely horrifying story, particularly the trans part of it, but it had a very similar narrative to Genesis P-Orridge, the punk rocker, in the way that Genesis and their partner tried to meet in the middle to try to create the same body. And so that part was just a funny narrative. I discovered that much later in life and then went back to *Black Kiss*.

SMW: Did all this villain material have any notable impact on how you thought about these characters?

LW: I would say that it had a lot of consequences. I think it radicalized me a little bit more. It made me sympathetic to villain narratives. So I brought that sort of stuff into my writing. It made me question where these villain narratives were coming from, and in a way I started connecting all those pieces in my brain when I was a young person. How I gravitated toward heavy metal and punk rock, and then more hard-core rap and hip-hop. I could see all these things were connected to the idea of anti-authority and how it all came under an umbrella with my transness. I didn't have an idea of what my transness was at the time. It was something that I instinctively started to slowly put together.

Art to me is about self-portraiture in so many ways. Even after I came out, I just started dealing with the idea of the consequence of coming out and how it felt to be this giant, nonpassing trans woman in the world. Like, how did that feel? I ended up painting these little ducks in lakes of blood and fire, and skies of darkness. The ducks keep on truckin' and they're happy; and this is the way I view myself in the world. I think that there's a lot of evidence that I was probably correct; especially in this country nowadays, it's not an exaggeration. The joy that I get out of being free of the closet outweighs the alternative.

SMW: So, out of this barren landscape of TV, you end up creating a beautiful trans character in Nomi on _Sense8_. Could you talk to me about your move to TV and the creation of that character?

LW: It was written probably seven years before somebody decided to make [_Sense8_]. We were fully in the Iraq War at that point, so we were very invested in calling attention to the crime against humanity that this country was participating in at that time. It wasn't that the crime had been dissipated any, but the fact that it was clearly written seven years before, we ended up having to rewrite a couple of the plotlines. That's how long the script sat around. At the time, Netflix was a handful of people, and they were just starting to get into television. [*Sense8*'s] co-creator, Michael Straczynski, was tenacious in trying to get it made and it just kind of popped up. We could see that there was this shift happening in the industry where the more interesting art was flourishing on television rather than in movie theaters. Because we had this prolonged relationship with Warner Bros., all they wanted was the next giant tentpole IP. So the idea that we could go make a TV show diverse and globally minded felt really interesting to us.

And then, in the making part of the first season of *Sense8*, I had a series of back-to-back-to-back productions where I went from *Cloud Atlas*, to post on *Cloud Atlas*, and simultaneously prepping *Jupiter Ascending*. Then I had the same experience on the back end of *Jupiter Ascending* where we were in post and prepping at the same time. It was this kind of grueling period of my work life. My professional life and my personal life started to grind, and during the end of *Jupiter Ascending* I started separating from my partner at the time and felt my life coming apart. Somewhere in that period before we started shooting *Sense8* I started medically transitioning and went on hormones. So the character of Nomi was this interesting component to that because, in a couple of ways, this was an artist's magic trick, where the artist can basically write or create out of thin air this magic rope that is attached to some unknown point in the future. The artist can use the rope to drag themselves along to get to that point in the timeline.

Lana [Wachowski] wrote a lot of amazing bits to that. Like the Pride speech, and when they're talking about art and being in the closet. Shooting those scenes, her character made me really reflect on the idea of how you can use art-making to speak about truths about yourself, truths about the world, and still make something compelling. The idea of how life and art create these parallels and mirrors between each other. I became more acutely aware of that paradigm, and I could focus my art in such a way that I can use it to work through shit a lot better than I used to. But now I'm sensing it much more when I work on stuff like *Sense8*. In *Work in Progress*, I'm able to explicitly investigate and analyze the things that are going on in the world and in my life.

There was this moment in *Sense8*, midway through the production, maybe a little bit further: We were in Berlin. We went out to dinner and Jamie [Clayton, who plays Nomi] saw me and was so excited to see me. She came over to me and we had this little quick sidebar where she was like, "Tell me what's going on with you." She was one of the first people I came out to professionally. I told her everything, the whole spiel. I said, "Fuck it, I'm gonna start hormones." She said, "Oh my God. Congratulations!" And just like that, radical acceptance. It just filled me up with warmth. Like the feeling that I could get that from people blew me away.

I needed to take a break and do something else. I loved everything that I've done, but I felt like I had missed so much. My work relationship became this bad time machine, where I felt like I was disappearing to some extent. So I took a break, did some painting, and went back to school for a little bit. And then *Work in Progress* sort of came along. Abby

[McEnany] is a friend of mine, she lives in my neighborhood, and I was trying to get her stuff in front of people. And then suddenly, people started taking notice. She and her creative partner at the time made the first pilot and took it to Sundance. It started getting a lot of buzz then. And then the three of us went out to Hollywood and pitched around town and Showtime bought it. And I was back. It took me a minute to recalibrate on what I was doing there. The main thing that I took away was the joy of getting queers, trans folks, and people of color all together making art and getting paid. I felt like that gave me more of a sense of purpose than I ever had. Before, my purpose was for me to make cool shit or interesting shit. I'm not saying that we didn't try to tell radical political stories or stories of transformation, but I feel like I recentered myself.

SMW: It also felt like a pretty radical genre shift.

LW: Yes, yes, that's true. I think a lot of our films always have an element of humor in them and you can see that kind of humor. Like most of the Coen Brothers' movies where they don't take themselves too seriously. And I don't think that our films did that either. There were always these moments where you could tell we were delighting in genre, but especially delighting in the mashing of genre. As I look back on it, I can say that is a particularly trans way of being as a filmmaker.

SMW: Going back to Jamie Clayton, and to this incredible moment you had with her, was that the first time that you had worked with an out trans actress?

LW: I think so. There were definitely trans people in some of the rave scenes in the *Matrix* films. I know Club Hell had trans folks in it. And then in the first *Matrix*, there was this bar called, like, the Hellfire Club or something like that, that we had shot in. That was with the leather and rubber community. There were trans people there, but they were in the background. Like us. It was exhilarating. I was also really afraid but exhilarated by these two things coming together.

SMW: Jumping back to *Work in Progress*, can you talk to me about working with queer and trans artists on all sides of production, especially in the second season?

LW: *Work in Progress*, in the very first season, was created a little bit by the seat of our pants. I had signed on as a producer with the creators Abby McEnany and Tim Mason. Showtime bought it right after we pitched, since they had a show fall out. To some extent that was a lucky break for *Work in Progress*. They needed a show, and *Work in Progress* was there. They said yes, and we ended up sort of banging out the season. We were doing this without a deal in place, because those things can take forever; the legal side is always impossible. You can end up writing an entire season of television before the deal finally gets done. So we ended up writing the whole season, and then they finished the deal and then we went right into preproduction.

For the writing process I let them go forward and then I kind of came back in after the fourth episode and did some polishing of the scripts. And there was a bit more back-and-forth between the three of us. And then the following season Tim directed, and there was a shift where Abby wanted a proper writers' room. One of the things about that writers' room was a focus on queerness that was not prevalent in the previous season. But in both of the seasons we wanted to bring in queerness and to bring in transness. We wanted to populate the show's DNA with that. Even in the music, we hired queer artists to put in our soundtrack. We hired as many speaking parts as we could. We tried to find trans people to put them in the backgrounds to populate our world with queerness and transness. We emphasized that even more in the second season. Out of the [ten] episodes, five are directed by trans people.

SMW: Was there anything that didn't happen in the first season that got to move into the second season because there was that sort of priority shift?

LW: The first season ends kind of dismally. It's a little heart-breaking. I think that thanks to the queerness and the trans-ness in the writers' room, from my perspective, and from Abby's perspective, there are different kinds of endings. One is sort of depressing. And the other one is like, oh, [Abby] did okay. But you know, she's done. Mercy. [In the first season] some of our notes in the studio were, "We have to hear Chris's [Theo Germaine] dead name." If there weren't a trans person in my position, and if I was just some cis person, that might have happened. And so you can feel the tenacity of transness and queerness repelling that repugnant idea. It's like a particularly cis point of view to think we deserve to know what the dead name is.

SMW: Were there any moments of on-set or in-production joy that you could tell me about?

LW: There's all sorts of stuff. There are these poignant moments where I'm on set, and we're shooting a scene where Abby is talking to her dead mom, cradling her box of ashes. While this scene is unfolding, there is a print or a replication of one of my mom's paintings in the background. And so there's this introspection that is happening in the piece itself, as well as this introspection that is happening in the moment of the creation of the art as well.

There's the riotous joy of seeing Abby and Celeste [Pechous], who plays Campbell, you know, those moments have these two human beings who have so much love for each other, and they're cracking up in the car. Those are some of the favorite scenes for Abby to shoot because there's nobody around except for her and Celeste, and they're just shooting the shit. Those kinds of things feel so good. It's funny because I've reached this moment in my career where I'm always discovering things. I didn't realize that if you have a bar scene in your schedule, the best thing you can do for yourself is put the bar scene as the last scene you shoot in your production schedule, so that you're finishing in a bar, and you can all go have a drink together afterward. So that's a good piece of advice that I will always give my future self. Move that bar scene into the end of the schedule. You're going to have a nice, warm drink, full with love, with your entire crew, and you've all participated in something special.

SMW: *Work in Progress* and *Sense8* were both canceled in their second seasons. Broadcast has always been kind of a difficult place to tell queer and trans stories, but streaming seemed like there was exciting art that was able to exist, especially at the advent. Now that we're kind of in this pendulum shift or swing back, how do you still make art through that? How do you still imagine these stories when you're seeing this pattern of cancellation?

LW: It's a problem. I feel like there's something that is happening in this industry that is happening in all modes of capitalism and around the world, where you can see these super conglomerates hoovering up smaller companies. The way that the profit structure is working in this industry, all corporate industries, oil, food, and tech, where you have this upward flow of profit, and I think that mentality is really exhibiting itself in ways in this industry like I haven't seen before. Yes, Warner Bros. was always interested in trying to hit home runs with their properties. Like the way that they go out and they buy *Harry Potter*, you know, they were hoping that *Jupiter Ascending* was going to be this thing. Especially in the film industry and TV industry, it's going to rely on breaking the back of that capitalist structure; that is what is going to have to happen for art to find its audiences.

I think it's gonna rely on the artists to take a stand. The unions have to do something. The artists have to come together in a way they haven't since the times of United Artists or Mary Pickford. Artists are going to have to regain control of the way that their pieces are exhibited and run, and the profit structure has to be realigned in a way. I'm thinking about it, and I'm invested in it, and I have an eyeball toward it. It's just a matter of when.[*]

Me and Lana had this project that we were working on where we interviewed all these folks that we were reading and watching at the time, who were talking about what was going on with queerness and imperialism. People like Cornel West, Sasha Harmon, and Naomi Klein. One of the people that we interviewed was Bill Ayers, who's from Chicago, and his wife, Bernadine Dohrn, who were in the Weather Underground. At the time, Bill was a teacher at the University of

---

[*] A few short months after this interview was conducted, the Writers Guild of America (WGA) struck from May 2, 2023, until September 27, 2023, when they secured a deal with the Alliance of Motion Picture and Television Producers. The Screen Actors Guild and American Federation of Television and Radio Artists (SAG-AFTRA) joined them on July 14, ratifying their own new contract on December 6.

Illinois in Champaign. We asked him, "How do you keep going? What is the thing?" And he's like, "Well, you know what, every day I wake up, I get into my car, I go about my day, and I try to bring down the empire. And you know, it's not easy, and it wears you down. And you get home and you say to yourself, 'How can I keep going?' And then you go, and you get a good night's sleep, and you wake up, and you get in your car, and you go and try to bring down the empire."

And there was something about the optimism of this unflappable state of being that you can do that, and the reparative nature of, like, getting a good night's sleep, so that you can come at the day again, with the same energy and tenacity. I think we have to inhabit our lives as queer and trans people. It's like we have to continue to try to defeat the empire and, you know, get a good night's sleep.[15]

Chapter 3

JUST A REGULAR JODIE: RECURRING, REGULAR, AND LEAD QUEER CHARACTERS

One of the most beautiful aspects of television is its serial format. Like radio before it (but with that nifty visual component), television returns to us, episode after episode. Though not all series are rolled out on a weekly basis, audiences still get to immerse themselves in the world of the show, hopefully long enough for it to grow into a fully realized destination. Of course, not all narrative shows' transportive qualities are created equal, but the best and brightest are well worth the hours of dedicated viewing—and well remembered not just for the world, but for the favorite characters who seemed to grow, or deteriorate, right alongside us.

These are the characters whose visage and dress are studied—nay, worshipped and emulated to varying degrees of success. Whose lines are so often quoted with an ironic zeal that they become sincere. These are also the characters whose motivations and inner psyches are dissected, decades after their series' end, to discuss why they did that thing they do. Whether that be cooking crystal meth, or murdering their godson, or pushing their lover in front of a train, or choosing to jump to their death to save their imaginary sister, these characters stay with us.

Of course, a character's lasting impression or potential to be truly intriguing usually depends on their showing up for more than one episode. Far be it from me to devalue the impact of a choice cameo or particularly memorable guest star, but the satisfaction or frustration of a character arc often relies on their importance to the series. We have to be persuaded to glue our eyeballs to the screen, anticipating and dreading what they'll do next. We have to want to give them our time, and a series has to give the character time to grow, flourish, and flounder.

As we've discussed, early, explicitly queer characters started out a little short on one crucial piece of the Important and Memorable TV Character equation: namely, they just didn't have the time. Coded characters certainly lingered long enough to become beloved, but out gay characters were largely one-offs (and one-offed), even if they did make for memorable villains or victims or PSAs of the week. Of course, by this time, we do have a cache of mostly gay and lesbian characters who managed to punch in and never punch out—the biggest names of whom are credited with changing hearts and minds all across America. But before the name of a gay character took up valuable real estate in the title of a network sitcom and the covers of *Time* and *Entertainment Weekly*, there were a slew of recurring and regular ones, and even a few ensemble leads, who were allowed to vie for a slice of the audience's attention.

Panamania

The first openly gay recurring character on American TV was gone in a blip, but it's hardly his fault. Cartoonishly named Peter Panama (character actor Vincent Schiavelli), a flamboyant gay Broadway set designer, was one of the mainstays of the first season of *The Corner Bar* (1972–1973), a *Cheers*-esque precursor summer replacement series that landed on ABC for a paltry two seasons. Panama was a gregarious, ascot- and loud pattern–sporting patron of the fictional NYC bar Grant's Tomb, and his status as an openly gay recurring character is one of the only reasons the series is even remembered today—and he didn't even survive the second season's complete retooling. Panama's inclusion in the show, though capital-G Groundbreaking, wasn't particularly well received, with Rich Wandel, president of the Gay Activists Alliance, calling Panama "the worst stereotype of a gay person I've ever seen," and *Village Voice* reviews considering his character just one "effeminate" among the series' several novelty demographics (Black, Jewish, and alcoholic among them).[1,2]

The Corner Bar is virtually impossible to watch now, with only a few clips of the first and second season's theme songs circulating the recesses of the internet. Chronologically significant as Panama may be, he does succumb to the age-old question: If a historically monumental gay character on a nonsyndicated television show falls in the forest and nobody has uploaded his episodes to YouTube, can we make any judgments on the quality of his character or how he might have changed the world? Not particularly, but unfortunately it would take three years before another recurring queer character had a better chance to stick around and make their own mark.

All in the Lear Family

Sitcom impresario Norman Lear's long roster, including *Maude* (1972–1978), *Mary Hartman, Mary Hartman, The Jeffersons*, and *Hot l Baltimore* (1975), is home to many a button-pushing character of all orientations, and his first sitcom, the critically hailed hit *All in the Family* is no exception. The series follows a blue-collar family in Queens whose bullheaded, bigoted patriarch, Archie Bunker (Emmy winner Carroll O'Connor), makes no secret of his longing for simpler times, often in direct, rude conflict with his Baby Boomer daughter and son-in-law and his Black, Jewish, and liberal neighbors and coworkers. Although critics were at first divided on Archie's plain-spoken boorishness, and whether Lear's satire was in fact a successful critique or simply offensive, *All in the Family* made a point of featuring the characters Archie was most vehemently prejudiced against and creating many landmark moments in sitcom history in the process.

One of Archie's most famous encounters with queerness is in the fifth episode of the entire series, "Judging Books by Covers," an episode so culturally impactful that then president Richard M. Nixon was caught on tape complaining about its "glorify[ing] homosexuality."[3] In the episode, Archie clashes with his daughter, Gloria (Sally Struthers), and son-in-law, "Meathead" Mike (Rob Reiner), over their metrosexual, ultra-fashionable friend Roger (Tony Geary), who eschews sports, has a dainty but eager handshake, and waxes poetic about his photographic tour of Europe ("For your information, England is a fag country," Archie says to needle Meathead).[4] Archie is rude to and disgusted by the oblivious Roger, but by the end of the episode, he discovers that it's his former pro ball player bar buddy Steve (Philip Carey) who's gay, not Roger.

The episode is a typical example of *All in the Family*'s tradition of showing up Archie by turning the tables on him, and Archie's idolizing of Steve is especially funny when it's so physical and homosocial (Archie makes note of Steve's muscles, his broad shoulders, his sports accomplishments). Carey plays Steve as extremely tongue-in-cheek; even though the bartender is clearly homophobic and tolerates Steve only because he's a tall, swarthy man who doesn't "camp it up" or bring his friends around, Steve hasn't exactly made his homosexuality a secret. In fact, he revels in Archie's shock and disbelief, as if his presumed heterosexuality crumbling before Archie's eyes is one of the funniest things to happen to him all day.

Notorious as "Judging Books" was, *All in the Family* didn't stop with one queer guest appearance. Beverly LaSalle (openly gay professional drag queen Lori Shannon) became the sitcom's first recurring queer character, appearing in a total of three episodes over seasons 6 through 8. In "Archie the Hero" (season 6, episode 4), Archie is introduced to Beverly by way of her passing out in the back of his cab. After Archie performs lifesaving CPR, she tracks him down at his home to thank him and reward him with a generous tip—and Archie is more than interested in something beyond the monetary from such a beautiful, elegant woman like Beverly. Unfortunately, his heroism and flirtatiousness are cut short when Beverly has to go to greatly impolite pains to communicate that she's not the woman Archie thinks she is, but rather a female impersonator,* ultimately tearing off her wig to Archie's befuddlement.

---

*   Beverly also refers to herself as a transvestite.

"Archie the Hero" expands the territory that "Judging Books" established. Beverly, like Steve before her, is more sophisticated than Archie by far, and her reveal of her "true" identity makes Archie (and Jean Stapleton as Archie's doting wife, Edith) into dopes. But rather than a wink and nod to the audience that Archie has once again been proven wrong right before the curtain closes, the last third of the episode follows Archie contending with the fallout his positive press might have now that his courageous rescue involves "those people." By then thoroughly clued in to the obtuseness and prejudice that pervades Archie's circle, Beverly convinces a nosy reporter that it was a truck driver who saved her life through CPR, not Archie, who merely pulled over to the curb to call for help. After she's successfully vanquished the reporter, Archie is forever grateful, shaking Beverly's hand with gusto and announcing, "I just wanted to say to you, Beverly, for a dame, you're one hell of a guy."[5] Beverly, of course, crushes Archie's handshake before waltzing out the door.

Some of the same hallmarks of pulling the rug out from under Archie carry over from Steve to Beverly, but even in her first appearance, Beverly has more screen time than Steve did and subsequently has the ability to affect Archie (and the audience) a little more. Now the focus isn't only on Archie's misconstrued and bigoted—though riotously funny, if the live studio audience is to be believed—worldview, but on the way even a relationship to someone else's queerness and gender deviancy can indict him in the eyes of his own pals and society at large. It's not as if any viewer would ever have a shadow of a doubt about Archie's proclivities or believe that Archie would ever have a hope of really understanding Beverly, but "Archie the Hero" is interesting because it goes beyond a singular punch line—something that is expanded the longer Beverly has the power and time to become a part of the Bunkers', and the audience's, world.

Though "Archie the Hero" is a marked increase in time and energy spent on a clearly queer character, an increase in episodes doesn't automatically equate to a suddenly equal authority. Much like her first appearance, in her second interaction with the Bunkers and their friends ("Beverly Rides Again"), it's very difficult to tell whether the audience is laughing at or with Beverly, especially as Archie makes Beverly wildly uncomfortable and even puts her in some danger. Each character either takes advantage of Beverly's generosity, looks down on her, or, like the mostly good-natured but utterly flappable Edith, just doesn't know what to make of her.

Edith's relationship to Beverly is highlighted most in Beverly's final appearance, "Edith's Crisis of Faith: Part I" (season 8, episode 13). By then, Beverly and Edith are shown to have a truly close and special relationship, though Edith still doesn't know how to refer to Beverly. It doesn't bother Beverly, though, who has come to visit and invites the Bunkers to her Carnegie Hall show. This designation adds a fun element to Beverly's character; not only is she a successful female impersonator, she must be at the top of her game as a performer. Carnegie Hall! After giving Edith a preview of her lushly draped and sequined costume, and Edith showing Beverly the photo album where she's saved every news clipping from Beverly's press, Beverly professes a deep familial love for Edith, who returns the sentiment with, "Oh Beverly, to me, you're like a sister. Uh, no, I mean brother. Oh, well, both rolled into one."[6]

Unfortunately, this—and a lighthearted prank they play on a still grumblingly homophobic Archie—is to be the end of their relationship. Beverly and Mike are jumped that night while Mike is accompanying Beverly to her ride, and Beverly passes away in the hospital from her injuries. Mike gets pretty roughed up, too, and confesses to a hysterical Gloria that Beverly saved his life by fending off a metal pipe meant for Mike's head. It's implied that the teenagers who mugged them likely became aware that Beverly was "different" and beat her far worse because of it. Beverly's death is a breaking point for Edith, who just hours earlier had argued with Archie over inviting Beverly to Christmas dinner. When Archie once again reflects his staunch separation from everything Beverly represents, Edith rebuffs him and his discomfort, delivering a line that practically rings as a clear moral center: "Archie, we're all God's children. God loves everybody, including Beverly, and He don't want nobody to be alone on Christmas."[*][7]

Crushingly, Edith's Christmas instead turns out to be the worst she's ever experienced, as continued in "Edith's Crisis of Faith: Part II." She's so devastated by Beverly's death that she refuses to go to Christmas Mass, can't stand to say grace, and sees her relationship with God crumble before her eyes. Jean Stapleton delivers an outstanding performance in the Christmas two-parter, grieving and nihilistic in a way so foreign to the openhearted and admittedly daft Edith that the usual levity of the sitcom can't lift her out of her depression and anger. Everyone except Mike has a difficult time understanding why Edith can't overcome Beverly's passing. Though Archie is given a few moments of uncharacteristic graciousness, he soon attempts to argue Edith out of her catatonia with a conclusion that "fags" either get killed or kill one another anyway. Edith refuses to accept that—it just fuels her disillusionment that her God would allow heinous, senseless violence against a sweet person like Beverly just for being "different."

While Edith is eventually pulled out of her mourning just in time for the last hours of Christmas, the bulk of the episode is devoted to her love for Beverly and the utter unfairness of Beverly's absence. Thanks to Beverly's charm, humor, and repeated visits, Edith's grief is believable and earned, and the audience is losing a guest who actually meant something to the heart of its principal characters. While depictions of violence toward and deaths of queer people would be a trend that *All in the Family* neither started nor ended, the magnitude of Beverly's death was highly unusual for the time. Beverly wasn't a thoughtlessly disposable character who came and went within the span of an episode; she had a photo album in the family's home and three sympathetic episodes in front of one of the largest prime-time audiences of the moment.

---

*   Edith's relationship to God is evocative of Norman Lear's own philosophizing; in a 2015 interview with *Variety*, Lear relayed, "We've become a culture or a nation that takes itself far too seriously. We believe we're God's chosen. Well, God's chosen is the entire human species and every other species."

Lear's Least Wanted

In the years between the success of "Judging Books by Covers" and
"Archie the Hero," another Norman Lear show brought not just one gay
recurring character, but a regular gay couple *and* a lesbian character,
alongside undocumented immigrants and sex workers, to sitcom audiences with the ambitiously raunchy *Hot l Baltimore* on ABC. Adapted
from the 1973 play *The Hot l Baltimore* by Lanford Wilson, the ensemble
sitcom took place in a rundown Maryland motel, with future stars like
James Cromwell, soap star Al Freeman Jr., and beloved character actors
Conchata Ferrell and Richard Masur among its staff and patrons. As
historian Steven Capsuto notes, in a cast of societally "unwanted" characters, fiftysomething white gays George (*Dynasty*'s Lee Bergere) and
Gordon (Henry Calvert) are the most stable, and lovingly snippy, romantic couple on the show, and when they break up in the series' fifth episode ("George and Gordon"), the entire hotel conspires to reunite them.[8]

Shockingly, this unusual representation of a committed, supported
gay relationship did not inspire appreciation in Christian morality
watchdog groups, who were coalescing around the same time to protest
any portrayals of deviant sexuality whatsoever. While they weren't yet
organized enough to singlehandedly sway the network (though they did
succeed in requiring a content warning label in front of every episode),
several local stations refused to air the series, and its middling viewership added up to a commercial failure for the network. ABC had
expected far more from a Lear production and canceled the show after
its first thirteen-episode season.

Another Lear series that was met with tepid ratings and mostly critical disdain was *All That Glitters* (1977), a syndicated satire that imagined
a world in which God created Eve first, and as such, women dominated
their environment, absorbing the social, economic, and chauvinist
qualities of men. The premise was absurd and too on the nose for male
critics, who despised the way they, through women, were being portrayed, and they subsequently advised audiences to skip this foray into
role-play.[9] Between the jokes about men being too delicate to drink beer

and women executives ogling young male secretaries' butts, the series includes the first, and one of glaringly few, regular trans characters on US television. Linda Murkland (played by future *Dallas* star Linda Gray) is a bright-eyed spokesmodel for the hyperfeminine "Wilmington Woman Ale" campaign who fears that outing herself may ruin her career prospects.

Unlike *All in the Family*, which is considered a breakthrough success to this day and is easily accessible through reruns, physical DVDs, and streaming services, *Hot l Baltimore* and *All That Glitters* have almost no viewable footprint beyond verbal acknowledgments of its gay couple or trans character that crop up in queer television think pieces. The series are largely scrubbed from the recesses of the internet except for a few eroded clips of its opening title, original theme music, and ABC promos popping up across YouTube. They are entirely unavailable for purchase, with *Hot l Baltimore*'s only tracked physical copies kept safe from physical damage in storage at the UCLA Library Film and Television Archive, and some *All That Glitters* episodes are archived by the Library of Congress. *Hot l Baltimore* is even bolder than *All in the Family* in its ensemble lineup of societal undesirables, and *All That Glitters* is a huge historical marker (a regularly appearing trans woman character! Who has a wedding at the end of the series!), but with their limited duration and disappearance from public access, it's difficult to bring new viewers to them for a tangible sense of connection or impact.

Unfortunately, this question of lasting impact and recognition isn't at all relegated to the semilost series of the 1970s. In 2022, the merging of many major media companies sounded the alarm not only for potential monopolies over production and unethical labor practices, but also for the shelving of projects that don't hit their new employers' profit margins (or their moral standards). Shows being canceled or going off the air isn't a new concept, but in the streaming age, one particular acquisition has led to a previously unheard of volume of slate-wiping that has canceled projects even after they fully completed the production of their ordered season and, even more confoundingly, has disappeared shows into the ether without a physical release or reason as to why they would be removed from the platform that produced them.

The 2022 formation of Warner Bros. Discovery (an acquisition that includes such landmark media brands as HBO, CNN, Turner Broadcasting's entire slate, and the Warner Bros. studio and catalog by Discovery, Inc.) has already shaken up the idea that a streaming catalog, once so promising in its endless access, is forever. According to Discovery, all "content" that doesn't perform well with the service's subscribers but has the potential for a partial tax write-off is up for removal.[10] It's too early to understand the full ramifications of a streaming service like HBO Max (renamed Max as of 2023) removing its own HBO and HBO Max Original titles from access (will they be shopped around to other networks and streaming platforms? Will they simply disappear?), but their lack of a physical release is, at the moment, an effective obsoletion of entire works.

The idea that only the most popular series will be given a chance to survive is a television history nightmare. One only needs to look at the inaccessibility of *Hot l Baltimore*, *All That Glitters*, *HeartBeat* (the first show to feature a regular lesbian character), and my premature gray hairs to understand the frustration of knowing about but being unable to watch shows that featured queer characters much earlier than quickly deteriorating cultural memory suggests. If we don't know what came before, how can we ask for better? If we can't see what came before, how long will its impact reverberate? If even series' creators can't access the work they put years into producing, how can we celebrate the art that *did* speak to previously untouched aspects of existing as a queer person?[*]

But enough about my mental breakdown. The next queer character to grace the small screen and actually make a dent in cultural memory did so in a show that *is* comparable to *All in the Family* in its undeniable

---

[*]   I'm not going to say explicitly that the answer is torrenting, but I'm not *not* going to say that the answer is torrenting a good queer show while you can. Who knows—you might save a cynical dyke TV historian's life one day.

influence on the succeeding landscape and its ability to be streamed or owned today. It's also one of the first examples of what can happen when a queer character sticks around long enough to actually have multiple storylines and develop a personality, for better or worse.

Before Jodie, After Jodie

Soap (1977–1981) is a cockeyed parody of daytime soap operas from one of the most prolific American television writers of her time, Susan Harris. Integral ensemble player Jodie Dallas (an affable Billy Crystal in one of his earliest breakout roles) is an even-keeled gay television director and son of lead Mary Campbell (Cathryn Damon), who laughs off the utterly bizarre antics of those soapy, overdramatic characters around him who never seem to know which way is up. Despite his calm and collected temperament against the background of the show's chaos and the intervention of entertainment-savvy gay activists, Jodie's seemingly stable sense of identity can't withstand the spaghetti *Soap*'s writers loved to chuck at the wall just to see if anything and everything could stick.*

In *Soap*'s first episodes, Jodie is introduced as a gay transvestite who considers a "sex-change operation" to continue his relationship with a closeted football player. This was the key issue gay advocacy groups like the National Gay Task Force (NGTF) protested: that Jodie's cross-dressing and serious consideration of transitioning conflated transvestism, transsexualism, and gay identity in a way that would further alienate cisgender gay men from acceptance into straight society. Though Harris was not exactly an outspoken advocate for transition, NGTF's advocacy stance hardly took transness seriously either.[†][11] If he

---

* Before *Soap*, the Norman Lear–produced *The Nancy Walker Show* also had a recurring gay character, Terry Folson (Ken Olfson), playing the bedraggled gay secretary and actor who just couldn't seem to catch a break.

† Harris was no stranger to television controversy, having previously written for *All in the Family* and penning *Maude*'s explosive abortion episode.

were to go down the path of hormone replacement therapy (the concept of which he cheerfully explains in the second episode), Jodie, like caricatures of gay men before him, would be far from a respectable vessel of representation for the upwardly mobile gay activist tired of being most commercially identified by stereotypes of effeminacy.

By the time *Soap* rolled around, network heads had already been quietly consulting with some of this brand of gay activist,* who had evolved from in-studio, organized "zaps" to continuing relationships with the executive suite. While NGTF and other organizations (some fabricated by members of the NGTF to increase their weight) threatened protests and demonstrations against ABC if Jodie were to remain the same swishy cross-dresser as had been threatened by the as-yet-unaired pilot, some protests were staved off by executives and producers meeting with NGTF representatives. As it turned out, they agreed to abandon Jodie's transition storyline and reassured these potential protestors that they would order a delicate handling of Jodie's character—minus the limp wrist.[12]

Members of NGTF, who were one of the few protesting groups to ask for changes to the script rather than outright cancellation on a basis of moral decency (think of the hapless soap opera–addicted children!), got what they asked for. After those first few episodes debuted to a rapt and sizable audience, Jodie scrapped his plan to regain his "latent heterosexual" boyfriend's affections through transition, instead remaining his kind, quick-witted gay self, and *Soap*'s derisive but lighthearted tone won over enough of the Nielsen pie that heftier protests from mostly Christian religious organizations didn't sway ABC. According to then ABC Entertainment president Lewis Erlicht, the show operated at a loss for all four of its seasons before its cancellation; the solidifying Religious

---

*   It is crucial to note that the degree to which network heads took activist groups seriously was wildly varied, especially in the years before they had a consistent national presence. Sometimes, a gay consultant could change an entire storyline. Often, consultants would work tirelessly only to have their efforts watered down to the barest change in the script and a network claiming their stamp of approval anyway—a practice that plagues consultants and sensitivity readers to this day.

Right claimed victory for reportedly warding away many sponsors, but ABC still, out of spite or pride or a love of Billy Crystal, gave viewers an integral gay character for seventy-seven episodes.[13]

Like Norman Lear's far zanier daytime soap spoof *Mary Hartman, Mary Hartman* before it, *Soap* was not particularly interested in producing realistic characters or scenarios, so it makes a certain kind of chagrined sense that an unequivocally out gay man could exist in a world where nothing is really supposed to be taken at face value.* Nonetheless, for a time, Jodie existed in this teetering environment with more gumption and good humor than almost anyone around him (aside from wisecracking butler Benson), forming the everyday homo archetype for which audiences still clamor and which some credit the much later *Will & Grace* with normalizing. As the friendly neighborhood gay, he spends many an episode calmly explaining his identity to the newest off-kilter dope who has never met a "home-o-sexual," before cracking a joke for himself and the audience that sails over his ignorant scene partners' heads. When discussing shows that made an impact on him as a young viewer, Stephen Tropiano specifically points to Jodie's groundedness: "He in some ways was the most normal person, in this cast of crazy characters, and I liked that. I liked the idea that you could be sort of the normalizer in a family of absurdities."[14]

Of course, living as a proverbial straight man in a crooked world doesn't guarantee a gay character happiness, and living on a soap spoof meant everyone had their manic ups and rock-bottom downs. Even though Jodie was a bright and seemingly grounded character, confusion, panic, and suicidal ideation make appearances, though Jodie's depression does lead to his making friends with another queer character and forming their own little refuge for a short time. He also tumbles through a number of questions of faith, as it were, becoming a parent after an ill-fated one-night stand, getting embroiled in a nasty custody

---

*   *Mary Hartman, Mary Hartman* closely followed *Hot l Baltimore* in its inclusion of two suspicious neighbor characters who happened to not be all that malicious at all—they were just a gay couple!

battle, and attempting to impulsively commit to women even though he, and everyone around him, knows he's as gay as the day is long. But, as Tropiano again notes, Jodie doesn't get walked over. He fights. The bottom line is that *Soap*'s writers put him through the wringer just as much as any other character. Jodie is able to stick around long enough to become an old Jewish man by way of botched hypnotherapy, and in the *Soap*-verse, that's just how the writers tell you they love you.

In the AJ (After Jodie) period, network television made room for guest appearances of gay male characters, often, though not always, using regular characters' ignorance for an occasional lesson around the treatment of gay people under law and common human empathy. A number of recurring and even regular and lead gay and bisexual male characters would make a splash on prime time between *Soap* and the oft-cited *Will & Grace*, but they were contending with an increasingly virulent presence from the morality police. Given a face by Anita Bryant and a voice by dozens of outraged televangelists, including Reverend Jerry Falwell and Reverend Donald Wildmon and his watchdog group Coalition for Better Television, the Religious Right was well on its way to cementing homophobia and anti-abortion activism as its main "decency and morality" calling cards. As networks navigated between rising conservatism and vocal opposition to even the mention of homosexuality, an incoming Ronald Reagan presidency, and increasingly organized gay civil rights groups, they presented gay characters so gingerly that one sometimes wondered if they were really gay at all.

Among the most notable were *Love, Sidney* (1981–1983), the NBC sitcom adaptation and continuation of the made-for-television movie *Sidney Shorr: A Girl's Best Friend*. *The Odd Couple*'s Tony Randall plays a lonely perpetual bachelor who adopts an actress and her young daughter into a makeshift family, and he *could* have been the center of the United States' first gay sitcom . . . if NBC hadn't decided to remove the word "homosexual" from the series, making Sidney Shorr the first officially and perpetually closeted lead of a sitcom. On the delightfully conniving prime-time wealth-porn soap *Dynasty* (1981–1989), Steven

Carrington (Al Corley, then Jack Coleman) was the gay or bisexual (definition dependent on whether one asked mega-producer Aaron Spelling or actually watched Steven's episodes) son of oil tycoon Blake Carrington (John Forsythe).* And finally, in 1984, premium cable took a stab at an openly gay lead character with *Brothers* (1984–1989), a sitcom about three brothers adjusting to a new normal when one of them comes out of the closet.

Brothers had been rejected by NBC and ABC before landing at Showtime, who approached creative team Greg Antonacci, Gary Nardino, and de facto showrunner David Lloyd (a veteran of *The Mary Tyler Moore Show*, *The Bob Newhart Show*, *Taxi*, and *Cheers* at the time) with their new mission to host programming of which network television would predictably steer clear. Thus began the tradition of cable, like Norman Lear's first-run syndicated series before it, adding homosexuality to its methods of distinguishing itself, outpacing network's comparatively strict and fearful adherence to standards and practices and the threat of losing its sponsors. At least, that's what *Brothers* was at first.

The pilot, "The Wedding," saw handsome youngest brother Cliff (Paul Regina) leave his bride-to-be at the altar and come out to his macho older brothers with the help of his new ticket to all things gay, Donald (Philip Charles MacKenzie). While his brothers react with disbelief and threats of violence at first, by the end of the episode middle brother Joe (Robert Walden) reverts to the heterosexual protagonist of "very special episodes" of years prior, reassuring Cliff that they'll always be brothers. Joe is apparently so evolved that, by the second episode, he's able to pretend to be gay in order to reassure one of his closeted pro football buddies Bubba (James Avery, who would find fame as Uncle Phil on *The*

---

* With *Dynasty* being a ratings smash, Steven Carrington is likely the best-remembered gay male character of the eighties, even if he himself was shuffled between gay and straight by the writers and was shown caressing and kissing his wives (plural!) far more often than he shared a tender physical moment with any of his male love interests, which, thanks to ABC's Broadcast Standards and Practices department, was never.

Fresh Prince of Bel-Air) that he's not alone in the world. Bubba confesses that, as a Black gay man (a demographic often relegated to a guest spot as white gay men had been in years prior), he was always afraid that that was all a tabloid reporter might see him for. Bubba reappears in later seasons for *Brothers'* attempts at commenting on the HIV/AIDS epidemic, with Joe standing in for the average American viewer who needed their fears quelled.

In many ways, *Brothers* is a prototype for *Will & Grace*, combining the "average" heterosexual viewer's viewpoint with the trepidation of a regular-degular gay man who's just like you but gay, and placing him opposite the flamboyance of a gay man who loves himself to spite his critics. Cliff and Donald are a template for Will and Jack a decade later, with Cliff often feeling embarrassed by Donald's faggotry, even as Cliff is hopelessly lost in the gay world without his guiding queen. The audience sees queerness through Joe's or Cliff's eyes, often as a scared, deeply insecure, and femmephobic gay man who distinguishes himself by not liking musicals or arts and by having been brought up in a man's world. Donald, effortlessly entertaining, witty, and secure, takes pleasure in rebuffing the ignorance and stupidity of the fragile straight, or formerly straight, men around him, a callback to Jodie, or even Beverly LaSalle's delight in pulling Archie Bunker's leg (and indeed, eldest brother Lou is exactly the Archie Bunker type). The specifically gay storylines that *Brothers* followed in its first seasons, introducing its characters to Donald's world, were tapered off in later seasons, perhaps in order to attempt easier syndication, but it had already proven too difficult to sell to most major markets. No matter—it had still made its mark as Showtime's most popular program to date.

Let's Hear It for the Girls

Though they appeared in guest arcs and brief mentions, white lesbian characters had not become quite as popular as recurring or regular characters as white gay male characters had, and bisexual women even less so. Short-lived and impossible-to-find CBS prime-time soap *Executive*

Suite (1976) had a proportionally short arc for two lesbian characters, one a guest and one a recurring character. Even in their brief time on this plane of televised existence, furtive couple Julie Solkin (Geraldine Brooks) and Leona Galt (Patricia Smith) managed to make their definitive impression on the lesbian canon. After an abused Julie confesses her love to the married Leona, Leona runs away! Julie follows her into the street and is promptly hit by a car and dies. Long live the lesbian death cult!

Another notable lesbian character appearance is that of capable psychiatrist Dr. Lynn Carson (Donna Pescow) in a four-episode guest arc on the legendarily long-running daytime soap opera *All My Children* (1970–2011). Despite gay characters making appearances on soap spoofs prior, Dr. Carson was the first openly gay or lesbian recurring character to appear on the real thing. Dr. Carson's orientation is depicted as more or less a nonissue within the world of the show; the bigger problem is that her patient, divorcée Devon McFadden (Tricia Pursley), starts to develop unrequited feelings for Carson. While Carson's arc was short, Pescow's appearance on such a ratings giant garnered noticeable attention—both nervous attention from ABC and messages of gratitude from fans of the series. As Pescow recounted in 2021 to *Entertainment Weekly*, "The thing I remember most were the fan letters. They were so extraordinary and would make me cry. People finally felt like there was a representation that fit."[15]

The first regular lesbian character on television arrived far later than Jodie's turn on *Soap*, and even four years after *Brothers* had premiered on Showtime. *HeartBeat* (1988–1989), writer Sara Davidson's women-led ensemble drama about a group of friends who set out to establish their own private practice outside the misogynistic barriers of the medical field, couldn't quite strike a consistent tone before floundering and disappearing after its second season, but its treatment of its lesbian protagonist is notable for its successes and failures. While nurse Marilyn McGrath (Gail Strickland) is a self-possessed, compassionate, and likable character whose sexuality has no bearing on the way her colleagues approach her within the script, ABC's discomfort with her sexuality was in direct opposition to *HeartBeat*'s attempt to assimilate her, like any of its otherwise marginalized characters, into its ensemble.

Marilyn is not the only queer woman on the series; she's in a long-term, committed relationship with her partner Patty (Gina Hecht), who appears in five of the series' eighteen episodes. In the first season's two-part finale, Marilyn and Patty are shown to be a real, lived-in couple with a good rapport. Unfortunately, "To Heal a Doctor" and "The Wedding" (hey, are we sensing a gay marriage panic theme here?) finds Marilyn and Patty in a crisis that they have little hope of controlling. It's Marilyn's daughter's wedding and, hurting from her perception of how Marilyn abandoned her when she and her ex-husband got divorced, Allison (Hallie Todd) doesn't want her mom to bring Patty along. Patty is understanding and soothing and even argues against Marilyn's guilt and impatience.

In their spacious, bright kitchen, Patty watches Marilyn fret about the unfairness of attending without Patty, emphasizing that "it's acting as though I'm ashamed of you, and I won't do that."[16] They've been bustling about the kitchen, conducting their argument over burning cake and trading garlic, grabbing oven mitts, and doing dishes, building tension until Patty leans against the kitchen counter opposite from Marilyn to make sure her partner can hear her.

PATTY

Marilyn, this is the first chance you've had to heal things with your daughter. It's a golden moment that may not come again. Be a little patient.

It's an emotional, well-delivered line that calls for a kiss, a tender handhold. Instead, Marilyn puts down her trivets, rounds the counter, and gives Patty an extremely standoffish hug from behind, positioning her body about as far away from Patty's as she can while still touching her.

ABC censors did not allow Marilyn and Patty to touch the way any of the other couples on *HeartBeat* did, and in doing so, the network created an obvious, unfulfilled vacuum where physical affection should be. Marilyn and Patty's relationship is so obviously wrong for television, not because of its writing or because of its obvious subversiveness (they're two white, feminine women living as each other's domestic partners), but because the very show that debuted them wasn't allowed to fully invest in the believability of their everyday touch. That absence was more glaring than holding hands would have been.

A Different Leading Man

Though there was a chunk of the eighties in which regular gay characters all but disappeared from the airwaves as homophobia-driven AIDS panic rose, by the end of the decade, it was no longer shocking to see a gay or lesbian character on television, with guest and recurring characters being somewhat commonplace. Regular characters were almost exclusively white gay men with one nurse practitioner exception, and you could count lead roles on one hand. You could then put that hand in an oven mitt and refuse to touch your partner with it. But even before *Brothers* and before the series protagonists and queer-themed series that would arrive in the 1990s and 2000s, made-for-television movies provided some queer characters with extended chances at playing the lead.

Though not broadcast in the United States, it would feel like an omission to exclude one of the earliest gay dramas broadcast on television in the UK, especially because it was based on a play by an American. *South*, adapted from the play *Sud* by Julien Green, was broadcast on ITV's *Play of the Week* program in 1959 to mixed praise and controversy based entirely on its subject matter. The understated production was directed by openly gay Canadian Mario Prizek, who brought the plantation period drama to life with the help of flamboyant and semi-out actor Peter Wyngarde in the lead role of exiled Polish officer Lieutenant Jan Wicziewsky.

Wicziewsky is initially just a casual observer of the Americans around him as he visits a wealthy family's Deep South plantation prior to the outbreak of the American Civil War. Over the course of the production, Wicziewsky devolves from an arrogant, unflappable presence to a lovestruck, tortured soul, thrown for a loop by the arrival of American Adonis Eric MacClure (Graydon Gould). Reserved as the drama is, Wyngarde imbues his character with an obvious, enthralling desire, confessing his love for Eric in everything but the word. Though ITV would not permit the producers to use the word "homosexual" explicitly, thanks to euphemistic writing, the intensity of Wyngarde's gaze and presence, and some very clever blocking that managed to put the lead actors in a number of compromising positions without technically pushing any censor buttons, the drama was absolutely clear and a heartbreaking love story.[17]

The most frequently referenced early gay television movie to have been broadcast on US airwaves is likely *That Certain Summer*, which aired as a 1972 *ABC Movie of the Week*. Directed by Lamont Johnson, the film told the story of divorced contractor Doug (Hal Holbrook), whose teenage son is coming to San Francisco to visit his dad and, unbeknownst to him, his dad's life partner, Gary (Martin Sheen). Much like the character that Jodie would become, the pair represents a purposefully sanitized, upper-middle-class white gay couple that was meant to evoke understanding and cautious sympathy toward a sexual class usually portrayed as effeminate and disruptive to traditional notions of fatherhood and family. Holbrook, who, in 2019, explained he was attracted to the project because of "the principle of fair play, honesty, decency," represents much of the ethos that went into its production and the reception that garnered the film critical acclaim and an Emmy.[18]

As with *Sud*, *That Certain Summer* was met with restrictions and revisions from its network around physical touch. Where *Sud* was burning with desire and its description of gay love as a sin was imbued with homoeroticism, *That Certain Summer* was miserable, describing homosexuality as a possible sickness at the behest of ABC. Reflecting on the film, Steven Capsuto characterizes the final scene—in which Doug weeps over the rejection of his son and Gary is censored from physically comforting him for the ease of the mass audience—as both cruel and nonsensical: "Imagine if a TV movie presented the same scenario with a straight husband and wife who never seemed to touch each other, even at a time of such great emotional pain. What conclusions would viewers rightly draw about the health, lovingness, and value of that marriage?"[19] This conversation recalls the heartbreak of *HeartBeat*—not so much a diegetic tragedy, but an indignation that strains the believability of the relationship.

The next notable made-for-television film, *The War Widow* (1976), was constrained to a certain threshold of allowable outright sexual language and touch, but like *Sud*, it leaned into the stifling tension of that and distanced itself from a narrative like *That Certain Summer* in almost every way, especially when it came to valuing nuclear family and propriety over freedom. Initially produced for Los Angeles PBS affiliate KCET's *Visions* series, and broadcast nationally with a disclaimer that it was funded by grant money rather than public funds, gay playwright Harvey Perr and director Paul Bogart (whose credits include the landmark gay film *Torch Song Trilogy* [1988] and a whopping ninety-seven episodes of *All in the Family*) created a sumptuously designed, carefully staged period piece of quiet despair being met by determination, in which upper-class, depressed, and harried mother Amy (Pamela Bellwood) is brought back to her senses by bold portraitist Jenny (Frances Lee McCain). Invited to write for a playwright-to-TV-writer program designed by TV pioneer Barbara Schultz, Perr penned the script while just out of the throes of the dissolution of his own marriage and temporary estrangement from his daughter, transplanting his coming out onto the pages of an aesthetically softer world.[20]

The War Widow is astounding for a number of reasons—not the least being that it devoted an hour and twenty minutes to portraying queer women in an unshadowed, admiring light. The film included more displays of queer desire than almost anything on television before it as well as for a period after, and it paired shining, vulnerable performances with wholly romantic dialogue like "This is my life I'm risking. This is my life I'm offering." Amy and Jenny share poetic, sincere conversations, and touch in dozens of forms—stroking each other's hands, arms, and shoulders; cupping each other's heads; drawing each other close while dancing and whirling about the room. Further, Amy and Jenny aren't isolated in their queerness. In one scene, Jenny brings Amy to an afternoon tea with two delightfully chatty older women who are novelists, artists, and, as they reveal in a sparkling moment praising each other's work, lovers. Overall, it's the kind of period piece that one could imagine seeing green-lit today, hopefully with a much larger budget.

The very next year, ABC aired the Golden Globe–nominated legal family drama *A Question of Love*, starring respected actors Gena Rowlands and Jane Alexander as a forcibly outed, working-class lesbian couple fighting for custody of divorcée Linda Ray's (Rowlands) youngest son. Based on a real case that was brought to ABC's attention by NGTF member Ginny Vida, the film moves beyond an after-school special in large part due to the unbelievable caliber of its performers, but it's also sensitive, realistic, and largely optimistic about the care Linda Ray and Barbara (Alexander) sustain for each other during their fraught public trial against Linda's ex-husband. While the language and attitudes of their families, colleagues, and neighbors are expectedly blunt, the film is a compelling and genuine love story, albeit one in which the ABC standards and practices board struck again, changing a kiss on the hand between Rowlands and Alexander into holding a hand against a cheek.

Most other landmark television movies that followed, including the Glenn Close–starring *Serving in Silence: The Margarethe Cammermeyer Story* (1995) and the Mario Lopez–starring *Breaking the Surface: The Greg Louganis Story* (1997), came out after queer characters had secured some sort of leading role in a series, but portrayals of bisexual and trans characters were more difficult to find than their gay and lesbian counterparts. In 1986, two made-for-television movies would air opposite each other: *My Two Loves* on ABC and *Second Serve* on CBS.

The former took up a familiar fascination with family dynamics and queer parents, but this time with a bisexual widow being pursued by two suitors, a woman (played by Lynn Redgrave) and a man, as her daughter disapproves of both. *Second Serve* was the biographical story of Renée Richards (played by Vanessa Redgrave), a trans woman and tennis pro, adapted from Richards's own memoir. All in all, 1986 was a fruitful year for one demographic in particular: the Redgraves.

Will & Grace (and Ellen, Too)

Between 1989 and 1997, when *Ellen's* by-now legendary "The Puppy Episode" aired on ABC, there were many watershed moments for queer representation. In 1989, *thirtysomething* (1987–1991) showed two gay men next to each other in bed, which reportedly lost ABC over $1 million in pulled advertising. In 1990, *21 Jump Street* (1987–1991) inadvertently introduced the "lesbian kiss episode," in which a queer woman and straight woman would lock lips, only for one of the women to never appear again. In 1991, rare bisexual regular character C. J. Lamb (Amanda Donohoe) would perpetrate a second lesbian kiss episode on *L.A. Law* (1986–1994), driving home the point that lesbian kisses existed for sweeps week. In 1993, Armistead Maupin's *Tales of the City* would drive PBS's highest ratings ever before subsequently getting pulled out of the United States altogether. In 1994, Wilson Cruz's portrayal of Rickie Vasquez on *My So-Called Life* would spark an awakening for queer kids of color who had never seen more than a hint of their reflection onscreen.

By the late nineties, the biggest shows on television—*Melrose Place*; *Friends*; *Seinfeld*; *Roseanne*; *NYPD Blue*; *ER*; *Mad About You*; *Sisters*; *The Golden Girls*; *Picket Fences*; *Spin City*; *Star Trek*; *The Simpsons*; *Cybill*; *In Living Color*; *Beverly Hills, 90210*; and more—featured recurring or regular queer characters. They hosted gay weddings, pregnancies, families, friends, trans aliens, and blatant transphobia, with a hefty helping of "not that there's anything wrong with it!" jokes to remind everyone that queerness may have been in vogue, but it still wasn't natural. This was the gay nineties.

None of these characters or shows represented abject failure and unexpected, mind-blowing success the way that *Ellen* and *Will & Grace* did, at *almost* the exact same time.

In April 1997, after at least a full year of negotiations with ABC and Disney, months of rabid media anticipation, and years of being semi-closeted in the public eye, Ellen DeGeneres's goofy onscreen persona, Ellen Morgan, leaned across an airport podium to Susan (Laura Dern) and became the first openly gay lead character in a prime-time series and the first openly gay actor to play a gay character on any American network comedy or drama. The episode would be viewed by forty-two million people and win a Peabody and an Emmy. The next season, heavily undermarketed and slapped with parental warnings despite its extremely tame lesbian humor, would be *Ellen*'s last. Ellen DeGeneres would find her career briefly paused, and Laura Dern would lose work and need to hire a security detail.[21]

In September 1998, just two months after *Ellen*'s final episode, a sitcom about a gay man and a straight woman, a classic combination since before the man could come out, premiered to modest ratings on NBC. Along came their pals, another gay man and a somewhat straight woman, as perfect foils to their starring counterparts. *Ellen*'s so-called curse was knocked straight out of the water—at least for gay men. *Will & Grace* made history for its title alone—no other out gay man had ever been a titular character on a network series (sorry again, Sidney).

Looking back, all the pieces were there to slowly put Will Truman together over decades. With Max Mutchnick and David Kohan's proudly politically incorrect, lighthearted, snappy scripts, veteran director James Burrows's (*Cheers*, *Friends*) watchful eye, and two odd couples with sparkling chemistry, it seemed that it was a perfect, tried-and-true recipe that hit at just the right time.

Will & Grace has been credited with changing then vice president Joe Biden's mind about gay marriage.[22] In a 2015 poll, Ellen DeGeneres was the top result as the celebrity who most influenced the American populace's opinion on gay marriage.[23] If I were a politician, I would also probably go back in the closet and then say *Modern Family* or *The Fosters* really taught me to think about the "LGBT" community in a whole new light. They're just like us! But for queer television, *Ellen* and *Will & Grace* aren't anywhere near the be-all and end-all. They're the culmination of a very specific lineage of queer characters, mostly written for straight people in majority straight series, with some gay input, to be palatable for as many viewers as possible. They're approachable, silly, welcoming, cis, and white, and they're finally, completely out enough to lead their own shows. But in the end, they're just an ordinary guy. For *Will & Grace*, that struck gold. For *Ellen*, with no thanks to her quickly bailing network, which fought her every step of the way and blamed her for making the show too gay, that struck lead.

After *Ellen*: The Beginning of the Queer Series

Enough has been written about both *Ellen* and *Will & Grace* that I don't have much more to add to that particular conversation—as a queer person or as a TV enthusiast. There's no debate that they've both left a mark. However, when you get to the demise of *Ellen* and the roaring success of *Will & Grace*, you also get to a timeline where queerness has now been used, even briefly, as its own hook. While prime-time network television would try to replicate the magic, widely approachable, and just gay enough combination that *Will & Grace* perfected, premium cable and narrowcast channels with specific age demographics in mind had started to agree: they didn't need to appeal to *everyone*; they just needed to retain a smaller portion of loyal, satisfied customers.

With that agreement, new types of queerness were able to make it to the screen. There were an increasing number of queer characters on networks aimed toward teens, with the WB picking up fare like *Buffy the Vampire Slayer*, *Dawson's Creek*, and Ryan Murphy's first show, *Popular*. There were difficult, messy queer shows aimed at more mature audiences, with characters that thrived when an audience couldn't always feel safe around them. As soon as they got revved up, it seemed like

HBO and Showtime were competing to see who could lay claim to the most layered, implacable, and maybe even unlikable queer character.

Even before *Ellen* fell, HBO had been experimenting with lesbian made-for-TV movies, and then in 1997 it launched its first one-hour original drama, *Oz* (1997–2003), a gruesome, violent look inside a fictional experimental men's prison unit that would take queer romance and psychological power struggles to twisted new heights and depressing nadirs. In 2000, Showtime launched their US reboot of the 1999 UK series *Queer as Folk* (2000–2005), depicting a sex-, drugs-, and more sex–fueled version of Pittsburgh that would have made the Philly-based characters of *Brothers* blush. HBO came back with some of the greatest shows and characters of all time with *The Wire* (2002–2008) and *Six Feet Under* (2001–2005). In 2004, Showtime, having bided its time in anticipation of the moment when, post-*Ellen* trepidation, lesbians could finally make their triumphant return to television, unleashed *The L Word* (2004–2009) on our poor unsuspecting souls. Finally, in 2005, Logo TV launched as a specifically LGBT basic cable channel, kicking off its reign with Patrik-Ian Polk's dramedy centering four Black gay friends, *Noah's Arc* (2005–2006).

While Logo turned out to be a disappointment, canceling the fabulously received *Noah's Arc* after two short seasons and shifting away from LGBT programming in 2012 in favor of mostly playing sitcom reruns and the occasional gay-themed dating show, network television was coming back around to gay viewing for the entire family. *Glee* on Fox and *Modern Family* (2009–2020) on ABC both debuted in the same year with multiple gay characters, quickly becoming ratings giants, with the former doing irreparable damage to high schoolers' music tastes.

In 2013, Netflix began its landscape-altering dips into original programming with a bang, with *Orange Is the New Black* (2013–2019) introducing the biggest cast of queer women characters since *The L Word* had gone off the air. Amazon Prime Video followed in 2014, releasing the game-changing but troubled *Transparent* (2014–2019). Both *Orange Is the New Black* and *Transparent* amplified conversations about trans representation and casting that had been circulating but gone largely ignored for years, but no more. In 2018, FX debuted ballroom drama and 1980s period piece *Pose* (2018–2021) with five trans women of color series regulars. And those are just the obvious landmarks!

Today, a queer series regular or recurring character is rarely treading new ground solely from their inclusion. With queer characters now presumably far freer than their one-to-three-episode guest star ancestors, the sky should be the limit. In some ways, queer characters—and, remarkably, queer series—have blasted into outer space, exploring far beyond the bounds of mere existence as a form of positive representation. But in the two decades since "The Puppy Episode" proved that even neutered queer characters are sometimes too much, there can still be hesitation around pushing the envelope and fear that a queer character who burns too brightly just won't last.

Queer & A: Jamie Babbit

Credits: *But I'm A Cheerleader, Itty Bitty Titty Committee, Popular, Nip/Tuck, The L Word, Drop Dead Diva, Brooklyn Nine-Nine, A League of Their Own,* **and many, many more**

Jamie Babbit is as inextricable from the contemporary queer television landscape as one director can get. Babbit first rose to the attention of queer audiences with the debut of her candy-coated, piercingly funny feature narrative *But I'm a Cheerleader* (1999), and like other independent queer filmmakers of the eighties and nineties, including Rose Troche, Guinevere Turner, Angela Robinson, Donna Deitch, Kimberly Peirce, Nisha Ganatra, and more, she soon found a home in television.

Babbit's résumé as a director is enormously long-running, crisscrossing through an impressive chunk of the series written about in this tome, as well as hugely successful series like *Girls, Nip/Tuck, Gossip Girl, Gilmore Girls, Alias, United States of Tara, It's Always Sunny in Philadelphia,* and so many more. Being able to interview her was like approaching someone with the keys to the queer TV kingdom, especially because one of Babbit's latest projects, the television adaptation of *A League of Their Own*, had just swept through queer viewers like a particularly welcome D'Arcy Carden–shaped wildfire. I was able to speak with Babbit about her own driving desire to work on any queer script that was sent her away, the importance of seeing queer possibility before you yourself can imagine it, and how she's continued to navigate the responsibilities of telling queer stories for queer audiences who aren't always receptive. This is an edited excerpt of our conversation.

SHAYNA MACI WARNER: Do you remember the first queer character you saw on TV, whether they were expressly queer or just coded?

JAMIE BABBIT: I think the first queer character that I remember on TV was definitely not overtly queer, but it was Jo on *The Facts of Life*. I certainly remember movie people like Kristy McNichol, who I always loved. And Barbara Stanwyck in *The Big Valley*.

SMW: When you were first moving into directing for TV, was the personal importance of queer representation something you were actively thinking about?

JB: I came to storytelling as a gay person who always wants to tell gay stories. My parents were really political when I was growing up, and I always thought if I got into any kind of storytelling, whether it was theater directing or movie directing or TV directing, that I wanted to tell gay stories and feminist stories. That's literally my reason for getting into the business. So any time queer content comes in front of me, I always say yes to directing it. It's my interest. It's what I like, it's what I know about, and it's what I care about so, yes, 100 percent.

SMW: One of your first big projects after *But I'm a Cheerleader* was *Popular*, Ryan Murphy's first show. Your credits are full of what we now know as huge queer shows—*The L Word* and *Looking*, to name just a couple. When you were making these shows, did you and your fellow queer filmmakers have the mindset that these were going to be landmark queer shows, or were they just another job?

JB: One thousand percent, on every one of those shows. We were a bunch of gay people making gay content, and we were really excited. We knew it was groundbreaking and important, and we cared a lot about gay representation. We wanted to tell stories that felt accurate for our community that we weren't seeing on TV. Certainly Ryan Murphy did. *Popular* was his and my first TV show. We got a lot of pressure from the network to cut a lot of stuff, but Ryan was very who he is and fought back, and I was fighting as well. We were able to push forward, getting things on TV that have never been on TV before. Especially for young people, because *Popular* was a show for young people.

I had started with *But I'm a Cheerleader*, which I also thought was like a G-rated movie. In my opinion, it was a teen movie for kids. When I got an NC-17 as its first rating, I realized the culture was way behind, so I just thought what a great thing if we could get some of this stuff on TV for kids. I knew with *But I'm a Cheerleader* people would steal the DVD and pass it around to their friends. But TV is a more direct venue to get to young people and bypass parental control, which, when you're a gay kid in the middle of nowhere without a lot of gay role models, that stuff is so important. It was really important to me.

For *Looking*, we really wanted to make a gay show that was about gay people in San Francisco, like right now, and starring gay actors. [*Looking* executive producer and lead writer/director] Andrew Haigh, who had directed so many great gay features, really wanted to talk about gay intimacy and living in the time of PrEP, and exactly what was going on in San Francisco with the tech bubble; otters and bears and all kinds of stuff that wasn't really talked about in shows like *Queer as Folk*. It was the first HBO gay show, so we were really proud of that and wanted to do right by the community with that. We had a full gay group of out writers and directors and actors, so it was a big leap forward for the community, in my opinion.

And then *The L Word* was always revolutionary. We never had lesbian sex on TV, written, directed, and acted with real lesbians. We got to define ourselves and have it be by women, about women, for women. Every single time I made any one of these shows it was a really big deal and we fought really hard to get things on television that had never been allowed before. Certainly my most recent show, *A League of Their Own* on Amazon, that is [adapted from] a film very beloved by the queer community. It's such a closeted movie, so we really wanted to overtly talk about all the stuff we wish had been in the original. I love the original movie so much, so this was just an exploration of the real gay lives of a lot of players.

SMW: Could you tell me a little bit more about the conversations that you were having when you were fighting to get things onscreen? Are there examples that stick out in your mind, conversations between you and an executive who is trying to dull something down a little bit, make it a little more sanitized for TV?

JB: Honestly, it's happened every single time. *Popular* had an episode about Lily [Esposito, played by Tamara Mello] and her lesbian relationship, and they told us we had to cut away before they actually kissed. We weren't allowed to see the actual kiss onscreen in that because *they had a young audience and it was the WB, people are uncomfortable and think that we were going to get canceled. Advertisers are going to drop, blah blah blah*—so, we just ended up trimming it down. We kept fighting to at least keep part of it, but we ended up having to cut the actual kiss out.

For *The L Word*, the studio was very onboard for all the sexuality, which was great. I think our biggest struggle was casting queer actors who were out. Basically, saying to the network that it is important to actually cast gay people and not just beautiful women who are palatable for the straight audience. We really wanted them to have authenticity and prioritized gay or bisexual or trans actors. Sometimes they were less experienced than other actors, who were really strong actors, but for example, butchy lesbian [actors] can't get agents, so they don't work as much, so they're not as experienced. You have to break the barrier of entry and actually give people a chance. We fought really hard on *The L Word* to be able to cast people who were less experienced than others because they were actually in the community.

On *A League of Their Own*, we had a lot of fight back from the sect of women ballplayers. There's only around fifty left, who are in their nineties, and I think there was a lot of reticence [around coming out] from the players who are alive. Certainly, the straight players didn't want to ever acknowledge the gay players. But the truth is there's also a lot of closeted ninety-year-old players in the league, too, who were nervous about coming out because they hid their whole lives and if they had come out when they were in the baseball league they would have been arrested. They would have been in mental institutions, lost their jobs, lost their kids. There were really serious consequences.

Thankfully, [original All-American Girls Professional Baseball League player] Maybelle Blair did come out at the premiere of the show. She's one of many, but the only out [player] I know of. Everyone's in charge of coming out on their own: we would never out anybody, but it's complicated because you're telling the story of the league and the queerness of it. We want people to know it's real; it's not a fantasy that we're making up. We certainly did our research, but I think there's still a contingent of players who are uncomfortable with that message being out there. It's tough to navigate because I don't want to alienate any of the players, but at the same time it's a new era, and I do think it's okay to be honest about what was going on. Especially today it's nice for players to know they're not the first gay baseball players out there, you know? They did exist.

Every single project has had its complications. Some of it is within the community; some of it is fighting to get the community to be accepted by outsiders. But it's complicated out there. I've pretty much fought every fight that there is. Convincing actors to come out, getting networks to let us tell stories, to have the confidence that though something doesn't test well technically, the whole point of television is to push the culture forward. You don't test to see if people are bigoted; you have the confidence and bravery to push people into empathy so that laws change. The whole point of storytelling is to have people watch a story and feel empathic for characters who aren't them, and then to actually give a shit about them and think, "Wow, maybe they should have rights?" I feel like storytelling can change everything. It is very important, and it's also been a struggle every single time.

SMW: From the viewing perspective, you can definitely see markers of change, which are pretty rapid and can be impressive. On

the maker side, have you noticed changes or trends in the kinds of stories you're being asked to sign on to as your career has progressed?

JB: Most of the stuff you get offered is definitely not gay. It's still few and far between that gay projects come along, and I definitely say yes to every single one that is offered to me. There are a lot of straight [shows] that I don't do because I'd rather do gay content. I wish it were a waterfall of gay stories; I do think it's better, but there's a long way to go. It's funny, I have so many co-conspirators on this path, a lot of whom are from a younger generation, who'll still say, "Oh, I have this great idea for a gay show! Do you want to direct it? Let's try to get it made." And I'll be like, "Yeah, sure," and then we try to sell and then they go, "God, why did everyone say no?" It's heartbreaking, and it's happened to me so many times. It doesn't mean I don't keep trying, but it's still pretty rough out there.

You look at networks like Netflix, or Amazon, or HBO Max, and there's definitely gay content, but I've pitched a lot of shows that I think are super commercial that people would really want to see and have gotten resounding nos over and over again for a lot of them. That's why I get so excited when something actually gets through. I will say there are a lot more shows, including the one I'm working on right now, where there's a gay character, but the main thrust is a straight romance. That has gotten a lot better.

SMW: Can you talk a little bit about the difference between working on something that's a gay show and working on something that has a gay character, gay theme, or gay episode?

JB: Of course I'd prefer to work on a gay show, but I'm not the one who works for the network. I don't buy shows. I'm the one who's trying to get people to buy them. I think in [network] minds, gay shows have a target audience of gay people. For them, the good thing about *The L Word* is that they were also targeting dudes; late-night Skinemax people. They were like, "Sure, lesbians can make the show and star in the show, but make sure they have a ton of sex and make sure at least some of them are hot." I mean, it gave us more freedom. And as someone who's more of a femme, I'm not offended for having femmes on a show, but getting legitimate lesbian butches was tougher. I think Showtime was excited about having it be a show that married couples and dudes could watch. So when we were like, here's this very masc-presenting woman, they were like, "Really? Where's more girls like Jennifer Beals?" I love Jennifer Beals, she's awesome, but there are different types of lesbians.

As far as shows with one gay character, in a network world, they think, "Oh, straight people can watch this. They'll have one gay character that won't offend anyone." It's all about the tolerance of the general public. With *A League of Their Own*, we sort of had a Trojan horse where in the pilot we just have one girl who's a lesbian who kisses this other girl who's married, so it's not that bad. As the show goes on, more people come out, and it turns out everyone's gay. I think it was crafty; done to try to lure people in. Even if you're not gay, you keep watching and maybe you enjoy it, or maybe you're mad that everyone's gay. I don't know. In an all-gay writing staff, with mostly gay directors, there was an excitement about having so many different kinds of gay people on that show, and trans and Hispanic and Black in all its generational grandness. We got to go into a lot of different facets of the queer community. It's very, very fun.

SMW: It's funny, Angela Robinson used the same phrasing of this Trojan horse to use a certain aesthetic or commercial appeal and sneak everything in and run before anyone notices you've done it. The writing staff that you're talking about sounds, at least from the outside, kind of like a rarity. Have you noticed a big difference in how writers' rooms are demographically composed throughout the years?

JB: There have always been a ton of gay writers. There were a ton of gay men writing on *The Golden Girls*. There have certainly been a lot of Hollywood writers and directors who are gay, but they weren't comfortable or allowed to write about their own lives. I think the main shift is that people are able to talk about what's really going on with them. If anything, more women are being allowed in the rooms and certainly more people of color. When I got into television in the nineties, and around 2000, when I had my first TV directing job, I was definitely one of the only women, and certainly there were very few people of color. I would say it would be more like 50 percent women and at least 10 percent people of color. But certainly the women have crept across both writing and directing.

SMW: Throughout your filmography you've had these very complicated, morally gray characters, which I personally think are a lot more fun to watch, but I was wondering if this conversation about how queer characters are portrayed is a conversation happening behind the camera as well?

JB: Definitely. We're always thinking how we're portraying the community. I have a wild streak in me, too, where when I first started out and I was making *But I'm a Cheerleader*, so much of the gay community hated my movie. They were older and just like, "How can you make jokes about gay conver-sion?" Very early on I didn't want to be a part of a community that I can't make fun of. It's my community, and I'm on the inside, so I can do whatever I want, so don't tell me, you know? And then I made this other movie that screened at the San Francisco Film Festival [Frameline]. It was *Itty Bitty Titty Committee*, this little movie, and a bunch of lesbians after the screening were like, "How could you have these les-bians smoking? You're killing our community." And I was like, I know a lot of lesbians who smoke. I'm asthmatic, I don't smoke, my grandmother died of lung cancer. I get it, but I'm also at a certain point holding up the mirror. I also know a lot of lesbians who cheat on their girlfriends and I hold the mir-ror up and it's not flattering, but it's our community. I'm part of the community, and if I don't tell the truth about what I see, I don't really know who it's going to be telling the stories.

That's literally the point of people in the community writ-ing and directing stories. We get to tell the truth about what's going on. Humans are messy, and I can't only be telling gay stories where no one smokes and no one ever cheats. It's just not the truth. I try to always love my characters even when they're complicated, and I always try to see their point of view and let them try to live their truth even if it's fucked up. Why do they do what they do? Why do they cheat? Why do they smoke? Why do they act badly? My mom was a thera-pist, so I always try to think like—I always care about why characters always do certain things. But I don't judge them.

SMW: I like that. Humans are messy, and queer people are humans.

JB: I admire a straight director who tells those stories, but I tell myself that I'm allowed to. I'm certainly allowed to.

Chapter 4

THE RAINBOW AGE MEETS THE GRAY AR

As many representations of marginalized groups do, contemporary queer characters face an unwieldy responsibility in their conception. While stereotypes have ranged from martyred and neutered to villain- ous and promiscuous and back again, a queer character never seems to escape the discussion of what they're actually allowed to be on a moral level—and, sometimes, whether a show has done enough to even confirm that they exist as queer! I want to examine queer characters breaking the rules in two ways: through the time-honored tradition of the morally gray queer villain or queer mess, and the historically treasured but con- temporarily frowned upon tradition of the subtextually queer character.

By 1998, when *Will & Grace* first aired, gay men, lesbians, bisexual men, bisexual women, and trans women had all been series regulars on at least one prime-time show—but only gay men and lesbians had secured leading roles. Trans men, nonbinary characters, intersex char- acters, asexual characters, and two-spirit characters had not yet secured their longevity in series—and as of 2023, two-spirit characters had not found more than recurring roles on US television. Nonetheless, there was enough of an awareness of queerness to see patterns form around identities that did more consistently make it to the small sc primarily as abnormalities in heterosexual worlds. *Will & Gr* (and to some extent *Tales of the City* and *Brothers* be to tweak that at least a little bit, offering gay ch in heterosexual worlds but who weren't the on kind. They were welcoming viewers into their w

As big splash as both shows, especially *Ellen*, caused among networks, advertisers, and viewers who were hostile to a show featuring out
gay people, it's not controversial to call the fictional characters on both
series extremely nonthreatening by most narrative standards. Ellen
Morgan might be a lesbian, but she's also a friendly, hapless sitcom lead.
Distasteful as Jack's (Sean Hayes) flamboyance could be to the more
straitlaced Will (Eric McCormack), his over-the-top effeminacy was a
source of mirth, comedic narcissism, and only occasionally a font of
anti-assimilationist wisdom. Queerness on television by way of *Will &
Grace* and *Ellen* built a bridge between daringness solely for its subject
matter and knowledge that their sitcom genre allowed the delivery of a
comedic, enjoyable gay-next-door package. No one was trying to scare
away a straight viewer.

After gay media advocacy groups had lobbied for so long to depict gay
and lesbian people with respect, Ellen, Will, and to some extent Jack
(though his flamboyance was protested by the same groups as playing
into stereotype) were major accomplishments simply because they were
"normal" and "respectable" gay people. Gone were the days of gay pedophile gym teachers, fraudulent and murderous dyke con women, and
bisexual men sociopathically infecting their lovers with HIV (though
trans women characters still used their feminine wiles to trap men into
dating them). Finally, gays were just like everybody else, if a little snap-
pier and more entertaining, and it was about time that major networks
platformed that view.

White queer characters had been presented as affable and unthreat-
ening long before *Will & Grace*, though they were often the only homosexuals within a fifty-mile studio radius. In the decades following, series
The Education of Max Bickford (2001–2002), *Dawson's Creek*,
Family, *The Fosters* (2013–2018), and *Andi Mack* (2017–2019)
followed *Will & Grace* in making their out gay, lesbian, and trans
characters nonstereotypical, likable, and integral to the show, arguably essential belonging to the fabric of modern American life
teachers, football players, parents, and children—and all

fundamental contributors to the contemporary family unit. In recent years, queer characters have even been cast as superheroes on *Supergirl* (2015–2021), *Black Lightning* (2018-2021), *Batwoman* (2019–2022), and the long-running *Power Rangers* (1993-) television franchise, stepping into the stretchy uniforms and ultimate emblems of American patriotism. All is well in the land of the good television gays.

Around the same time that network television had shut down *Ellen* but supported *Will & Grace*'s meteoric rise, premium cable continued their own platforming of queer characters. However, cable networks, with their lack of dependence on advertisers, relaxed censors, and determination to distinguish themselves from their competitors, began taking a different, more controversial approach to writing queerness into American life. Beginning with *Oz*, HBO's explosively graphic first foray into hour-long original dramatic series, queerness had the opportunity to morph into something more aggressive and at times far more sinister than that of its friendly network counterparts. But these weren't the exaggerated villains of camp fare like *Lost in Space* (1965–1968) or the single-minded, one-note vengeance seekers of incontestably homophobic early network depictions. Instead, as premium cable built queer series and series in which queerness was an implicit fact of life, explanatory and assimilatory queer characters were matched by morally ambiguous, messy, and, yes, unforgivably villainous gays. Queer characters were finally getting enough screen time—and interest in their characters beyond their intrigue to heterosexual viewers—to exist in the rich, fascinating gray area between dully, righteously normal and downright perverse.

So Good Being Bad

Before tracing some of the most memorable evolutions of the lying, pathetic, villainous, scheming, or just messy queer character ac[...] decades, I want to foreground this section with a question: Why i[...] exciting to see queers being bad? Historically, depictions of quee[...] acting despicably have been met with strong opposition be[...] were the primary manner in which straight people interfac[...]

the idea of a queer person. Television and film could reach far more people than your average out queer person, and when those depictions or reports of queer people were based in violence, shame, and stereotype, they continued to serve as evidence for reasonable hatred of queer people. Off-putting queer characters were argued to be obstacles not only to successful assimilation but also to mere existence.

In many ways, shades of this argument still hold merit. Mass media depictions of queer people still do serve as a miseducation for straight people. Repetition of some tired inaccuracies—especially those deliberately portraying transition as genital mutilation, depicting myths about hormone replacement therapy and other aspects of medical transition, and calling into question the general legitimacy of trans people and the proven benefits of young gender-expansive people receiving trans-specific healthcare—continues to put queer people in tangible danger. Nonfiction programs and news media are still extremely culpable in this case as well, lending clear relevance to organizational guides that today caution media workers away from stereotype.[1]

When it comes to the moral responsibility and likability of fictional characters, continuing to advocate for storytelling that prioritizes only the upright homosexual citizens of the world encourages even queer audience members to evaluate storytelling (and queer people) on the basis of box-checking. If avoidance of stereotype is the premier rubric, television loses its possibility to tell interesting stories with queer people at the center. The only real winners are the straight people who are uncomfortable with queer characters that diverge at all from widespread notions of an acceptable, largely harmless gay character or person. In many cases, writing that harmless queer character to improve the chance that straight ʻiewers will accept them, and by proxy queer people, is an impossible ʻchmark anyway—just look at what happened to *Ellen*.

ʻmedian, actor, writer, and *TV, I Say w/ Ashley Ray* host Ashley ʻrris names this desire for morally upright queer characters, those who appear in reboots of older shows and seem to be ʻrectly to the sins of their past, as an unwitting "queer sanctity."[2] Building off Kobena Mercer's 1990 theory of the "burden of representation" that Black artists were forced to carry by serving as automatically assumed spokespeople for Black culture in its entirety, Ray-Harris points out that queer sanctity traps characters. By being hyperaware of the potential consequences straight people might take away from negative representations, shows write in an underlying need to believe that the sometimes "holier-than-thou" queer character is always right. As in life, central queer characters, especially of marginalized identities that haven't been as frequently represented, *have* to be fundamentally brave, righteous, and true, or else they reflect poorly on an entire (extremely diverse!) population.

Ray-Harris describes the further difficulty of finding Black queer characters, especially Black queer women characters, who have escaped the constraints of moral perfection to arrive as their own distinctive, human, messy selves onscreen. It's easy to recognize these morally gray, unpredictable, fully developed white men as some of the greatest characters in modern television history. Take, for instance, *The Sopranos* (1999–2007), *The Shield* (2002–2008), *Deadwood* (2004–2006), *Mad Men* (2007–2015), *Breaking Bad* (2008–2013), *Sons of Anarchy* (2008–2014), even *Seinfeld* (1989–1998), *Curb Your Enthusiasm* (2000–), and *BoJack Horseman* (2014–2020) as contemporary shows that understand the attraction of a supremely polarizing, selfish human (or horse) at the center of a serial narrative. Ray-Harris points out that white women have also gotten in on the antihero action, with explosively successful series like *Sex and the City*, *Weeds* (2005–2012), *Girls* (2012–2017), and British American co-production *Fleabag* (2016–2019) shining an inquisitive flashlight into the more embarrassing aspects of human existence.

Though fewer in numbers, straight Black women have had a significant history of outsize bitchiness and poor decision-making in prime-time soaps like *Dynasty* (1981–1989), *Scandal* (2012–2018), and *Empire* (2015–2020); playfully insipid or chaotic comedic performances in sitcoms like *227* (1985–1990), *The Fresh Prince of Bel-Air* (1990–1996), and *Living Single* (1993–1998); and more recent landscape-defining staples like *Insecure* (2016–2021) and British limited series *I May Destroy You* (2020) that make the case for messy Black women. But central Black, women-centric, *and* queer stories are still few and far between, with some of the best remembered, positive portrayals being fan favorites Sophia Burset (Laverne Cox) and Poussey Washington (Samira Wiley) on *Orange Is the New Black*; squeaky-clean family matriarch, wife of a cop, and vice principal Lena Adams Foster (Sherri Saum) on *The Fosters*; highly principled soldier Tasha Williams (Rose Rollins) on *The L Word* (2004–2009); aforementioned superheroes on *Black Lightning* and *Batwoman*; and the Emmy-winning "Thanksgiving" episode on *Master of None* (2015–2021), in which best friend character Denise (Lena Waithe) comes out to her mother.

Central Black queer women characters who could be considered even slightly antiheroic or morally complex are notably few. Among them are *The L Word*'s short-fused, biracial power dyke Bette Porter (Jennifer Beals), who, despite her cheating and hypocrisy, is still a politically admirable series protagonist; manipulative pansexual law professor and catastrophic bad-luck magnet Annalise Keating (Viola Davis) on prime-time soap tycoon Shonda Rhimes's *How to Get Away with Murder* (2014–2020); prickly house mother Elektra Abundance Evangelista (Dominique Jackson) and prideful foil Candy Ferocity (Angelica Ross) on *Pose* (2018–2021); sexually fluid, fiercely independent, and sometimes self-destructive loose cannons Nola Darling (DeWanda Wise) on *She's Gotta Have It* (2017–2019) and Nova Bordelon (Rutina Wesley) on *Queen Sugar* (2016–2022); and troubled unreliable narrator Rue Bennett (Zendaya Coleman) on the hugely popular teen drama *Euphoria* (2019–).

As Ray-Harris explains:

> There are so few of us that often the writers behind these shows think: if we're going to give [Black women] that representation and show them, it has to be in the best light. And it's because we're still being used as tokens. We're still not the center of our own

stories. At the center, it's normal to be a complex character. When you're at the center, people understand, "This is a character I will like sometimes and dislike sometimes and that's okay." You can exist in that morally gray ground. But when you're just a secondary character to someone else's story, it's a lot harder to get that through.[3]

Ray-Harris's longer list of shows in which difficult white people thrive adds two essential elements to the case for imperfect gays on television. The first is strength of character: when queer characters are unquestionably good, they—and their stories—don't have as much room to grow, despite their longevity as series regulars or recurring favorites. They don't have complicated backstories, hidden traumas that center on something other than their queer identity, or the option to engage in that magnetic journey toward antiherodom. As a direct example of one such character who makes mistake after mistake, and whose increasingly pronounced desperation is hypnotizing, Ray-Harris points to Don Draper (Jon Hamm), the universally acclaimed protagonist of multi-Emmy Award–winning and long-running series *Mad Men*. Draper is a fraud, serial philanderer, absent father, and selfish prick whose fractured past concretizes him into a million-dollar liar and master storyteller. In short, he's the perfect ad salesman for his firm and for AMC.* Well-written, heavily invested-in "bad" characters are just good for television.

The second aspect of this argument for queers running amok is the concept of tokenization—not just of a character but of an audience demographic. Underdeveloped queer villains of the sixties, seventies, and eighties were certainly capitalizing on straight fear and ignorance, but simple, flattened, *good* queer characters are also capitalizing on a

---

* One of the few queer women characters of color whose series longevity, hidden backstory, and womanizing could even be slightly comparable to Draper's is Kalinda Sharma (Archie Panjabi) of defining CBS hit *The Good Wife* (2009–2016). Panjabi earned a Supporting Actress Emmy in 2010 for her portrayal of the seemingly ruthless badass, but ultimately even her character is proven time and again to have a remorseful, sympathetic moral compass.

heterosexual need to regard queerness as one-dimensional. Easily consumed, easily digested, and easily discarded. In order to reorient toward a queer story and a queer audience, queer characters must have the option of being fully developed as liars, cheaters, self-obsessed hypocrites, and insecure assholes.

Thankfully for viewers craving dynamism and unpredictability out of queer characters, since 1997, premium cable started to approach the possibilities of catering to a different audience and the draw of queerness morphing into something magnetic, difficult, and sometimes reprehensible onscreen.

Be Gay, Do Crime

Unsurprisingly, our first dive into despicable but fascinating queer characters on television begins with premium cable dipping its toe into original programming. Two original HBO series produced two mesmeric gay male characters—*Oz*'s Chris Keller (Christopher Meloni) and *The Wire*'s Omar Little (Michael K. Williams)—who were incredibly good at being bad. Impulsive, intelligent, and at times without mercy, Chris and Omar were two fully realized, sometimes (often, in Chris's case) reprehensible queer characters who still serve as references for originality in layered villainy.

For HBO's very first hourlong narrative drama in 1997, playwright and *St. Elsewhere* and *Homicide: Life on the Street* (1993–1999) writer/ producer Tom Fontana swung big. Joined by *Homicide* executive producer Barry Levinson, Fontana aimed to push past the events of the familiar police procedural by introducing a steel-and-concrete world in which men were utterly dehumanized, authority was both grossly inept and corrupt, and anyone could die a grisly death at any time. This was *Oz*, short for the fictional Oswald State Correctional Facility, where Fontana sequestered his tortured gangs of philosophizing inmates in an experimental über-Panopticon nicknamed Emerald City. Guided by paralyzed inmate Augustus Hill's (Harold Perrineau) fourth wall–breaking narrations, *Oz* paired meditations on faith, power, and love with brutal rapes, race wars, casual murders, medical horrors, and a twisted gay romance of operatic proportions.

Tobias Beecher (Lee Tergesen) enters Oz as the audience's everyman: a deeply regretful lawyer sentenced to fifteen years for drunkenly hitting and killing a nine-year-old girl with his car. Meek and melancholy, he quickly becomes a target of violent physical and emotional abuse and forms a lifelong nemesis in the terrifying neo-Nazi leader Vern Schillinger (J. K. Simmons). By the end of the first season, Beecher loses his mind and his passivity, vowing revenge on Schillinger. The two continue to torture each other throughout the series, whittling down extremities, family members, and hope in a yearslong battle. One of the more sadistic long games that Schillinger devises in season 2 introduces a new inmate to Oz: Chris Keller. Explosively violent, mercurial, and charming, Keller is tasked with seducing, and then destroying, Beecher, which he does handily. Unfortunately for Keller and Schillinger, Keller also genuinely falls for his target, though not soon enough to keep Beecher's limbs intact.

Keller and Beecher's romance is often passionate, dangerous, and tumultuous, with Keller pulling the rug out from under Beecher (and almost any other character he takes a passing interest in) on multiple occasions. As the quadruple-married-and-divorced Keller, Meloni is a simmering pot of poison, switching loyalties with barely a warning blink. He's a self-hating serial murderer of other queer men and a chronic, intentional heartbreaker who enjoys playing with his food; but somehow he manages to find genuine tender moments with Beecher, and in his ultimate betrayal, he would rather give up his own life than that of the man he loves. In an ensemble of standout characters, Keller dominates the screen and remains an original, memorable deviation from one-off queer villains and long-running straight placations alike.

Calling Oz positive queer representation is kind of laughable. The series is infrequently positive about any group of people, and only a few individuals really find redemption. Despite the obvious corruption and authoritarian abuse inmates suffered, in Fontana's imagining of a prison system (which he wasn't initially invested in abolishing), everyone was guilty of something, and it didn't really matter what the initial crime was.[4] Given the violent, oppressive pressure cooker they were thrown into, the inmates would continually return to their guilty ways or find new ways to fall apart. This was certainly a boon for character building, but it also jostled uncomfortably with the many deeply political sentiments the characters espoused, particularly Kareem Saïd (Eamonn Walker), a Muslim leader and "political prisoner" whose fight to free Black men from all forms of carceral violence often found itself invalidated by his own selfishness.

Other forms of violence were crucial to Fontana, who believed the main issue with violence on television was that it was too sanitized and therefore inured an audience to its actual consequences—a framework that some critics bought and some viewed as a thin excuse for sensationalism. The series depicts sex in particular at its most destructive and nonconsensual, humiliating, dangerous, and deceptive, but the many queer recurring and background characters, including out gay and unspecified trans or gender-nonconforming inmates, were not portrayed as either moral or immoral for engaging in consensual sex.* Where *Oz*'s Aryan gangs used anal sex, sodomy, and male gang rape as tools of torture, unexpected queer love and the "gay gang" of Emerald City found their ways to survive, die, and murder with the rest of them.

Oz, with its body count upward of fifty characters by the end of the series, piled Shakespearean tragedy on top of tragedy, shivving, poisoning, and burning its characters as agonizingly as possible. Everything, as Fontana told writer Elon Green in 2015, was done in order to "keep the audience off balance" and consistently overturn expectations of good and evil in an unjust world.[5] Because queer people were a given in

---

* One of the more quietly moving deaths on *Oz* was that of Nat "Natalie" Ginzburg (Charles Busch), an inmate sentenced to death row for a contract killing of another inmate. While nothing is explained in plain language, Nat spends what is to be his last night dressed as a woman and passes away, presumably from complications from AIDS, in his sleep. In the morning, resident nun Sister Peter Marie (Rita Moreno, one of the series' many Broadway legends) breaks down because she hadn't finished painting his nails, and she does so postmortem.

Fontana's world, and character was more interesting to the writers than total accuracy or political soundness, they were also able to join the rest of the *Oz*'s ranks as some of the most fascinating and unmanageable characters on television at that time. *Oz* also, arguably, laid out the red carpet for premium cable's embrace of antiheroes altogether.

Though *Oz* was less critically and commercially venerated than *The Sopranos* or *The Wire* (and with good reason—*Oz*'s theatricality and commitment to hyperrealism sometimes overwhelmed its plot), both later shows certainly took pages from the ur-text of HBO dramas. *The Sopranos* improved on the cartoonishness of *Oz*'s Italian American crime syndicates (and poached *Oz* cast member Edie Falco) to create one of the most well-regarded dramas of all time, which in its fifth season began laying the groundwork for a gay Mafia member's subplot. From 2004 to 2006, made man and longtime ensemble member Vito Spatafore (Joe Gannascoli) embarked on his own complicated journey, beginning with a blow job at a construction site and ending with a brutal murder and rape that was fashioned after the ends of real Mafia gays.[6] What was perhaps most interesting about his character was not his surprise fellatio, or his frequenting of leather bars, but the fact that he simply could not work up the desire for a normal, monotonous nine-to-five and the unperturbed gay love life it guaranteed. Vito couldn't fathom existence outside the family or his true self (a blackmailer and organized assassin), even if it meant his certain end.

The creators of *The Wire* were more explicit in naming *Oz*'s influence. David Simon, a former police reporter whose book was the basis for *Homicide: Life on the Street* (1993–1999), noted that *Oz* was ultimately what pushed him to forego *Homicide*'s home network of NBC and take *The Wire* to HBO instead.[7] Aiming to expose the layers of corruption and devastation wrought by the ongoing, so-called War on Drugs, *The Wire* treated addicts and dealers, Nixon's and subsequent presidents' public enemies, as full, complicated people with sometimes impressive interiority. With excellent performances from a sprawling ensemble cast (many of whom also appeared on *Oz*), *The Wire* boasted a host of memorable, difficult characters who broke with expectation. None is more synonymous with the show's desired subversion than Omar Little, a gay, shotgun-toting, drug kingpin–robbing stickup man whose whistle was enough of a warning to send the neighborhood running.

Omar wasn't the only queer character on *The Wire*, nor was he the only long-running, entrenched, and complex antagonist. On the other side of the law, Baltimore Police Department detective Kima Greggs (Sonja Sohn) is openly lesbian and less proudly devolving into workaholism, much to the chagrin of her girlfriend. Beginning in the third season, Snoop (Felicia Pearson) is a new recruit-turned-cold-assassin and trusted member of one of Baltimore's warring gangs, whose sexuality is casually acknowledged and has no bearing on her far more enthralling (and repulsive) string of murders.* All are fascinating, and Omar is rightfully remembered as a standout of the series and a breakthrough for depictions of queer men of color on the small screen.

The Wire made a splash with Omar's deeply devoted relationships to other Black queer men and queer men of color, three years before the premiere of *Noah's Arc*, Patrik-Ian Polk's far lighter *Designing Women*– and *Sex and the City*–inspired fare that put queer Black men in conversation, community, and romantic relationships with one another. Where *Oz* made physical relationships between Black men violent and purely attributed to sociopathy or prison power plays, Omar is driven by a strict moral code, impeccable survival instincts, and love for his "beautiful boy." That love is subject to particularly malicious external violence, with Omar's first onscreen love, Brandon (Michael Kevin Darnall), withstanding torture and choosing death before giving up any information about Omar's whereabouts.

---

*   Alongside *The Wire*, the crime family series *Power* (2014–2020)—and its many ensuing spinoffs—is one of the few hubs to find a number of ethically complex or downright villainous Black queer women characters on television, including Anika Noni Rose as merciless dirty cop Jukebox. But she gets only six episodes in the original series before she meets her maker and respawns as a teen in the prequel *Power Book III: Raising Kanan* (2021–).

Brandon's murder sets Omar on a course for vengeance, which takes an at-first puzzling turn toward Omar becoming a confidential informant for the Baltimore PD. It's here that the audience gets a taste of Omar beyond his robberies. Performer Michael K. Williams's unblinking, unnerving stare and smooth delivery makes for one of the most terrifying presences in a show full of very real threats. However, when he's put on the stand to testify against members of the gang who killed Brandon, audiences are treated to Omar's unexpected charisma, stinging wit, and ability to calmly push anyone toward utter frustration and madness simply by finding their weaknesses and needling them with a butter-wouldn't-melt smile. Though fearsome with a shotgun (in later seasons, his reputation for bloodshed so precedes him that he can't even go out on an errand for the Honey Nut Cheerios his lover finished without being treated like he's on the warpath), the series displays early on that Omar is often the smartest in the room.

Omar would go through several lovers throughout the series, many of whom are targeted by gang leaders in ways both common to *The Wire*'s world and distinctly homophobic (many characters are put off by Omar's "faggotry"). Omar is rarely shown to have any sort of compunction about his sexuality, instead flaunting any aspect of himself that might throw his enemies off balance. Williams initially had reservations about his role, but when he realized Omar was a distinctly nonstereotypical portrayal of a gay man, the actor reportedly fought for more physical intimacy for his character. According to Williams's memoir, he and scene partner Darnall improvised their first unscripted kisses, pushing the script's tentative treatment of queer Black men's physicality and sexuality to a tangible onscreen space. Thanks to Williams, Omar and his sexuality were real, which would have crumbled if the script continued to balk at the idea of showing queer male intimacy. Omar is a multidimensional, interesting, cruel, smart, handsome, and complicated antagonist who in many ways set a precedent for queer antiheroes and antagonists to participate in really nasty, violent exploits—and not because they were tortured by their own sexuality like in previous iterations.

Echoes of Chris Keller and Omar Little can still be heard across the more successful contemporary iterations of television's queer villains. These characters are driven, cunning, and, unlike the heterophobic killers before them, are not flatly motivated by their hate for their own queerness or the unfairly lucky, unbothered straight people around them—though that may still be a part of their lore. Like Chris and Omar, they play entirely by their own rules and often are motivated by their fierce, borderline-obsessive love. Above all, whether chilling, charming, chaotic, or a combination of all three, they are enrapturing, often providing their actors with delightful material and a dedicated fan base.

If we continue to embrace the category of villain, queers can really do anything! We can be sardonic, lawless, sexually fluid vengeful vampires willing to upend tenuous social contracts to avenge a staked lover, or similarly warped blood drainers trapping our soulmates for all eternity (*True Blood*, 2008–2014; *American Horror Story*, 2011–). Straight-up murder is still an option, too—as long as it's creative and done in the name of the greatest love story ever told (*Jane the Virgin*, 2014–2019; *Killing Eve*, 2018–2022; *Harley Quinn*, 2019–) or if the murderee really deserved it (*Chucky*, 2021–). Of course, if the pursuit of traditional romance is less your speed, there's always the option to fatally abandon your partner in order to fulfill your true destiny as a Chechen crime magnate (*Barry*, 2018–2023) or callously betray everyone you've ever claimed to love in the name of assuming political power in ancient Rome (*Spartacus*, 2010–2013). Or if something as simple but effective as bullying insufferable theater kids (*Glee*, 2009–2015) is just a little too pedestrian for your tastes, you can always opt for trading in your morality to become a homophobic talk show host or an off-kilter brainwashing, kidnapping mastermind or the leader of a suicidal free-love zombie cult—maybe even on the same show (*Search Party*, 2016–2022). Or maybe you're just misunderstood and continue to have really bad, gruesome days at work—you can't help it if you're the boss (*Shrill*, 2019–2021; *Ratched*, 2020).

The preceding are only a few of the explicitly queer villains in the Rainbow Age whose fuckery has disarmed and decapitated the affability of assimilationist queer characters who came before, but they aren't the only archetype to complicate the rise of the friendly neighborhood television gay. Thanks again to premium cable, all-out villainy wasn't the only avenue a queer character had to take in order to expand past the constraints of self-censoring cleanliness. Sometimes, a queer just has to dip their toe somewhere between moral perfection and murder to get a little bit messy.

Be Gay, Be Dazed, and Be Confused

On the heels of Russell T. Davies's (later of *Doctor Who* and *It's a Sin*) short but successful UK *Queer as Folk* series, Showtime and its Canadian-based co-network Showcase turned to two seasoned television writers to Americanize the explicit antics of a group of twenty- and thirtysomething queer friends. Ron Cowen and Daniel Lipman, who had already made significant queer television strides with the made-for-television AIDS film *An Early Frost* in 1985, expanded Davies's eight initial episodes into a twenty-two-episode first season, filled to bursting with storylines about sex, drugs, porn, teen homelessness, class tensions, queer bashing, physical insecurities, assimilation, age gaps, HIV/AIDS, and one of the most miserable lesbian relationships ever put to screen. It was a sensation, becoming Showtime's number-one series by its first season finale.

Pittsburgh-based *Queer as Folk* revolves around five main gay characters, with plenty of idiosyncratic recurring characters, who make giant mistakes as they proceed on their crusades for or against love. The very first episode throws a wrench into the life of Michael Novotny (Hal Sparks), when closeted high school senior Justin Taylor (Randy Harrison) somehow cruises his way to losing his virginity with Michael's best friend and perpetual crush, the all-desired ad executive and notorious one-night-stand enforcer, twenty-nine-year-old Brian Kinney (Gale Harold). Michael, flamboyant jack of *some* trades Emmett Honeycutt (Peter Paige), deeply insecure accountant Ted Schmidt (Scott Lowell), and struggling lesbian couple and new mothers Melanie Marcus (Michelle Clunie) and Lindsay Peterson (Thea Gill) find themselves wrapped up in caring for (and berating) Justin, who manages to break Brian's one-night-only rule through his fraught coming out and relentless pursuit of a life outside his homophobic household and school.

QAF split its focus among many contemporary storylines, giving significant time to each of its main gay characters and their hopes, dreams, and neuroses—and the ways those driving motivations affected biological and chosen kin alike. Built into the glittering, Elysian club scenes and graphic (though somewhat tame compared to its UK originator) sex scenes were sniping conversations, disappointments, and deep hurt. Though they cared for one another, characters were thoughtless and selfish and struggled with the expectations of modern gay life, and with the exception of the empathetic, zaniest arc-prone Emmett, they were often fairly unlikable. Ted was self-hating and outwardly judgmental; Justin was naive; Michael could be whiny, codependent, and sometimes even less mature than Justin; and Lindsay and Melanie were so ill-suited to parenthood and monogamous partnership that one wondered how they ever got together in the first place. No singular character elicited as much vocal grief, however, as Brian Kinney.

Handsome, confident, slutty, and self-absorbed, Brian was consistently the subject of not only his friends and lovers' disgruntlement but also sometimes the chatter of the entirety of gay Pittsburgh. His promiscuity was legendary, and his lack of emotional attachment even more so. Though Justin would eventually change that after seasons of wearing him down, Brian was, in his own words, not kind or available. He had the option to move through the world as a superficial object of ultimate white gay masculine desire as well as an assimilatory straight-passing man, but he was never shy about broadcasting the commonly undesirable parts of himself, to both the gay and straight worlds. Nonetheless, everyone around him ignored his plain signals in favor of hearing and seeing what they most desired.

QAF seemed to be well aware of the conversations it was instigating with such potentially divisive characters, with Cowen reflecting to *Entertainment Weekly* in 2018 that he and Lipman saw the series as "an opportunity to address a lot of issues that had never been shown on American TV before."[8] Most obviously, this meant sex and sexuality, but with fully developed, distinct gay characters, it also meant plunging into differing attitudes *about* sex from a queer perspective. In *QAF*'s primarily gay world, there was room for and encouragement of a range of unpopular opinions and characters who couldn't see past their own bullheadedness.

Though the first season dove headfirst into different approaches to heterocentrism in dating, raising a family, and public outness, a second-season storyline took an incredibly cheeky stab at the assimilation conversation. In season 2, episode 3, "Hypocrisy: Don't Do It," Brian is the recalcitrant nominee of the local gay and lesbian center's "Hero" award for having saved Justin's life—that is, until a local journalist and fellow awardee writes a hit piece on Brian's sexual indiscrimination and his relationship with the then-underage Justin. The episode details the various hypocrisies that each member of the *QAF* gang, and their employers and critics, engage in—from corporate shilling to extramarital affairs to barebacking.

The situations range from satirical to sobering, and they're all foregrounded by a pointed opening, in which the gang is gathered at a gay bar for a weekly viewing of the ultra-sanitized, respectable fake TV show *Gay as Blazes*. When Brian switches off the TV during a commercial break, he's met with a wave of protest from the gathered audience, which quickly turns into a transparent conversation about *QAF*. As most of the gang fawns over *GAB*'s dreamy actors and reviews proclaim it as "the most honest look at gay life ever portrayed on television," Brian bites back at its utter blandness and complete lack of "sucking and fucking."[9]

TED

Even you have to admit, it's important that the straight world sees realistic portrayals of us.

BRIAN

You call that realistic? And who gives a flying fuck what straight people think?

Written by Cowen, Lipman, and queer cult horror screenwriter Karen Walton (*Ginger Snaps*), the episode once again gives Brian plenty of real estate to be an asshole, but the bar conversation is a hat tip to the strength of his character and a giant wink toward the queer *QAF* audiences. The sex, narcissism, vulnerability, and otherwise socially impure choices made by their characters are all aspects of real queer life. Though you'd be maligned by straight people and antagonizing your own community alike, "bad" behavior (and venomous sarcasm) is integral to many queer experiences.

Just a few years later, a similar focus on queer community, and the many petty sins therein contained, arrived on Showtime. From the moment Shane McCutcheon (Kate Moennig) sloped her way across the screen—no, from the moment Jenny Schecter (Mia Kirshner) and Marina Ferrer (Karina Lombard) sensually whispered their favorite books into Alice Pieszecki's (Leisha Hailey) ear—no, from the moment Bette Porter (Jennifer Beals) first screamed at a male guest star—no, from the moment that Jenny spied Shane fucking her hookup against the wall of Bette and Tina Kennard's (Laurel Holloman) sparkling outdoor pool, something fundamentally shifted in the lesbian universe.

Suddenly, queer women had the same permission as queer men to throw their lives, and the lives of their friends and lovers, into utter shambles. *The L Word* was an oasis for lesbians making the wrong choices, largely revolving around the concept that queer women, far from being sanctified, sexless humorists, were enormous emotional and sexual sluts. At least, they had the *choice* to be so. They could also be deeply vulnerable, conniving, ambitious, self-destructive, breathtakingly stunning, and utterly incapable of taking their own advice. For as many criticisms that were rightly leveled at it, *The L Word* laid the blueprint for queer characters—women especially—to continually fuck up and still be rendered as human beings.

Modern Messes

Thanks to *Queer as Folk* and *The L Word*, it's difficult to imagine a television landscape barren of the complex queer series that gave its characters so much room to start as imperfect, sometimes deeply unlikable, characters—especially if they were having any sort of sex. The licentious but mostly good-hearted queer surgeons of *Grey's Anatomy*, hapless incarcerated dykes of *Orange Is the New Black*, adult toddlers of *Broad City* (2014–2019), idealistic but selfish romantics of *Looking* (2014–2015), delightfully hateful titular difficult person of *Difficult People* (2015–2017), identity crisis–laden ice-cold femme top of *Vida* (2018–2020) anti–inspiration porn but pro–little white lie protagonist of *Special* (2019–2021), not-so-smooth womanizers and late-in-life chaotic bisexuals of *Harlem* (2021–), absurdly funny and miscellaneous randy lesbians of *A Black Lady Sketch Show* (2019–2023), or the deeply oblivious, celebrity-obsessed millennials of *The Other Two* (2019–2023) and *Hacks* (2021–) could all compete for "least together television queer" to make us all feel a bit better about our lives. Competing with the worst of them were the utter messes that were the inescapable, often detestable Pfeffermans of the greater Los Angeles area.

You probably already know a few key facts about *Transparent*. First, it was conceived as showrunner Joey Soloway's therapeutic unraveling of their feelings about their own parent transitioning; therefore, the show is about Maura (cis actor Jeffrey Tambor), matriarch of the fictional Pfefferman family, navigating her transition and about Maura's children navigating their own feelings around their new mother and their traumatized pasts. Second, Tambor's scandal-ridden departure from the show after harassing his trans coworkers ran the show aground before its time, giving it one episode in which to tie up the whole four devastatingly caustic but imaginative seasons. Diving past that brief and obvious introduction, *Transparent* is very much about queerness, and its second season even dives into the historical transness and queerness that the Pfefferman family inherited but never knew existed. It's populated by incredible trans performers and writers, many of them without extensive prior credits. But above all else, *Transparent* is about the Pfeffermans, a family of utter basket cases.

Transparent was so enthralling precisely because it was grounded in more than Good Trans Representation or Good Queer Representation. It challenged tired notions of queerness by having its core family commit almost every sin in the book and either grow or flail while doing so—and more often flail. They hurt one another, and other queer and trans people, in mind-bogglingly insecure, insensitive, and believable ignorance. While figuring themselves out, they use other people and toss them aside. Eldest daughter Sarah (Amy Landecker) explores her attraction to women and sadomasochism in some of the most irresponsible scenarios imaginable, leaving her partners abandoned, emotionally devastated, or unconscionably horny. Middle son Josh (Jay Duplass) works through his molestation at the hands of a childhood babysitter by unwittingly projecting onto every woman and romantic prospect with whom he comes into contact, displaying an especially headshaking lack of introspection with on-again/off-again girlfriend Rabbi Raquel (Kathryn Hahn) and enigmatic dancer Shea (Trace Lysette). Youngest kid Ali (Gaby Hoffmann) is the most empathetic but finds themselves linking every marginalized struggle to their own internalized growth. And throughout it all, the series is incredibly specific, despicable, and funny. Watching an episode of *Transparent* is like daring someone to get a rise out of you and being satisfied when they do.

There was no shortage of issues on *Transparent*, key being its conception of Maura as Mort first—a fallacy that Soloway has since expressed as an "original sin."[10] At the same time, it gave us charismatic, narcissistic, daring queer characters and trans storylines that mattered, which made Amazon Prime Video's decision to shutter it before it could take a chance on a complicated trans and queer story without a cisgender, recognized actor at its center even more disappointing. And yet, we'll always have the Musicale Finale.

The Other Gray Area

If you've had enough of difficult queer representation, I understand. Let me entice you to continue reading by presenting you with an utterly uncontroversial and universally beloved aspect of queer television history: subtext.

When I first began an attempt to think critically about queer media, I thought that, in this decade, writing subtext without it evolving to main text was cowardly. Characters who don't kiss when they should were beneath my critical praise or verbal attention; storylines that were mere metaphors for the monstrous belonged in a different book, but not in mine! Of course, what I was doing was an attempt at righteously indignant scholarship—casting my gay gaze on the media that was worthy of mine and others' attention. If queerness—not just hints of it, but textual queerness—was beneath hypothetical executives and showrunners laughing at me (laughing!) for prizing onscreen representation, then I would turn my nose up at them.

Unfortunately, I was fighting a fictional enemy and denying one of the biggest reasons I got into entertainment in the process. When I was a teenage television fanatic, subtext was my bread and butter! I was obsessed with the nineties fantasy and sci-fi series that wove teen angst and repressed sexuality into supernatural menaces. One of the most visceral thrills I got from a genre show was the charge between two women who were mortal enemies and could never admit they needed to fuck each other's brains out, so they came at each other with chain saws instead. A legion of fan fiction writers and theorists were right there with me: as frustrating as it might have been to never see that tension resolved, it was equally as gratifying to resolve it on your own terms and to tune in each week to lightly wonder if your genius would be reflected back on the screen.

I was also unwittingly ignoring the history of queer television. Sure, some of that imagined disdain that heterosexual lenses had for homosexual viewers was real, but that did not in any way stop queer viewers from identifying coded characters as lifelines. That executives fought tooth and nail to get as much subtext as they could off the screen, too, as in the cases of *Cagney & Lacey* (1981–1988), *The Odd Couple* (1970–1975), and the planned spin-off to *The Many Loves of Dobie Gillis* (1959–1963), didn't even occur to me. Television hadn't always been about dropping crumbs to desperate queer viewers, as the discussion du jour had me believe; sometimes, it came from the other side—from performers, writers, and costume departments that were desperate to drop as many hints as they could, like a tin can wire from one side of the screen to the other. It wasn't until I stepped out of my hyper-contemporary focus that I realized: to dismiss subtext would be to dismiss the historical, the layered, the connective, and the potentially delicious.

For an abstract notion that could have earned me the title of least fun at parties, subtext has now transformed into one of the most delightful aspects of queer television. In so many interviews conducted for other chapters, subtext became the most fruitful topic, from many more angles than I had ever read between—and not just as a nostalgic recognition. Today, when we expect a character to be explicitly named, the next frontier of queer representation might just emerge in the gray areas, especially those that can't be flatly included in the name of ticking a box. In the spirit of a holistic look at queer television history, let's take a gander at some of those perspectives, discussing queer subtext through the lens of connection, subtlety, tension, and a change in the television landscape that can both accept explicit, named queerness and appreciate what isn't said.

A History of Wrong Girls on Motorcycles

On November 19, 1980, Jo Polniaczek (Nancy McKeon) rode her motorcycle onto *The Facts of Life* (1979–1988), a spin-off of *Diff'rent Strokes* (1978–1986), and into the hearts of burgeoning dykes across America. With her hardscrabble, tomboyish, all-denim exterior and a constant scoff aimed toward Eastland Academy's resident teen narcissist Blair Warner (Lisa Whelchel), Jo presented a perfect alternative to the preppy, blonde, spoiled center of the series. From their first episode together, Jo and Blair immediately hit upon the classic dynamic of frenemies: diametric opposites who shine when the other pratfalls, whose squabbles could be the basis of an episode's drama, and who could still bond together against a common enemy when the going got particularly tough.

"I just read her and Blair as totally in love," venerated writer, director, and all-around lesbian film icon Angela Robinson (*D.E.B.S.*, *Professor Marston and the Wonder Women*) relays.[11] Robinson, who spent her early life watching straight characters through a queer lens and forming her viewing muscles around what she resonated with rather than a writer's strict intent, is far from the first person to find a kindred spirit in Jo's tomboy character or to read Jo and Blair's bickering as a front for their true feelings. Alongside Kristy McNichol on the film side, Jo Polniaczek is one of the most frequent namedrops in the pantheon of early queer characters that film dykes watched out for.

But from her first appearance in "The New Girl" parts one and two, Jo was strictly, emphatically, all about men. She'd been sent from New York City to Eastland by her mother to get her away from her boyfriend, and after being thoroughly turned off by the prim, virginal nature of her fellow Eastland students and their schoolgirl crushes, Jo decides to take matters into her own hands, stealing the school van and heading toward the local bar to meet some real men. Blair tags along to prove that she has more experience and elevated taste than Jo expects of her, which backfires predictably, and they both end up in trouble. Their punishment turns them into unwilling roommates, and thus the classic frenemy tension continued throughout the series, never to be resolved. At least, not in the way that queer viewers may have dreamed of.

The Facts of Life actually point-blank featured a lesbian panic arc in its very first episode, and she, too, runs headfirst into conflict with the flouncy, ferociously feminine Blair. However, Cindy (Julie Anne Haddock), the reedy tomboy of the house, was gradually written off the show around season 2, making only a few appearances in later seasons and never amassing the same following or self-recognition that Jo did. Though Jo never got her own lesbian-curious moment of reckoning, she continued to sing strongly to queer viewers who would be far less comforted by Mrs. Garrett's insistence that one should never jump to conclusions based on another person's looks. Why, though, after many seasons of storylines that revolved around no-good boys and a definitive insistence from the creators that Jo was not in any way gay, could queer viewers privately hold out hope, even just in their imaginations?

"I don't think [the creators] intended it to be [queer]. I believe their sincerity. I just think a lot of people claimed it," Robinson says. "To me, it doesn't matter. There were no queer characters really on television at all, so it wasn't really a question of being able to read characters as queer. You had to read it as such. You had to be able to reinterpret."[12]

Speaking about tomboy characters like Jo and another oft-cited coded inspiration, Kristy McNichol, who played the hardscrabble tomboy Buddy on the sitcom *Family*, Jenni Olson describes the importance of that visual kinship, even in cases where neither the character nor the person watching is certain of its meaning. She explains:[13]

> For queer people who grow up feeling alone, we're not necessarily recognizable to one another. Even though you look at pictures of me as a kid and you could see twenty miles away that I was queer, somehow I was not figuring that out or connecting with others. We are uniquely alone, and so it is uniquely that much more powerful and important that we see ourselves onscreen, in whatever context. "Oh, my God! Kristy McNichol has something to say to me!" Something that's meaningful to me for a reason I'm not sure of yet, but there's something there that's desperately important to me because I'm otherwise alone.

Jo is the paragon of a distinct type of coded character, one that, despite insistence from those creating her, is continually claimed because she speaks to queer imagination. Not only that, she was a long-running central character queer audiences could get invested in. She wasn't siloed into one-off episodes in which her sexuality was the moral lesson of the week; she was a fully rounded, tough-talking, capable soft butch who could hold her own against bullies and boys alike. She had longevity, avoided stereotype, and was guaranteed her own adventures—as long as she stayed firmly out of impunity's way and far back in the closet.

Why So Gray?

Although a refusal to label a character as queer can still strike at a queer imagination, subtext now has the potential to utilize a different function, especially when it's employed in series that already accept queerness as one of those pesky facts of life. It's a bit of a Swiss Army knife of a tool—no longer forcing characters into the closet but providing ways to escape the expected, to hint at a world unseen, or to lend flexibility to audience interpretation. With the latter, subtext can sometimes be about not only a character's uncertainties but also an audience member's.

As Princess Weekes, multidisciplinary critic and assistant editor for *The Mary Sue* explains, "We can sometimes forget that it takes people decades to discover who they are. It's important to show that people can have queer attraction and move in very queer ways while not having fully figured out themselves. That can be its own arc."[14] A perfect example of this type of label-less arc comes in narratives of older characters exploring their sexuality but feeling as though they may have missed the boat when it comes to dropping into a ready-made identity or community. One such consuming example is *Mrs. Fletcher* (2019), the HBO miniseries that sees venerable talent and frequent onscreen bisexual Kathryn Hahn play long-divorced middle-aged mom Eve Fletcher finally attempting to explore her long-dormant desires through the world of internet porn now that she's an empty nester.

Without ever using language to describe her own sexual orientation, Eve finds eroticization in the previously mundane. Most of the sex Eve fantasizes about (at least that we're shown) is fairly vanilla, but with Hahn's absorbed gaze it still carries an air of previously untouched, dangerous possibility. The series eventually includes one of the most empathetic and well-directed threesomes to hit the small screen, but the scene I keep coming back to is all talk, and nothing is particularly exclamatory.

In the fourth episode, "Parents' Weekend," directed by celesbian extraordinaire Carrie Brownstein, Eve and her senior center coworker Amanda (Katie Kershaw) hang out after an emotionally exhausting day. They're blowing off steam, Eve using a proffered weed pen for the first time, and they end up in Amanda's neighbor's hot tub, drinking and talking. Amanda, an openly queer woman, talks about her past relationship ending, the very complicated dyke threesome she's had ("my ex and her ex"), and, for the first time, asks Eve what exactly her deal is. At first, Eve balks, but eventually she opens up: she's been having "crazy" fantasies— none she'll ever act on, she claims, but a weight seems to lift now that she's finally admitted to having an active inner life.[15] Amanda's response is one of interest and newfound respect—encouraging Eve to actually follow through on those fantasies and good-naturedly calling Eve a pervert.

There's something uniquely resonant about two women, one comfortably queer, one unable or previously unwilling to voice her queerness and desire, sitting in a hot tub and casually, directly engaging in a conversation about desire. It's flirty and hot and heady and high, but it also strikes at the way people feel unable to speak to their own queerness. There's a rigidity, passed down from generations of heterosexual panic and overcorrection, to the way new queers are taught to label themselves: to boldly claim one label, to never touch another if it isn't assuredly theirs. And here, Eve Fletcher is called a pervert in an encouraging way for finally raising the desires she's discovering but could never, ever voice—because it's not her space. It's never been her label. But "pervert"— that's a word that screams queer, and bequeathed by another queer woman, it screams welcome, it's okay, lay your burden down. You can fuck, be fucked, love, be loved, and be absolutely filthy, and you only need one word for it.

On the other side of the coin entirely, Weekes also argues that a less declarative sort of queer representation can be immensely valuable to audiences who aren't questioning but rarely see themselves represented—including asexual and aromantic viewers who still identify within queerness but see their sexuality and relationships in entirely different presentations. As Weekes points out, that's a bit of a steep, representation-less curve for those who have a difficult time finding "queer" storylines that actually match up with the way they experience their own identity. In this case, a character who's not actively consummating a relationship or labeled as queer stands as a possibility for an ace or aro representation.

From the Outside Looking In

Another function of nü-subtext is the sometimes unfortunate, sometimes neutral imitation of life itself, especially when it comes to depicting relationships between queer people and the straight people who love them. It's wonderful when a queer character is surrounded by people who deeply intuit and understand them, but what happens when a character inhabits a space where gender and sexuality are open topics but are hardly seen from the same perspective? What if a family isn't fully understanding but isn't rejecting? What happens when a smart, confused kid becomes an assured queer adult when you weren't looking? What happens in the side conversations, the quieter moments, the unbridgeable gaps? What does love look like when you never fully know a person?

Pamela Adlon's excellent slice-of-life dramedy *Better Things* (2016–2022) is a show unlike any other in many ways, but it deserves a spot in this chapter for its provocation of these questions. Throughout the series, Sam Fox (Adlon) is tasked with raising her three kids as a single mom, and the joys and pains of contemporary motherhood are most frustratingly prominent when interacting with her middle child, the too-intelligent, often combative, and deeply introspective but untouchable Frankie (Hannah Alligood). Over five seasons, Frankie is clearly on some sort of queer journey, but the audience's perception of who Frankie is mostly relies on what Sam picks up.

One of the episodes that demonstrates the two different languages Frankie and Sam are speaking while still trying to love each other is season 5's "Ephemera." While taking a tour of Hollywood Forever Cemetery, where Sam's father, Murray, is buried, the tour guide gives his pronouns. Sam is thoroughly amused by this, making jokes about her own pronouns ("mine are trans and fat!"), which Frankie ignores.[16] Later, during the car ride home, Frankie confronts Sam with a lot more patience than Sam would probably give Frankie credit for: Frankie's best friend, and one of Sam's honorarily adopted children, Jason, "is they/them." Sam can't really process that at first, taking it like another joke and making a familiar fake-confused argument. *Is Jason multiple? Is Jason Legion?* When that doesn't get a rise out of Frankie, Sam switches gears. Hypothetically, might there be an identity that Frankie's not letting her in on? Does she still have three daughters, or two daughters and a child, another major obstacle of a concept?

Frankie doesn't give the straightforward answer Sam wants—there's nothing Frankie wants to let Sam in on (understandable, given the way the conversation about Jason is going), but hypothetically, Sam would still have three children. After all, as Frankie questions, why does everything have to be so labeled and "genderized" anyway? Can't Sam recognize that her children's gender isn't about her?

This is one of the conversations that makes Frankie's journey on television, and Sam and Frankie's relationship, so unique. Both of them wound each other, frequently. In lighter moments, they insult each other for sport, but Frankie is often rude and willfully disinterested in Sam's needs and backbreaking physical and emotional labor as the single mom of three strong-willed kids (and the financial support for one pathetic ex-husband). Sam is often flip, diminishing Frankie's desire to change the world and sense of personhood with her need to turn everything into a joke. They're two of the most intelligent characters on the show, extending support and understanding toward almost everyone but each other. In the rare instances when they aren't at opposite ends of generational arguments, they show each other love without speaking, mostly in the form of cooking, one of *Better Things'* most sacred rituals. The love they have for each other is inescapable and, in its most sincere form, nourishing, but they can't trust each other not to weaponize what the other doesn't understand about the facts of life. In short, they're a mom and kid who are more similar than they'd like to admit.

Better Things is so adept at telling queer stories from a different angle because it has such a strong sense of itself, its mundane crisis-laden characters, and its ordinary chaos. Life is messy, it purports—so how could a mom perfectly understand her kid? Why should a young person who is constantly misunderstood by authority figures be forthcoming about their identity? By spending time with both Frankie and Sam and their flaws and genius, we get multiple perspectives on the same queer existence. Like the characters themselves, they're not all flattering or open-minded, and their shifting POVs allow Frankie to evolve without having to fully define who they are to the audience or to Sam's qualifications.

As frustrating as that is to Sam, it presents a sort of freedom to Frankie that rarely appears on television. Frankie can be inconsistent, have private revelations, and grow in the zigzag pattern that neither parents nor linear storytelling easily approve of. Their queerness is often implied and discussed with confusion by the people who don't understand a younger generation's embrace of gender nonconformity, but the show is content not to force them into one label or another. Sam's approval of other labels she understands makes the show an even safer place to experiment with this sort of identity exploration. Frankie isn't in danger of losing family or friends, and Sam isn't a homophobe or traditionalist, but the show sees that there are further nuances to queer experience than just acceptance or flat-out rejection.

Getting Textual

The final use of subtext that I'll describe here is right back to the basics: the kind that most often emerges when two attractive actors make googly eyes at each other in a pining, or chagrined, romance that can never be. This, surely, is no longer needed when we have actual queer couples dotting our screens, the likes of which Xena and Gabrielle could only have dreamed of (and according to Lucy Lawless and some of *Xena: Warrior Princess*'s (1995–2001) more hand-wringingly sapphic episodes, dream they did). From Kirk and Spock to Watson and Sherlock, this kind of tension has been deemed queerbaiting, fool's gold, and ultimately a tired remnant of bygone eras best served by fan fiction and nothing more.

However, there's a curious, and sometimes delectable, development in this type of subtext now that queerness is, by numbers alone, alive and well in so many more series. A character now has the legitimate chance to take up the gauntlet thrown down by the clues fans pick up—a choice made by many shows for which queerness isn't a laughable concept. From the hard-won battles for *The Legend of Korra* (2012–2014) and *Adventure Time* (2010–2018) to include confirmed queerness in their young adult programming, to the series-long game of *Person of Interest* (2011–2016), to the decreasingly dramatic coming outs of *Broad City*, *Dead to Me* (2019–2022), *Ted Lasso* (2020–2023), *Harlem* (2021), *P-Valley* (2020–), or *The Morning Show* (2019–), characters who had previously only been explicitly defined (though they may have hinted otherwise through their admiration of or tensions with other characters) as heterosexual took the small leap to queerness.

Of course, not all fans are on board with newly canonical pairings unless their specifically desired couplings are realized. As Weekes points out using the example of the highly shipped, never realized couple of Kara Danvers and Lena Luthor in *Supergirl*, even with a series that had multiple queer and trans characters and depicted loving, communicative, consummated relationships between queer women, sometimes a letdown is inevitable when all the provided canon representation is "not as important as two white femme characters kissing."[17] It may throw portions of the audience into convulsions, but in some cases, the dreamed-of couple being thwarted is the best thing that could possibly happen to the series.

In codependent stoner buddy comedy *Broad City*, for instance, Abbi's (Abbi Jacobson) coming out to herself is a watershed moment. After five seasons of only dating men, and little by little opening up her tightly repressed heterosexuality, Abbi reflects lightly that the only reason she hesitated in asking for her hot emergency room doctor's number is because said doctor (played by a cheekily cast Clea DuVall) is a woman. Simple as that! After five seasons of thirsting after her best friend's soul, attention, and ass, it's not so simple for Ilana (Ilana Glazer), who is physically torn between being thrilled for her bestie hooking up with a hot dyke doctor and absolutely devastated that she's not Abbi's introduction to bisexuality. Abbi and Ilana's trampled potential for subtext-to-text is crushing in a way that actually moves them forward. They're not a long-shipped couple that creatives or producers just refuse to consider; they're already soulmates.

Of course, in a queer series that already tacitly respects its audience, a little unresolved sexual tension between friends is hardly the worst thing that could happen to two attractive characters. As with queer villains, queer messes, and even queer deaths, if a series breaks the rules of respectable representation in order to make a story more complex, full, and/or even torturous in its refusal to promise a happy ending or pairing, then it may just set the queer imagination alight and make the show even more worth watching.

Queer & A: Jessica Sutton

Credits: *The Kissing Booth*, *Motherland: Fort Salem*

One of the most fascinating recent examples that I've encountered of unspoken but tangible queer subtext on television is found across three seasons of a little genre show that could, Freeform's *Motherland: Fort Salem* (2020–2022). As the mishmash title suggests, it's your standard woman-driven sci-fi historical revisionist supernatural military drama. The premise is simple. What if, around the time of the Salem Witch Trials, the United States government had made a pact with a witch: they would let her and her kind live if she would pledge her allegiance to them as the head of their armed forces? The answer is Eliot Laurence's (*Claws*) max-imalist, backstory-laden, matriarchal world of ritual, spirituality, occult espionage, and paramilitary witchcraft.

Into this ecstatically complex environment steps a main trio: the brooding healer Raelle Collar (Taylor Hickson), perfectionist natural-born leader Abigail Bellweather (Ashley Nicole Williams), and enthusiastic, naively openhearted Tally Craven (Jessica Sutton), all bound together as rookie conscripts in the hugely powerful Witch Army. Within the first episode, Raelle finds herself falling into an ill-advised romance with the secretive Scylla Ramshorn (Amalia Holm), setting up a delightful star-crossed-lovers plot that becomes a sincere heart of the series. From the outset, *Motherland* is explicitly queer (and steamy!), using Raelle and Scylla's connection to guide much of the first season's intrigue and betrayal.

The pair remains a couple throughout the series, and *Motherland*'s world, laden with dense lore around bloodlines, ancient enemies, and sex as a tool for power boosts, became a predictably fertile ground for veteran shippers everywhere. It would have been a largely standard example of contemporary fandom, if not for two actors, Jessica Sutton and Lyne Renée, diving headfirst into fandom culture as soon as they were aware that their audience had picked up on an intense chemistry between Tally and the ultra powerful and aloof head of the army, General Alder (Reneé). Sutton and Reneé had a curious, burning dynamic onscreen that never quite culminated into a canonical couple, but as fans learned, it wasn't for lack of trying.

Sutton was particularly hyper-engaged with fans of the show, giving interviews in which she discussed cut scenes and lines between her character and Renée's, providing insight into the production with an enthusiasm that many fans were stunned by. The two even formed an alternate canon as the episodes aired, posting photos of themselves kissing on set as the series drew to a close. Given the long history of queer fans creating their own comprehensive worlds out of heterosexual media, I was fascinated by the same thing happening in a series that was clearly queer, this time aided by its actors as it was airing and not just as a revelation after the fact à la subtextual predecessors. Neither was it begrudgingly engaged with out of a polite appreciation or contractual obligation, or outright ignored, like more recent, super-popular noncanonical queer obsessions in the same general sci-fi/fantasy realm, including *Once Upon a Time* (2011–2018), *Supergirl*, and *Supernatural* (2005–2020).

Sutton's participation represents a new era of responsiveness to queer audiences—cast members who actively court and endorse an LGBTQIA2S+ interpretation of their characters when said characters' sexuality isn't confirmed in explicit words or actions on the show. Not coincidentally, other actors and writers who have chosen a similar path in recent years do so on shows that are also, from the outset, invested or nonchalant about existing in a queer or sexually fluid world. Curious to hear what might have sparked Sutton to choose that direction personally, especially on her first principal television role, I was lucky enough to spend a few hours chatting about her delight in the community that formed around *Motherland* and the unique glee that came from an audience picking up the subtext that she was so painstakingly laying down.

This is an edited excerpt of our conversation.

SHAYNA MACI WARNER: You seem like a performer who has a really holistic sense of what they're bringing to the screen, not just in terms of craft, but in terms of backstory, chemistry, and thinking about almost every angle of what's happening in your story. It's very exciting to talk to you about how that translates to audiences!

JESSICA SUTTON: I think every artist has a desire at some point to have critics and audience approve of them. That's not why we choose to put ourselves out there but inevitably, there is that sense that once it's out, it no longer belongs to me. Inside, it feels like I'm literally putting everything that I have out there on the floor, but what it feels and what it looks like are two vastly different things. It's really humbling, because you have almost no control over it. Then there's also that added thing of how somebody's going to perceive it and receive it, and that always just fascinates me. So what are you getting back from my performance, what you've seen, just, you're rocking my world.

SMW: I'm happy to hear that. Something that really drew me to you, other than just watching _Motherland: Fort Salem_ for its central queer relationship, was the way you engage with fans. I hope somebody has mentioned to you that it is pretty new for the center of a noncanonical queer couple to so consistently interact with fans of that pairing in a way that gives a lot of access to your process, to what conversations you've had with your fellow actors, and to what conversations you've had with production. Why do you give that access and engage in these conversations, not just on journalistic platforms and publications, but directly through fandom Discords, YouTube channels, and multiple other direct venues?

JS: I think it's just my love and my joy of sharing, which comes to the power of storytelling. Acting has always just been a medium for me. It's become a love affair and a practice that I am devoted to develop throughout my years but it isn't the only thing that satisfies that. A conversation can do pretty much the same . . . it's a joy, basically. I'm a creature of habit. I love to follow the things that bring me delight and draw me closer to life in a really intimate way. I'm not somebody who indulges much in small talk. I like going the depths and the distances, very much like [Tally].

I wanted to engage because this is just so fascinating to me. This is the other part of my job that I don't get to control but I get to participate in if I choose to. I don't know why other actors don't. I think maybe with the social media, you see people engage, but you forget that they are people. I always find it really hard to have a conversation online. Like, is that the best platform for me to go and really dig in there? I don't know. So I've always kept it at a distance but so many things have changed now with my understanding of the power of community and the community online that embraced the show. It led me to engage with them further in a really personal way. The conversations that we've had around the show and around representation have left me with a profound . . . I want to say remembrance. I don't want everyone to forget this, that so many people have so much in common; that feeling of lostness, invisibility, these unanswerable questions that we take into the showers and into the car as we sit and ponder our life in traffic. I want to remember every day that how we see, how we choose to see ourselves, each other, the world, is really the only power that we have.

Something that resonated with me about Tally was her immense capacity to empathize and to meet anyone at the threshold of understanding. And how she never settled in her certainty; there was just this immense courage to keep stepping up and asking questions. I think by season 2, we see her humanity and her insecurity and her fear, and there's the element of despair creeping in, and self-doubt, and that just makes her three-dimensional and really human and really relatable. I saw her clinging to a certainty, I saw her seeking the answers, as if her very life depended on it, because it did, and the bigger picture just kept eluding her. And by season 3, it's just this devotion to faith, in a way, like "trusting the Mother." Which is a line we get to hear again and again, repeated, and it's like, "No, man, just give me the answer!" That's how I was feeling and probably how Tally was feeling. That sense of "why are you withholding the answer?" For it to slowly dawn on her, that the whole point of this thing is living the question? And maybe you lean into an answer, but maybe not. At the end of the day, it's just down to trust—trusting yourself and trusting those who you love.

It's interesting because Tally represented so much of my sentimentality, the childlike side of my heart, my enthusiasm for life, my innocence and trust in the goodness of things and people. I've called her my love letter, because it feels like through playing her, it was really cathartic to expose a side of myself that I was kind of healed [through]. It wasn't like I ever lost my childlike side, but I think when you're an adult, you kind of have this idea that you need to "fake it till you make it." And it's great to have a character like Tally who is just a mess, and she doesn't pretend to be anything else. She just rocks up at the party with all her questions and all her uncertainties and her quirkiness and her uniqueness and her strangeness and she just participates, like a charm is almost in her.

SMW: I want to talk a little bit more about this idea of uncertainty in a character. We've had this history of queer characters often being seen in subtexts or for a very brief, expository, educational arc, and then they're gone. They don't really get any development or complexity. We come up to right now, contemporary television, and you almost expect that there's going to be at least one queer character in each show. But that subtext still exists and can be in a delicious tension of not saying explicitly what's happening on the screen. In *Motherland*, you do have a very specific central queer relationship. But then we have Tally and Alder, who are never named but have that subtext built over three seasons. I would love to hear what is so satisfying about playing that subtext and if there are any frustrations on your side with knowing that it is just going to be subtext, even after you may have given some requests to see a little more text come through on the screen?

JS: Lyne Renée, who plays General Alder, and myself, as artists and actors, we share a similar love for process. Our process is pretty intense. We discovered that through three seasons of basically playing a very intense tennis game. What actors are doing in a scene can look pretty invisible, actually. We're just watching two people speak across a room. That can seem quite unextraordinary. But I like to give the metaphor of tennis because there's so much energy and intention and preparation that goes on behind the scenes and when you step onto a set and are preparing to go into a scene, I mean, you're up to serve. A scene is really only interesting to watch when two people don't want the same thing. They're wanting a similar thing, but there always has to be some kind of tension, some kind of conflict. It doesn't have to be explicit, it doesn't have to be a fight per se, but this push and pull.

I learned from one of my first acting coaches, this idea of point and counterpoint. You know, "I love you, but I'm terrified of who you're becoming." You can want two things almost contradicting each other, and it makes for life being so complex. What we want, and what we think we want, can be at odds with what we need. So Lyne and I, we love the implicit and, like you said, the subtext: what is not being said. I liken that to the silence between notes. What makes music is the silence just as much as the noise; in fact, if it was just a note, you wouldn't hear it as you do.

So acting opposite somebody like Lyne Renée, who is a master at her craft, was that funky strange alchemy of your performance being so much about the other person that they become your performance. What they're giving to you, that serve, is the thing that you're gonna hit back. But you're not hitting back if they're not serving anything. We took these characters and we were just peeling back layers. We kept finding ourselves through season one and two, in particular,

really back in more or less the same room having more or less
the same conversation, and we couldn't help but find more
layers. I think then what inherently started to happen was
that the writers were writing us more and more into the same
rooms having more or less the same conversations, but what
was happening was really interesting. It was almost like they
were picking up on . . . I don't know if we can claim it.
Chemistry is also such a funky beast. I just played off what
Lyne gave me.

But we also never really had a destination in the scene.
We never really spoke about what we were trying to do to
affect each other. I just came in with my goal, she came in
with hers. I went in with a lot more lover intention with
[Alder]. Most of the time, there was this obstacle between us.
But the intensity when I met her eyes . . . I realized that so
much of the craft is in the connection with your scene partner. How present can you be in the moment? Can you let all
that preparation go and just be in this moment, connected to
another human being? And not break eye contact, because
that's also about the power dynamic in the scene.

By the time we reached episode 8 in season 2, the writers
were writing this quite sexualized, dark, fantasy nightmare
between us. We were like, okay, this is interesting. I got some
ideas; Lyne had some ideas. So there was just that element of
being able to play, and then to have the audience respond and
pick up on the subtlety. I always say subtlety is sexy. I'm the
kind of actor where if I can show it, I don't want to say it.
Like, give me a shot at showing it rather than saying it. If you
can, as a filmmaker, trust your actors to deliver. I think
silence is needed. Nowadays I see a lot of films with cascad-
ing music and there's not one beat, not one pause, not one
moment of silence. Everything is overwritten. There's just
this element of breath in life that we, if we're really trying to

depict life in all its complexity, need in order to let things breathe. And sometimes, it's just a pause where two characters are looking at each other.

I think Lyne and I started to just organically put more and more of that breathing, that pausing in it. And then we were indulged in our play, we were throwing things up there to the directors, and they were like, "Oh, that's great!" and the studio liked it, too, and you start to realize that that's the collaboration. The best of collaboration is when everyone is kind of putting things on the table, and obviously, you have one person who gets to dish up their plate. That is an actor's job, is to serve the story, first and foremost, to take direction from the director. You can have a say, and it's nice to be heard, but that is not a given. And that's also not your job. I had to learn to restrain the part in me that wanted to be in control of the story and to not overreach. That was really important.

Three years being a lead on a TV show will teach you so many things, and one of the most important was understanding that, in order to balance the dynamic of a film set, there are so many people, experts, professionals, artisans bringing their craft and energy and spirit and humanness to the circus every day, and you're making this thing but no one really knows what it's going to look like, how it's going to be received. You just have to trust the process, but it's really important to also know your place. So the times when we were able to give a suggestion, and the suggestion was able to be heard and then approved, were awesome.

We did push for season 3 to have it a little bit more explicit, because we had been face-to-face, forehead-to-forehead, seasons 1 and 2, and so we thought it might be cool to just have a smidge. And Lyne was all for it. By that point, we'd also had this upswell of the audience shipping. That was the first time that myself, and Lyne, had ever been shipped before by an audience, and I was very excited and super enthusiastic about it.

Lyne and I have started to talk about, beyond chemistry, how beautiful the relationship of a mentor is and how powerful it is. That, I think, is something that maybe the studio wanted to keep refined when we were trying to advocate for the smooch. The relationship was so ambiguous, complex, and very hard to pin down because there's so much loaded into it. I always just thought that Tally saw Alder, especially in the first season, as somebody she wanted to be but then found out who she really is, as a human being—fully formed, flawed, questionable, deeply questionable—to realize her own humanity. They wanted to make that connection to be like, it could be mother, but also lover. Which also brings back into the theme that our show explores so beautifully, but also implicitly, about sexuality and the power of it.

SMW: It's sometimes difficult to get a complex, queer relationship on TV in this world because it has to be presented in a very specific way in order to get network approval. So the idea of some of the layers in this relationship that many fans were picking up on being almost a hindrance to tipping into text across the screen is really interesting.

JS: At the end of the day, I think it's interesting, right? If we had gotten the approval, it would have totally changed the dynamic. What makes something interesting is that tension. Okay, so then how do you keep that tension? It's like a held breath. So the kids would have an exhale and a release. We feel that all the time, and the different relationship dynamics, especially between [canon queer couple] Raelle [played by Taylor Hickson] and Scylla [played by Amalia Holm]. We're just holding our breath until they're together again. It's almost a variable. But once you get the release, you crave the tension again; it's a really strange thing.

I've had so many conversations with friends about this idea of happily ever after and how we are desperate for everyone to be shipped together and sail off into the sunset, and that there is still that idea, right? Yes, we all want to be there, but maybe not for too long, because we would want to have some kind of tension, something to catch us off guard, the surprise element. I'm really interested in that, because I know that I seek that in my life. I'm not a creature of comfort. I'm a creature of curiosity. And that has led me to very different places, and very different ways of what I find attractive, and why I want to have conversations and never really stopped having them. Because a conversation is a really uncomfortable place, you have no idea where it's going, you have no control over what the other person is going to say or how they're going to take what you've said.

So Lyne and I, we were like, "We want the release." Well, now it's on us to really try to just keep this band taut. The three days when we shot in the ice cave [season 3, episode 8, "Petra's Favorite Pen"], that really felt like we could bite our teeth into a closure. It wasn't going to be a smooch. But it would have to be something maybe even better, which was if we could land that moment of really seeing each other, which was basically the whole of season 3, for me. It was these moments when you're seeing two people who are like, "Oh, there you are." Not as mother and daughter, not as general and soldier, not as sister, it even goes beyond that. You're really taking in the whole human being, and that's true recognition and acknowledgment. I felt seen through making this, and then to hear how the audience was feeling seeing themselves was just the most beautiful mirror, because how many times in life are you finding that alignment with your inner world being so beautifully reflected outside of you? It becomes really spiritual in that way. But we've been talking about it a lot. I've been having so many conversations about contentment and comfort.

SMW: Which I think is exactly what an audience was picking up on. Not the contentment at all but the discomfort, that tension.

JS: That's what makes things sexy. It's really weird. It's a full-body experience of that. We want things that pull us on the edge of our seats, that draw us closer, that almost, almost . . . and then maybe you pull back. In a way, this is why I've always preferred thrillers to horrors, because I really get off on that feeling of being on the edge of my seat, not knowing. I think I've chased that feeling my whole life. Being an actor is not comfortable for me; giving interviews is not comfortable for me. Social media is not comfortable for me. I've immigrated countries; that's not comfortable. I've started to realize, I think you have that pursuit of happiness, and I have a pursuit of discomfort. Because I'm really interested in the mystery and what's behind the discomfort, and believe me, there is a world behind that discomfort.

What I've discovered is, once you put yourself in the way of discomfort, inevitably, you're poised to grow again, to begin again. Whether we know it or not, consciously or unconsciously, we're just beginning again, in our lives, but there are many conversations that people have where they're bored, like chronically bored with their relationships, with their job, with their life. And I also think that's just so intriguing. I'm like, okay, let's dive into that. Because I have to say, boredom is not something that I feel in my life, and I wonder if it has a connection to do with my pursuit of discomfort? I don't know. I don't know!

Chapter 5

EVERYBODY DIES

Queer characters have long had a history of early mortality rates, with some of the earliest sympathetic portrayals of such characters hinging on their deaths to evoke that sympathy. Queer character deaths have mattered in some way to straight characters for decades, whether serving as a sorry example of life's leftovers or temporarily dismantling straight characters' lives and bringing them face-to-face with God. That is, before the straight characters inevitably return to life, an improved person with a new lust for living. While at least beginning with the intention to break through stigmas surrounding the inhumanity of gay people, some shows spun queer death into a blessing.

In his memoir *Even This I Get to Experience*, television godfather Norman Lear reflects on the many difficult-to-approach feelings that *All in the Family* aimed to confront between its characters and viewers alike. Chief among them was a basic but somehow polarizing building block of human experience: empathy. As he writes:

> Empathy, like silence, is another sound that can't be measured in decibels. Nothing caused our live audiences to "shout" their empathy more loudly than Edith's reaction to the news that a transvestite who'd become her friend was murdered by a street gang simply for being a man in women's clothes. Grief-stricken and unable to see how a just God could allow that, her faith was threatened. The audience was near tears.[1]

It's an impassioned reflection from one of the most determined and prolific television producers of all time, who managed to shoehorn sympathetic, smart, and entertaining gay characters (and many other targets of conservative scorn) into almost every show he ever oversaw, from 1968 through 2020. Of course, Lear's audiences were connecting with Edith, not the murdered transvestite Beverly—and Lear isn't writing his heartfelt appreciation with Beverly in mind. Rather, Beverly's importance is in how she makes Edith fall out spiritually with the God she's never before questioned. The catastrophe goes one layer further, to the most immovable and homophobic core of the family. Beverly's life, through her death, and mainly through Edith's crisis of faith, finally touches proud curmudgeon and bigot Archie Bunker.

When going through the TV firsts, I wrote about how unusual it was to see any core character care about an out queer person on television—especially not across more than one episode. Revolutionary as the concept of a blue-collar conservative caring about the destruction of a cross-dressing fag was for 1977, in the great arc of queer television deaths, it's quite easy to point to the ways in which even this groundbreaking, violent offscreen waste of queer life serves to narratively benefit the straight people left to continue. The goals of empathy and sympathy are noble, and "Edith's Crisis of Faith" centers only two people; neither of them is "the transvestite." Lear's honoring of his contribution to the queer death canon is equal parts remarkable and laughable. The most important episode—that centrifugal silence as a void where a female impersonator once stood sucks the air out of the studio audience's lungs—is still a variation on a common theme and even an extremist goal. Queer people must die so straight people can really, truly live.

Maybe Beverly's death was best for Edith, but taken in context of a laundry list of sympathetic dead queer characters, that emotional reflection starts to feel a little . . . well, past its prime. The justification for a queer character's death can feel especially irritating when looking at the scope and breadth of dead lesbians littering American television. For most of American (and a good scope of international) televisual history,

the introduction of a queer woman to a series came with a tacit expira-
tion date. While there are some notable exceptions, after the outspoken
dykes of *The L Word* (not without its own casualties) left the air in 2009,
the average life of such a character was short—not just in the number of
episodes.

In 2016, immediately following the airing of episode "Thirteen," of *The
100* (2014–2020), in which much promoted lesbian character Lexa (Alycia
Debnam-Carey) bit the bullet, Riese Bernard, then CEO of *Autostraddle*,
compiled an astounding initial list of sixty-five (now crowd-sourced and
updated to 230) dead queer women on American and international
television.[2] To supplement, then managing editor Heather Hogan created a subsequent list of only twenty-nine queer women to that date who
had survived their series and/or character arc. The article gathered a
virulent, grief-stricken, and, thanks to social media, enormously visible
collection of audience reactions and harsh criticism denouncing this historical treatment. To these primarily queer-identifying audience members, the problem was clear: television creators needed to stop treating
queer women characters like cannon fodder and instead consider them
as real, viewer-and-writer-invested characters.

But is the root of this outrage an altogether fair accusation? Why
should a writer be required to take sexual orientation into account when
fictional characters of any identity are killed off all the time? A writers'
room should have free rein and total creativity with any character's arc,
especially when considering genre shows, where the stakes are often life
and death and very possibly extinction of the entire human race, right?
Sure, sometimes these arguments sanctifying the showrunner as some
sort of untouchable, mega-brain creative who must be allowed to murder queer female characters for the good of the show aren't as unbiased
or objective as their proponents claim, but what would television be if
there were a true moratorium on killing any demographic?

Two years after Lexa's cataclysmic offing, I organized a panel for
NYU Cinema Studies called "Mom . . . I'm a Slayer: Coming Out in '90s
Fantasy Television." Unavoidably, the subject of Dead Lesbian Syndrome

and *The 100* came up. As asked by a self-described straight male audience member, shouldn't we be able to forgive *The 100* for killing Lexa, if she was just one character in an arguably diverse cast of characters? Panelist Heather Hogan took up the answer. Hogan explained that Lexa was "symbolic in a way that the show will never recover from," and that despite whatever redemption *The 100* sought in other areas, the trust between show and queer audience who had simply had enough was broken.[3] Maybe the best way to ask for a queer audience's forgiveness—and, by direct connection, their continued ratings—might have been in not killing their much-awaited and highly advertised avatar of that audience.

While many queer viewers have been aware of the fatalistic, often violent destruction of their fictional selves for decades, the outcry provoked by Lexa's death had finally attracted mainstream media attention, and journalists and fans weren't the only people putting intense scrutiny on the way queer women characters exited their series.* Creators, showrunners, and writers of shows such as *Jane the Virgin* (2014–2019), *Brooklyn Nine-Nine* (2013–2021), *Wynonna Earp* (2016–2021), and *Killing Eve* (2018–2022) were caught up in the conversation, with fans flocking to their shows in the hopes that their queer women would survive one way or another, as bulletproof, immortal, or the gal left standing with the gun. But now that the #LexaDeservedBetter fever pitch has quieted and the shows caught in the cross fire of its immediate aftermath have ended, what does the landscape look like? Am I lesbophobic for wanting us to kill a few queers every now and again? To answer this and other brave questions, this chapter explores the history of dead queer women on television, looking at their varied treatment on heterosexual and LGBTQIA2S+ series alike, in order to give a fuller

***

* As discussed in Rebecca Beirne's introduction, "Queer Women on Television Today," in *Televising Queer Women: A Reader*, the advocacy group known as Lesbian Feminist Liberation, Inc., rallied to send a message to television networks in 1975, demanding that there be "no negative portrayal of lesbians on television until 12% of all the women represented on television are portrayed as lesbians."

picture of queer death on television and still argue for its necessity in queer storytelling.

(Precursors to) The Stray Bullet: 1976–2001

That the very first recurring lesbian character, Julie (Geraldine Brooks) on the soapy *Executive Suite*, lasted only three episodes before being hit by a truck was part and parcel with *The Celluloid Closet*-coined inevitability of burying one's gays/Dead Lesbian Syndrome.[4] The same could be said about a 1992 episode of the acclaimed series *Northern Exposure* (1990–1995), in which guest character Cicely (Yvonne Suhor) takes the fatal bullet intended for her wife, who is also subsequently written off the show, even though both characters are identified as instrumental in founding the town. Even in some of the kindest portrayals of mentally balanced, generally likable lesbian characters, the unwritten rule was plain as day: recurring queer women had about a fifty-fifty shot at meeting their maker before the series was out and were fair game in any genre.

For every lesbian wedding in *Friends*, there was a bisexual death in *Seinfeld*: recurring character Susan Ross (Heidi Swedberg), whose dating a woman causes massive panic in her on-again, off-again ex George (Jason Alexander), ends her twenty-eight-episode run in the preposterous manner of licking and succumbing to toxic envelope glue. Moving from sitcoms to procedurals, a clearly shot and backpedaled-the-next-episode kiss between bisexual lawyer C. J. (Amanda Donohoe) and heterosexual Abby (Michele Greene) on *L.A. Law* could be matched by *NYPD Blue*, in which another Abby (Paige Turco), this time an out lesbian police officer, survives a home invasion, only to mourn the murder of her longtime partner, Kathy (Lisa Darr). Even in the historically progressive waters of fantasy and sci-fi, one kiss in *Star Trek: Deep Space Nine* is countered by a destructive sleeper personality on *Babylon 5* (1993–1998), a lab-rat experimentation gone wrong on *Dark Angel* (2000–2002), and an alien blast on the very same *Deep Space Nine* a few years later.

As white gay male characters were finally propelled into slightly tolerable and then more and more favorable recurring and then principal slots with *Brothers*, *Doctor Doctor* (1989–1991), and *Will & Grace* and began to more fully populate the airwaves in more than one-off bit parts and comic relief in the wake of *Oz* and *Queer as Folk*, queer women characters continued to flounder. The closest hits were in the form of recurring bisexual neighbor Nancy Bartlett (Sandra Bernhard) on *Roseanne* (1991–1997), harried lesbian couple Lindsay (Thea Gill) and Melanie (Michelle Clunie) on *Queer as Folk*, and eventually the decisive coming out of Kerry Weaver (Laura Innes) on her latter seasons of *ER* (1994–2009). It wasn't until a pop-culture phenomenon in the form of everyone's favorite monster-as-metaphor-for-childhood-trauma series that a lesbian romance was afforded any type of continued, sensitive spotlight—which made the death of one-half of the partnership a tragedy still talked about today.

Buffy the Vampire Slayer was a beacon of nineties prime-time television for many reasons—not the least of which being the fantasy dramedy, starring daytime soap star Sarah Michelle Gellar as a poppy, pun-wielding vampire slayer with equal propensities for kicking demon ass and interpreting *Seventeen* magazine spreads, takes teenagers seriously. The concerns of the average American high schooler are blown up to monstrous metaphors, with such topics as first times, inter-friend group romances, and what to wear to prom given the same narratively engaging treatment as more "adult" concerns like abusive relationships, suicidal ideation, familial abandonment, and financial insecurity. The series certainly drew its negative criticisms for its tonal and narrative fumbles with any non-white character and a few universally awful episodes (search the backstory of the failed anti-alcohol PSA "Beer Bad" for a laugh and grimace) while it was airing, and the public uncovering of creator Joss Whedon's misogynistic on-set attitudes lingers over its rewatches. Yet it remains the most-discussed television program in modern academia and retains an enormous fan base and a spot in American television's Hall of Fame. Unfortunately, it also deserves a section in this chapter not for its brilliance but for its dead lesbian.

In what would become the most fashionable way of killing off a notable queer woman character, the stray bullet that pierces Tara Maclay (Amber Benson) in "Seeing Red," in *Buffy*'s sixth season, was a shot heard across the airwaves, affecting viewers of all orientations. The tender, exploratory relationship between college witches Tara and Willow Rosenberg (Alyson Hannigan) flowered over three seasons, with Whedon and primary writer and eventual showrunner Marti Noxon hiding the sexual components of their love in downright cheeky magic euphemisms. From the outset of their very first episode together—season 4's "Hush," which is widely regarded as one of the best of the series, they move a vending machine with the force of a meaningful glance and their joined hands. After this explosive introduction, but before the two became a canonical couple, they conduct glitter-strewn spells in which they telepathically pluck the petals from a single rose and collapse at each other's feet in what can only be described as sweaty, postorgasmic afterglows.

Over the seasons, their visual subtext and euphemism gave way to a genuine, adoring relationship that resulted in the first breaking of the nineties tradition of the "lesbian kiss episode," in which two women characters kiss, usually in order to garner some press during sweeps week, but are unable to pursue a relationship further. In Tara and Willow's case, their first onscreen kiss in season 5's "The Body" is driven by grief, solidarity, and comfort and is a show of the strength, rather than the conclusion, of their romantic and emotional connection. Even after cementing their status as a couple and flouting convention with their kiss, the show continued to take advantage of its fantasy universe's rules to portray queer sexual desire and intimacy.

In season 6's impressively justified musical episode "Once More, with Feeling," Tara's sweet rhapsody to their relationship culminates in her literal levitation off a bed, with Willow just offscreen, presumably performing cunnilingus as her girlfriend sings her praises. Though there are arguments, such as scholar Edwina Bartlem's, that the show's equating lesbian sex with magic is a negative reinforcement of the allegation that lesbian sexuality simply doesn't exist without a male presence involved, Tara and Willow's skirting of censors was, by and large, a calculated avenue to depicting a love that had been absent from airwaves for so long.[5]

Along with thwarting the "lesbian kiss episode," their relationship endured many of the tropes that had troubled queer women's relationships in previous shows, including the return of Willow's ex-boyfriend Oz (Seth Green), the brief appearance of Tara's witch-phobic family in an attempt to reclaim and reconvert her, and, in tropes specific and beloved to *Buffy*, all number of vampiric, zombified, and evil-scientist antagonists. Despite fights, breakups, addiction, deaths in the family, and the second coming of the apocalypse, Tara and Willow's love overcame almost all, presenting a bright thread amid the many troubled relationships in the rest of the Scooby gang. The love with which Tara and Willow regarded each other was the equivalent of a floodlight, and the kind of relationship they demystified should never be able to be stuffed back into total darkness by overly fastidious network sensibilities.

Tara and Willow's relationship was a monumental step forward both in the portrayal of queer women characters as a whole and in celebrating young queer identities, but they may be most remembered for Tara's death, which came not at the hands of a supernatural force but at a bumbling shot from a mere mortal, only minutes after Tara and Willow reunite from a breakup. This method of murder, which Whedon has commented on as a metaphor for the overwhelming power of gun violence, was a particular affront to many who considered it a remark on Tara's dispensability. After all, with Willow and Tara's love having survived torture at the hands of a literal god (the delightfully sadistic and off-kilter Glory, played by Clare Kramer), it seemed mundane, and even disrespectful, for a witch as powerful as Willow, and a love as resonant as theirs, to be undone accidentally, without any magical or medical cure.

While there may have been plans to revive Tara at one point, a concept that Whedon claimed to have worked on but never informed Amber Benson of, *Buffy* ended without ever bringing her back—a conclusion that Marti Noxon expressed regret over in a 2018 interview with *Vulture*.[6] Narratively, Tara's death was meant to crack Willow, throwing her fully into the unhinged destruction of dark magic, but Noxon admitted that she was uneasy and even unsatisfied by the show's decision, wondering why the sweet, shy, and resilient Tara, "of all people," had to die. The same was asked by scores of message boards, but at the time, it was swept away by Whedon as a narrative necessity, and the show continued for its final season with only the memory of Tara.

Post-Stray Bullet: 2002–2016

After Tara, the onscreen death toll continued to climb. From 2002–2016, queer women were victims of impalement (*Smallville*), asphyxiation (*ER, Orange Is the New Black, Van Helsing*), stabbing (*Rome, Black Sails*), stabbing with a cursed blade (*Charmed, Supernatural*), car crashes (*The O.C.*), intentional vehicular manslaughter (*Agents of S.H.I.E.L.D., House of Cards*), bombs (*Queer as Folk, Battlestar Galactica, Home and Away*), overdoses (*Orange Is the New Black*), suicides (*Private Practice, The Following, Strictly Confidential, Blindspot*), murder-suicides (*Spartacus, The Vampire Diaries*), serial killers (*American Horror Story, Jessica Jones, Scream Queens, Law & Order: Criminal Intent, Pretty Little Liars, The Killing*), brutal beatings (*Deadwood, Spartacus, Hemlock Grove, Teen Wolf*), cancer (*The L Word, Private Practice, Code Black*), heart attack (*Under the Dome, Mistresses*), childbirth (*Heroes, Masters of Sex*), poisoning (*The Vampire Diaries, Defiance, Empire, American Horror Story*), and Ilene Chaiken (*The L Word*), to name just a few of the most memorable deaths. Most popularly, however, they were the victim of a bullet, stray or intentional (*24, The Wire, Battlestar Galactica, Torchwood, Sons of Anarchy, All My Children, True Blood, Boardwalk Empire, The Walking Dead, Agents of S.H.I.E.L.D., American Horror Story, Ascension*).

From this mere sampling of deaths of regular and recurring queer women characters, it almost goes without saying that on shows with primarily heterosexual ensembles and storylines, the guest-starring queer women characters had a much higher chance of being killed off than their straight guest-starring counterparts. But zooming out of these individual deaths, the resulting blow to this entire demographic of fictional characters can be seen in the fact that, between 2002 and 2016, only fourteen out queer women characters (who could be generously described as recurring or regular) in these heterocentric primetime and daytime shows, survived their entire series and were given unquestionably happy endings. Even then, the surviving couples and individuals of *Once and Again* (1999–2003), *Buffy the Vampire Slayer*, *ER*, and *Hannibal* (2013–2015) were matched by deceased queer women characters on their very own shows. That whittles the mostly straight shows in which queer women characters survived and were awarded a happy ending between the deaths of Tara and Lexa to only *South of Nowhere* (2005–2008), *Hart of Dixie* (2011–2015), and the heartfelt but sans kiss or developed relationship in animated kid's cartoon *The Legend of Korra*.

As could be expected, more recurring and regular queer women characters found their ways to implied offscreen happiness in shows densely populated with queer characters, such as *The Wire*, *Queer as Folk*, *Glee*, *American Horror Story*, and, yes, the lesbian playground of *The L Word*. Expectedly, these shows contained an excess of dead queer women characters, with *American Horror Story* and *The Wire* racing each other to total body count trophies. Many of the deaths in *American Horror Story* and *The Wire*, both of which fall into anthology styles, were motivated by their high-tension premises, which promised an eyeful of violence, or at least the setup to some truly shocking and heart-wrenching events, in almost every episode. And *The L Word* was eventually accepted (or bravely rejected) as an imperfect beacon of lesbian culture and that the best thing to do was unanimously mourn the inexplicably swift passing of Dana Fairbanks (Erin

Daniels), religiously defend or refuse to spend much grief on Jenny Schecter (Mia Kirshner), and regard the explicit hijinks in between with some gratitude and some befuddlement.

As filmmaker and *Autostraddle* senior editor Drew Gregory points out in relation to the deaths on *The L Word*, there's more than one way to kill a character. Even while Dana's death was so regrettable that *The L Word: Generation Q* spent entire storylines dedicated to resurrecting Dana's memory, her melodramatic death from cancer wasn't as painful to Gregory as Jenny's total character annihilation *and* death. Gregory explains:

> We're watching [Jenny] her entire queer journey. We've learned that she dealt with abuse as a young person, that she clearly struggles with mental illness. The original *L Word* is sort of like a dual storyline; there are Bette and Tina as the established lesbians who want to have a kid, and Jenny is the new lesbian. To take that character and to kill her, and to not just kill her but to do so by turning your sixth season into a murder mystery in this very flip way where you're having to justify why every single character in your cast would kill her is so brutal to me and so cruel. From within our community, it feels so brutal.[7]

These queer women deaths pre-2016 constituted a terminal exhaustion. With some of the most prominent characters in these series, merely surviving their run was cause for celebration, regardless of how they were treated during that survival. The baseline was this: survive and outwit the Dead Lesbian Syndrome, and all else will be lukewarmly forgiven if not forgotten and subsequently grumbled about by unsatisfied viewers for years after. With the number of queer women characters being so low in the first place, every guest appearance and minute implication was scrutinized for what it was, but those complaints were largely kept as an in-community sigh.[8] So, what changed? Why, after ninety-five deaths over four decades on American television, did one fictional leader of a dystopian alliance of barbaric "Grounder" clans break through this inundation to inspire a national turning point?

Stray Bullet Part II: 2016 as the Turning Point

The 100 is not, at its core, a reprehensible show. Neither is the CW sci-fi drama series about young apocalypse survivors muddling through the politics and perils of dystopian fallout a particularly extraordinary or innovative show, relying on TV's oft-employed stereotypes of tribalism, exoticization, white savior complex, and every science fiction trope in the book to produce a gritty, plot hole–filled but entertaining adaptation of the young adult novel series by Kass Morgan. If not for the hype generated by the show's publicity team, and by showrunner/developer Jason Rothenberg in particular, around the promised star-crossed-lovers-style pairing of series lead Clarke (Eliza Taylor) and recurring character Lexa in the third season, the show may well have escaped critical scrutiny and overwhelming backlash altogether. However, as Maureen Ryan of *Variety* pointed out in March 2016, mere days after the descent of Jason Rothenberg from new hero of LGBTQIA2S+ representation to PR nightmare, the show's team did not seem to understand a relatively straightforward argument: do not tout commitment to a viewer base if you are planning to kill off the best-established representation from that demographic.[9]

What was most incensing to the emergent #LexaDeservedBetter movement was not that Lexa, whose actor, Alycia Debnam-Carey, was openly signed to another show, is killed. Lexa's status as a fan favorite was certainly a factor in the disappointment surrounding her exit, but more unforgivable was the way in which the character, who had been explicitly promised as a queer love interest and promoted as appearing in the season finale, is killed off mid-season, mere minutes after she and Clarke repair their fraught relationship and consummate their love for the first time. And, lo and behold, Lexa is done in by a stray bullet meant for Clarke. Fourteen years after Tara, Lexa, an all-powerful commander of six armies and a casually, canonically queer woman (having been involved with another woman in a previous plot) who had survived assassination attempts, physical challenges to her throne, and the literal apocalypse (again!), accepts her fate at the hands of an everyday weapon. Lexa dies in Clarke's arms while asking Clarke to abandon all notions of getting help and only reappears to Clarke as a hallucinatory vision in the season 3 finale.

Fans were (sometimes personally, insultingly, and threateningly) furious, voicing their sense of betrayal to Rothenberg and episode writer and television veteran Javier Grillo-Marxuach alike, but no one had envisioned what frenzy would come next. Perhaps the mirror-image callousness in offing a queer fan favorite in yet another popular sci-fi/ fantasy drama could have been enough. Perhaps Jason Rothenberg's multiple interviews and Twitter feed full of effusive praise for *The 100*'s commitment to representation prior to that fateful episode could have been enough. Perhaps the total delegitimization of the consistent inter- actions between fans and the show's social media, in which the audience was told to trust the writers' intentions with Lexa on a series that had little compunction about killing most characters, would have been enough. Perhaps Clarke and Lexa presented an easy-to-root-for, beauti- ful cisgender couple whose slow-burn storyline was lifted from a thou- sand fan fictions, and snatching away the promise of this coupling would have been enough. Or maybe Riese Bernard, whose decision to compile a list of every single dead lesbian and queer female character on television provided fans with the concrete knowledge of television history to back up their intense emotional discord and refute the argument that Lexa was only one character, would have been enough. In any case, dayenu. The combination was enough to start a movement.

In the days after the airing of "Thirteen," #LexaDeservedBetter became a nationally trending hashtag, but the outcry was soon far larger than just Twitter, *Autostraddle*, or the typical individual blogs on sites such as *Wattpad*, *LezWatch.TV*, and *LGBT Fans Deserve Better*. *Variety*, the BBC, the *Washington Post*, *Seventeen* magazine, *Marie Claire*, and *Cosmopolitan* picked up the story, interviewing fans and public commentators with a previously unapplied spotlight, and dozens of smaller media outlets published their own coverage.[10] The ratings for *The 100*'s next episode dropped dramatically, and showrunners, including Jason Rothenberg, took notice. Three weeks after giving a *TV Insider* interview in which he defended his "beautiful" choice and painted the conclusion of Lexa's arc as a "good story," Rothenberg took to *Medium* to self-publish an apology.[11] Unfortunately for Rothenberg, his description of Clarke and Lexa's relationship as a "positive step of inclusion" and defense of *The 100* as a show with "a bisexual lead and a very diverse cast" rang false for fans who had closely watched his social media in the days following Lexa's death, and many responses to his note centered around accusations of continued attempts at queerbaiting, even after the termination of *The 100*'s most anticipated relationship. Rothenberg's claim that "burying, baiting, or hurting anyone was never our intention. It's not who I am" was soundly rejected.[12]

Although Rothenberg could not find his way back into the good graces of *The 100*'s queer following, the concept of #LexaDeservedBetter rippled outward with a force that far exceeded the reach of a single representation. The wave of media coverage resulted in connections across the queer internet, with fans congregating across platforms and eventually generating upward of $160,000 in donations for LGBTQ+ youth suicide prevention nonprofit the Trevor Project in Lexa's name. Three of these fans, Holly Winebarger, Nicole Hand, and Emily Maroutian, went a step further, creating and hosting the first annual ClexaCon, "the first and largest multi-fandom event for LGBTQ+ women, trans and non-binary fans and creators," in Las Vegas, Nevada, on March 3–5, 2017.[13]

Initially organized as a gathering for somewhere around a hundred people, the con gained enough word-of-mouth and social media traction to become a veritable event, attracting fans, writers, and industry professionals alike. The first ClexaCon was no slouch, boasting a roster of performers and creators from such queer favorites as *South of Nowhere*, *All My Children*, *Person of Interest*, and Canadian American co-productions and imports *Carmilla* (2014–2016), *Lost Girl* (2010–2016), and *Wynonna Earp*. The first conference was such a success that the subsequent guests for its second, third, and fourth installments included creatives and executives from almost every lesbian television arc of note; a roundup of independent queer cinema and web series; authors, editors, and publishers of lesbian fiction; and perhaps most relevant to this chapter, Alycia Debnam-Carey and Amber Benson—the original recipients of the Stray Bullets—and Javier Grillo-Marxuach, the scriptwriter of "Thirteen."

The existence of ClexaCon seemed to be evidence of a changing focus from those behind the scenes. That acknowledgment not only from the queer creators in the independent film industry but also from executives and showrunners of Hollywood and Vancouver television industries was remarkable. Considering that ClexaCon was started by women entirely outside the industry in order to cater to grieving fans who were channeling their frustrations with every devastating, violent, or lazy death into establishing a physical venue for what was previously only virtual interpersonal community support, its success established an overwhelming sea change with how queer fans and those who portrayed their favorite characters interacted. Perhaps as a direct result of that support, and *The 100*'s disastrous turn with social media, American television began to experiment with a new extreme: the immortal, the bulletproof, and the resurrected queer woman character.

Stray Bullet Redux: Will They, Won't They (2016–2022)

Jane the Virgin, the heartwarming, satirical send-up of all things telenovela, picked perhaps the most inopportune (or brilliant, depending on how you read it) time to flirt with the death of a beloved lesbian character. When sociopathic, face-switching, master of all devious trades Rose/Sin Rostro (Bridget Regan) was strangled, to the horror of her neurotic, alcoholic, basket case lover Luisa Alver (Yara Martinez) in February 2016, I was about as disappointed as anyone. Here, I thought, was just another example of a show recycling a tired trope—a real letdown with a series as inventive and purposefully, exaggeratedly skewering of all number of romantic and dramatic archetypes as *Jane*. I wasn't giving up on the show by any means, but when the Lexa movement emerged a month later, I certainly began to regard it in a different, less forgiving light.

I had the good fortune of attending a talk with two of the show's writers and executive producers, Amy Rardin and Jessica O'Toole, in April 2016. When it came time for the Q&A, #LexaDeservedBetter was conjured in the third audience question, and both Rardin and O'Toole were obviously uncomfortable. They were cagey with their answers, only expressing that showrunner Jennie Snyder Urman was positively horrified that Rose's death lined up with such a hurricane of visible grief and that she had no intention of aligning with Rothenberg or the "bury your gays" trope. Rardin and O'Toole also made a plea: keep watching. Those in the audience who were familiar with the question, including the audience member who had asked, were clearly unsatisfied, but at that point there was an air of finality and a lid placed on that particular conversation. Every show, no matter how interesting or purportedly feminist, had to pay its dues and kill at least one of the queer women in its supporting cast.

For a few seasons, I was proven wrong. I watched with shock and delight as *Jane* completely upended begrudging expectations that a lesbian, once buried, would stay buried. While fans were processing the unearthings of every queer woman character ever killed, neither Snyder Urman nor her writers' room would give anything away, which cost some ultimately unearned blowback. But in a classic telenovela fakeout, the second season's finale reveals Rose to be alive and well, in disguise (and with a completely new face) as Susanna (Megan Ketch), Luisa's new love interest. With the panache and melodrama typical of *Jane*, Rose announces to Luisa, "Ours is the greatest love story ever told." Right before she kidnaps Luisa, of course, in the name of their great love story.

Jane is not the first television show to resurrect its dead lesbians— SyFy's archeological camp fest *Warehouse 13* (2009–2014) excavated and briefly reunited the flirtatious H. G. Wells (gender-swapped and bisexual as played by the perennially gay-for-pay Jaime Murray) with her crush Myka Bering (Joanne Kelly), although the pair never became canonical. And superhero Sara Lance/White Canary (Caity Lotz) was shot through with (what else?) arrows on *Arrow* (2012–2020) before being resurrected by the mysterious Lazarus pit the next season, and just in time for a spin-off of her own with *DC's Legends of Tomorrow* (2016–2022). Both of these series, especially *Legends*, which found myriad opportunities for Sara to hop through time and seduce every historical lesbian she encountered, deserve nods for their subversions, even if Sara was less of a surprise with the announcement of *Legends*, and H. G. Wells's resurrection occurred shortly before she exited the show altogether. But *Jane* is especially notable for announcing a queer woman as the mechanic of her own fake death, masterfully manipulating characters and viewers alike and providing for a truly jaw-dropping plot twist driven by (twisted) queer love.

But *Jane* didn't stop there. In its penultimate season, after three years of a complex adversarial-turned-intimate-friends tension between Jane Villanueva (Gina Rodriguez) and Petra Solano (Yael Grobglas), the previously straight-identifying Petra finds herself falling for her unerringly smooth lawyer, Jane "J.R." Ramos (Rosario Dawson), who eventually returns her awkward affections. In the season finale, while defending Petra and wrestling a gun from an offscreen assailant, J.R. shoots the unknown attacker seconds before the season's end, prompting an iconic shot and inverse cliffhanger decades in the making: "J.R. shot who?" While it may not be as talked about as *Dallas*'s original watercooler moment of the year, *Jane* did stumble into a new inversion utilized in a post-Lexa landscape: making queer characters bulletproof in their indispensability, or the character to hold the gun.

Canadian American supernatural Western horror series *Wynonna Earp*, another SyFy entry and one of the earliest shows to make a full-slate appearance at ClexaCon, deals most directly and nail-bitingly with the inversion of the Stray Bullet. In the show's first season finale, newly romantic but as yet private couple Waverly Earp (Dominique Provost-Chalkley) and Sheriff Nicole Haught (Katherine Barrell) are caught in a supernatural brawl and hostage situation that involves a gun as the weapon of choice. Given the show's moody, swaggering aestheticization of Western conventions, guns, holsters, and other cowboy-related weapons are at least well within reason. When unhinged, envious family-member-turned-nemesis Willa (Natalie Krill) outs the couple, she shoots Nicole, but not a minute later, Nicole rips away her blouse to reveal a bulletproof vest. For a show that delights in gritty, messy deaths in combined styles of classic Western shootouts and explosive exorcisms, showrunner Emily Andras's sparing of Nicole was hugely gratifying to its fans, and she addressed them directly on social media and in interviews to reassure them that she specifically understood their frustrations with the landscape.[14]

Brooklyn Nine-Nine escaped an untimely death of its own when it was canceled by its parent network, Fox, and picked back up by NBC after a massive letter-writing, tweeting, and celebrity-endorsed campaign for its renewal. A large part of that surge of enthusiasm and protection has to do with the critically and popularly praised out bisexual actress Stephanie Beatriz. Speaking directly to the Dead Lesbian Syndrome in an interview with *Entertainment Weekly* in 2017, Beatriz noted that her position on the show as a principal character, and as a detective, allowed her to think of exploring her character's sexual orientation with a "safety net" underneath.[15] With an awareness of her emerging power as a queer creator, and the hindsight of the trope, Beatriz said of her representation as a bi character, "I know it's out there, but often times it's written in a specific way. 'Let's introduce a gay character and quickly kill them off' . . . It's not like [Rosa's] going to come out and then get hit by a car and get killed off." Indeed, Rosa remained a fan favorite—and alive—until the series' close in 2021, adding to *The Fosters* and *Adventure Time*, whose lesbian characters survived their runs.

In the forty-plus lesbian characters who have died since Lexa, some have caused more of a stir than others. One of the more recent additions to the canon, the BBC America/AMC co-production *Killing Eve* did its fair share of running over queer women with cars, as well as exuberantly murdering as many characters as possible with electrified glee. The central relationship of this cat-and-mouse thriller is the tempestuous, obsessive, brazenly sexual hunt between pencil-pushing MI6 agent Eve Polastri (Sandra Oh in a career-defining turn) and Villanelle/Oksana (the remarkably chameleonic Jodie Comer). Theirs is a fascinating relationship, an all-consuming spiral that reflects a stunning battle of wills and consuming desires in two morally gray, complex, and flawed individuals. Villanelle's bisexuality plays a factor in her origin story, and her attraction to Eve is not merely implied—it is explored in depth, made explicit as a motivation, and exploited as an Achilles' heel. Rather than limit her sexual orientation to an obsession with Eve, Villanelle picks up lovers of multiple genders throughout the series, without so much as a bat of the eye. Of course, she also kills other queer women, most notably her ex, Nadia (Olivia Ross), and, in a far more morose turn, effects the suicide of her earliest obsession, Anna (Susan Lynch).

Villanelle's characterization is a well-wrought, multilevel depiction of a queer woman, who, despite her murderous tendencies, offers a figure that somehow invokes sympathy and secret cheers. Eve's own orientation is somewhat of a muddle early on, even as she protests, after having described Villanelle in sweeping, poetic imagery to a hapless police sketch artist, that her attraction is purely, obsessively professional. However, as Eve uncovers more pieces of Villanelle's luxurious, violent, and recklessly indulgent world, she begins to fall into the same sensuality that makes Villanelle so committed to her job. Murder is at the heart of this story, with Villanelle and Eve both holding weapons of their own, occasionally on each other, but their relationship is so integral to the plot that it would be impossible to continue the series with one of their deaths. Logically, this is why fans had to wait until the very last episode to see Villanelle murdered.

At the polar opposite side to Andras, *Killing Eve* never promised a happy ending or dangled any social media morsel to entice a queer audience's belief in the immortality of the character, yet queer women flocked to the show in droves, hoping for the pair to become a real item, despite all that murder around them. When Eve and Villanelle finally seemed to have gotten together in the last episode of the season, improbably venturing toward a happily ever after, only for Villanelle to be shot and killed minutes before the final credits rolled, Twitter was once again up in arms.

Some, like Drew Gregory, regard that outrage with some skepticism. As she points out, the landscape between 2016 and 2022 looks markedly different for the sheer number of queer women onscreen—for its 2016–2017 season, GLAAD's annual *Where We Are on TV* report calculated 161 lesbian and bisexual women characters across prime-time broadcast, cable, and streaming, as compared to the 284 characters of the same orientations in the 2022–2023 season.[16] Even with a long history of dead lesbians, sometimes the comfort of a checkbox like "bury your gays" just doesn't encompass the varied ways to tell a story about death—especially in a genre show like *Killing Eve*.

"Villanelle is such a developed character that I'm more bothered by something where it just doesn't feel necessary. But Villanelle or Eve had to die; that just feels like the obvious conclusion of this operatic tragedy," Gregory says, further advocating for both of them to have died if the show wanted to really reach the full potential of its tragic climax. "But," she acknowledges, "I am also sympathetic to the fact that people don't go into a TV show with a blank slate. You go in with the media that you have. Even if you didn't have the experience of growing up watching these shows as they aired, there's still a general awareness. I feel like there's somewhat of a level of removal that happens, and of being primed for disappointment."[17]

A similar question arises when looking at the final curve of Rose's contorted arc on *Jane the Virgin*. It would have been improbable for Rose and Luisa's relationship to survive the length of the series. No matter how much Rose had displayed a cockroach-like impermeability, she was the mustache-twirling villain of a telenovela, and the only fitting end for her was to be fooled by her lover taking "cyanide" (a Tic Tac), accidentally pushed through a trapdoor, and impaled on a giant spike below, in a mirror image of how the show had depicted her earliest sadistic kill. Though some viewers were left hopeful that Rose would reemerge, a deranged lesbian kraken from the deep, this time, she was really, truly dead.

Did *Jane* fool us yet again? Did they take queer viewers for a joyride and dump us on our asses, confounded and horrified? Yes. And I loved it. Like Villanelle, Rose had made her way through almost the entire series, plotting deed after horrifying deed and backstabbing with relish, all in the name of the woman she loved. In a show of absurdities, Rose's survival would have meant either a betrayal of her character or a betrayal of form—both of which could have been possible but deeply strange. Sometimes, in order to make good television, one of the villains has to die a gruesome death so we can imagine their descent into the exaggerated flames of soap opera hell. Sometimes, that conniving, magnetic, long-running bane of the by-comparison milquetoast protagonists' existence just happens to be a lesbian.

Death as the Beginning

Detective Rosa Diaz, Sheriff Nicole Haught, and Eve Polastri are all card-carrying members of law enforcement or vigilantism in some way. Does this trend posit that queer female characters must legally own a gun or be employed in a notoriously anti-LGBTQIA2S+ arm of government in order to ensure their survival? On the other hand, Villanelle/Oksana and Rose/Sin Rostro are mentally unstable supervillains whose bloodlust is outmatched only by their obsessive love for their counterparts—is there really any question that they could have had a generic chance at survival? Why not simply make their deaths (and lives) as motivated and thrilling as a TV character's could be? New representations of bulletproof queer women characters are not enough to dismantle a decades-long (centuries-long, if one considers the literary canon) trope; however, the increase in numbers presents a new way of questioning queer women characters' construction, presentation, and eventual ending, without dismissing them as the victims of an unstoppable, long-running patriarchal force that dominates even when their writers are also women.

These character extremes are, more often than not, soaked in histories and associations with violence, and in many cases they hearken back to that Stray Bullet as the model to which all other queer female characters must conform or alter. In the age of screenwriting panels and filmmaking workshops hosted by ClexaCon encouraging new queer creators, increasing visibility and ownership is nothing to scoff at, nor is it something to take at face value. As is often repeated, to level the playing field, one must introduce enough players—in this case, some that can take survival for granted and assume that they are absolutely integral to their series, and more that can exist as characters who stand on their own as villains, heroes, or something entirely outside a checkbox.

Of course, the conundrum of the Immortal Lesbian is just one view of queer death—specifically queer women characters' deaths—onscreen. The possibility of death can be a basic building block to ensuring that your genre show has teeth, but it also comes into play for telling resonant queer stories across narratives. One of the most obvious categories of queer stories that would be rendered moot by a dismissal of death are personal narratives concerning HIV/AIDS. As is to be expected, those fictional storylines began on a path of straight moral enlightenment and myth busting, with medical drama *St. Elsewhere* being the first to broach such a topic in the 1983 episode "AIDS and Comfort." More about dispelling rumors of contagion and assumption, which the episode considered deadlier than AIDS itself, queer death didn't play as more than an underlying implication.

Two years later, just a month after Rock Hudson's death made headlines, AIDS-related queer grief would take a much more central thrust with *An Early Frost*. Future *Queer as Folk* showrunners Ron Cowen and Daniel Lipman's 1985 TV movie is the first and, next to HBO's *Angels in America* miniseries in 2003, one of the best-remembered television narratives to meaningfully cover the epidemic, two years before then president Ronald Reagan would even utter the word "AIDS." It spends a good chunk of its run time focused on the varied reactions of successful thirtysomething lawyer Michael's (Aidan Quinn) straight family to the double whammy of Michael, in the span of one visit home, coming out as gay and as having contracted HIV. As soon as the narrative has established his family's difficulty with Michael's double diagnoses, as it were, Michael himself moves through his own reckoning, with one of the most integral steps to his journey being the befriending of Victor (John Glover), an AIDS ward patient and fellow gay man.

Flamboyant, hilarious, and sickly, Victor is an even less respected member of society, and in some ways his pain does for Michael what Michael does for his own parents, adding an element of bitter understanding and empathy that isn't organically built between straight and gay characters. Victor's death doesn't magically cure Michael of his depression or revivify him; rather, it gives Michael a chance to mourn and grieve someone outside himself. Though *An Early Frost*'s purpose was primarily explanatory, characters and audiences alike are given, through Victor and Michael's relationship, the necessary space to acknowledge the suffering that was so often ignored or viciously belittled. When purposeful, thoughtful, and connected to other queer characters, queer death could provide a necessary container for sorrow, growth, and scorching emotion not previously played out on television with any degree of care for a queer audience.

Decades later, 1980s-set ballroom drama *Pose* would tackle the same acknowledgment of a period of unfathomable grief and enter the contemporary conversation about burying gays when delightful semi-antagonist and fan favorite Candy Ferocity (Angelica Ross) is murdered by a john in the fourth episode of the series' much anticipated sophomore season. Airing in 2019, well after the awareness of Lexa had settled in, Candy's death was a divisive point for audiences. Brutal and tragic, Candy's passing was tied to two epidemics—the by that point established history of New York City's fight against AIDS inaction and the still underacknowledged epidemic of violence against Black trans women.

Candy's death was devastating. It also falls into a fascinating repetition of a decades-long onscreen pattern, not just a queer woman dying, but a trans woman dying so that a Black gay man, in this case Pray Tell (Billy Porter), who could not previously acknowledge his own diagnosis of HIV, can live. While communing with said trans woman's ghost at her funeral, said man admits that he always gave her such a difficult time because Candy represented all the things he was afraid to be: unapologetic, Black, and femme. Pray Tell isn't the only character who gleans inspiration from Candy's untimely passing—her entire family, biological and chosen, is summoned by her ghost so that she can pass on to the next life with a final quip for everyone.

Candy's death is so interesting because, though it's still symbolic and follows some similar queer-death-by-numbers instructions, *Pose* is, especially in its second season, filled to the brim with other queer and trans characters who now get the chance to grieve—and each of them is strengthened by Candy's passing in a way that fully considers the importance of their character. Not only that, but Candy sticks around as a ghostly, deeply felt presence for two episodes after her murder and is the star of her own death, closing out her reign with a full-length, glittering lip sync to "Never Knew Love Like This Before" in a ballroom of adoring fans. In her death, Candy finally achieves what she needed but could never quite grasp in life, and *Pose* made a case for treating each queer show, and each queer death, like it had the potential to be an entirely new artistic and political experience.

It can be tempting to look at the history of queer death onscreen solely as a set of statistics. A few hundred dead lesbians is a weight that can be communicated more precisely than that of a personal emotional toll. But quantifying storytelling in this way can be disingenuous, too. How can numbers distinguish between a callous offing and a death that serves as the foundation for a new queer journey? Consider the death that opens *Vida* (2018–2020), one of the best queer series of recent memory. Or the resurrection and near-death misses in *Harley Quinn* (2019–), which push its queer characters toward one another. And say we separate that out so that your *Buffy*s are in one corner and your *Vida*s are in another—should we advocate for the correct, limited circumstances under which a queer character can die?

Queer death, like queer immorality and queer subtext, has an indisputably bad rap when we look at its past, but consuming it as if it's solely an equation and not a deeply human experience cuts us off from its potency within storytelling. Without death, loss, or grief as a possibility, how meaningful is a queer character's life? The "bury your gays" trope may always haunt the way we look at a queer character's passing, and it may always feel hollow to consider a character's legacy as merely having survived or not. But avoidance of a trope doesn't have to be an instruction for how to write, or how to watch, television. Death doesn't have to be the end. When queerness is central to a piece of art, death, like anything else, could be just the start.

Queer & A: Stephanie Beatriz

Credits: *Brooklyn Nine-Nine, BoJack Horseman, The Legend of Vox Machina, Encanto, In the Heights*, and many more

If Stephanie Beatriz's comments on Rosa Diaz's survival seem particularly well-informed and pointed, it's likely because the actor was intimately aware of the impact of queer representation, or lack thereof, on her own life. Since coming out nonchalantly in 2016, Beatriz has embraced the "true joy" of being her full self and even used her role on *Brooklyn Nine-Nine* as a map to navigating some of her own family relationships. I was able to sit down with Beatriz in 2023 to ask her about her small rebellions, the hints she dropped while Rosa was still effectively in the closet, and her reflections on being embraced by those who found a lifeline in her character. This is an edited excerpt of our conversation.

SHAYNA MACI WARNER: Can you remember the first ever queer character or person you recognized as queer on TV?

STEPHANIE BEATRIZ: No. Memories are tainted by the stories that you hear over and over, whether that's family stories that you hear, whether it's the way your friend group remembers an event; somehow, those colors start to wash your own memories of things. So for me, the first memory I have of a queer person on TV is conflated with the very public moment that Ellen [DeGeneres] came out. It was this big cultural moment. And what I remember thinking at the time was, "Oh, no, the show's gonna get canceled." That's what I remember thinking! Because even at that age, I knew that people didn't want to hear that; people would have an adverse reaction to that. Audiences at the time were more likely to think that that was strange, different, outside of the norm, because it was.

And I was afraid for Ellen. I remember that feeling. I was afraid because I liked the show, and I remember thinking, this is not going to feel fair if this gets canceled because of this. But I don't necessarily know that that was my first queer person that I ever saw on TV. Like I said, it's colored by the sort of cultural zeitgeist moment that that was for so many people.

I remember having clear feelings about people I saw on TV. That came very early on. I was watching really popular stuff like *Beverly Hills, 90210,* and then I was also obsessively watching *Seinfeld,* because I was really fascinated and interested by comedy. And I remember having very queer feelings about different people on those shows. It sort of ran the gamut, you know, even things like *Saved by the Bell,* which we use as a kind of funny touchstone joke in *Brooklyn Nine-Nine,* but those were real feelings that I had. I remember watching *Saved by the Bell* and ultimately thinking multiple people in that cast were super cute! So it's more the feeling that I had about: I think that I think that that guy is cute, but I also think that that girl is cute on the same show.

It was less about aligning myself with a feeling of seeing a bisexual person, because at the time, there wasn't really any rep for me, and my TV watching was very monitored by my parents. So the things that I was allowed to watch, I imposed my own feelings, my own journey of my sexuality, my own identity. Melissa Fumero [Amy Santiago on *Brooklyn Nine-Nine*] and I talked about how there was so little Latin representation in the television that we watched. So we would look for anything that we could grab hold of, and for a lot of times, that meant characters who had brown hair. It was just enough that we could maybe imagine that someday we, too, could be a part of it. It was the same kind of thing with bisexuality for me. I would just look for just enough. Maybe there was just enough little flirtation between characters that I could maybe imagine that bisexuality—and I didn't even really have a name for it at the time—but that what I felt could be real, in a world that was just make believe.

SMW: Do you remember any of those characters that you gravitated toward?

SB: The character that I really glommed on to was Elaine Benes [from *Seinfeld*], because she wore glasses, she wore cowboy boots, she wore big blazers. As a kid, I didn't know that some of that was to hide some of [Julia Louis-Dreyfus's] pregnancies. So looking at Elaine and the way she dressed and the way that she held her own in this very, you know, masculine energy group—she was just as funny, she was just as cool. She had just as vivid of a sex life. She was tough. One of her bits was that "get out" bit where she would push a dude halfway across the room. All of those blazers and glasses and that mound of curly hair, it was everything at once! I had brown curly hair, I liked to dress kind of masculine sometimes. I wore glasses, I was funny, I could hold my own with any group of people. That's who I identified with by the time I was in high school and knew more about my own bisexuality.

Looking back on it, it's a bit of a reach. But you know, when you're queer, you're like a starved vegan and you're at a buffet. And you're like, "I know there must be something here, what could it be? Could it be these cheese rolls? Well, there's cheese in them but maybe I could eat around the cheese." You're just looking for anything. Something, anything.

SMW: Oh yes, the crumbs. Going back briefly to *Ellen*, do you remember if seeing the really adverse reaction and the cancellation, compounded by having nothing else to see, had an impact on how you thought about your own identity, especially going into entertainment?

SB: Having nothing to see was hard. One of the first times I remember a bi character—a female bi character—was *Chasing Amy*. I remember being really excited to see it and then feeling so disappointed by it, and I haven't seen that movie since I watched it in high school. I remember feeling really disappointed because I just felt like, this isn't it. This isn't me. And when there is so little rep, your feeling about who is representing you becomes so hyperimportant, because it's going to be the introduction of that sexuality to people who don't know anyone. I mean, I'm talking about myself, but you and a bunch of your friends went to the movie theater together, and you know that this is maybe going to be the start of a conversation with you and your friends. And then turns out the character's kind of awful and uses sex in a way that you don't ever want to and is a disaster. And then you leave the movie theater, and you and all your friends are sitting at Denny's deconstructing the film. You, Stephanie, are going to keep her little mouth shut about who she is. Because now all of your cool alt friends have decided that they know who "that kind" of person is. And that's a really scary thing.

I think as a teenager, you want to be accepted by your friends. You're desperate for a community. And if your small community has decided that that's not the kind of person they want to be around, that's not the kind of person they want to align themselves with, even if it's based on something as silly as a movie, it's really scary to decide to step forward and say, "Actually, I'm bisexual. And this is what it's like." Because you might not even really know! And you don't have any rep to explain to you that all these feelings are normal! You can be this way!

It certainly didn't usher in a new age of freedom for me; it was quite the opposite. It really made me think to myself, "Well, if I want to retain my friend group, if I want to continue to be loved and accepted by these people who I love and adore and make me feel at home in every other way, then I don't think I will come out as bi because bi seems kind of like the villain. Bi seems like the bad guy. Bi seems like a disaster, a mess. And I don't want my friends to think that about me." These are all really "juvenile" thoughts that you're having when you're seventeen. But they're very real. When you're seventeen, the stakes feel really high for you. I think Ellen coming out and the subsequent cancellation of her show did the same thing for a lot of people. I think it made us feel like, "Well, see, someone tried, someone stepped forward, bravely stepped forward, and was rejected. So I think I'll just sit back and wait until it's safe." You know? That was hard. I mean, this is such a stupid comparison to make, but do you remember when Keri Russell cut her hair?

SMW: For *Felicity*? Yeah.

SB: There was such an adverse reaction to Keri cutting her hair. You know, now, when I think back on that, here's this woman who's decided to do this and maybe had a discussion with her producers about how it reflects the growth of the character. Maybe that's the move that they're making in the arc of the show. Maybe it wasn't even her decision. I'm sure you could do ages of research and find interviews where she and lots of people talk about it. But what I remember at the time, prior to the wave of social media, was just magazines and gossip at school: "Ugh, what a horrible decision that was, she looks awful." Everyone rejected it outright. And that was similar to what happened to Ellen. It was like, "We know you as this. We don't want to know you as this. If you show us this other side of yourself, we no longer want anything to do with you."

I remember Keri Russell doing that and thinking, "I'm gonna cut my hair short." I think it was this weird connection in my mind of like, "Everyone's calling her lesbian. Everyone's calling her gay because she cut her feminine long hair off. I'm gonna fucking chop my hair off." It was this weird, pseudo baby step toward coming out. Not that short hair has anything to do with anything. Well, sometimes it does! You know? So all of those things became conflated for me in this pop culture moment of a tiny foot coming out of the closet in a way. And I did. I cut my hair super short the last year of high school. I got so much commentary about it at school, but it was the one thing that I could do that felt safe but still felt outside of the box. A signal, in a way, to people that I'm not necessarily who you think I am. But I'm not going to give you the ammunition to completely take me down.

SMW: That comparison of a haircut as this tiny bit of rebelliousness to grab on to is so legitimate! There's a history of women leads cutting their hair and then getting in a lot of trouble with networks and with execs, or getting recast for looking too "butch."

SB: To continue on that little hair journey, one of the things that I insisted on when I was building the character of Rosa Diaz was that she keep this long feminine hair. I was really interested in this idea of the juxtaposition of toughness that you see in her costuming, which is primarily black, very well fitted so she can move really quickly, and these tough leather jackets, and also this über-feminine hair. Those juxtapositions are part of the makeup of my queerness. For me, it's the ability to put both of those things on, sometimes individually and sometimes simultaneously.

I'm just connecting the dots right now in this conversation, but it is a little bit of Elaine Benes. It is this long, curly hair mixed with this angular sort of toughness, all mixed into one character. It was really important to me, so much so that in the pilot, you can see there's one scene where Rosa pulls her hair back. After the pilot, I pretty much insisted I don't want that hair pulled back ever. There's maybe one other episode where I'm hungover and it's pulled back in a ponytail. In the final episode, I'm wearing a bonnet to sleep, but that's pretty much it. It's very long and very feminine over the course of all the seasons, because I didn't want people to put the character in a box. I didn't want anybody to be like, "You know what, if the actor comes out as bi, let's cut her hair!" No! It doesn't have to be that, and that's not what this character was.

SMW: My next question was: before Rosa came out, did you play her as queer, and I'm already hearing a confirmation of that. Can you talk about that a little bit?

SB: When I got the audition, I originally auditioned for both characters, both the Amy Santiago character and the Rosa Diaz character. Rosa's name was different in the beginning. It was not specifically a Latina. The character's name was Megan, she was described as like very fiery, hotheaded, maybe of Irish descent, lots of brothers in the force. They kind of switched those characteristics over to Amy. So in the audition process, I had multiple callbacks. There was a screen test with Andy Samberg [Jake Peralta on *Brooklyn Nine-Nine*] where we did some improv together, and during the improv, I felt this buddy relationship between our characters. I had this thought: I bet these two have gone out and sat at a bar, been like, "She's cute. Yeah, she's cute, who's gonna go over and talk to her?" That's what kicked it off in my imagination.

There are episodes in the very beginning where I'm slightly signaling, or I did some improv that maybe didn't make it into the show where I say something that makes it obvious that I'm queer. I really, really tried to work with physicality to make it obvious. I think out of anybody in the series, my signaling was really clear with Gina, Chelsea Peretti's character. Especially early on in the series, you can see that, physically, Gina and I will be in the same space, and I'm taking over much more space than you normally would with like a friend. Maybe my arm was around the back of the couch that she's sitting on. Maybe I'm leaning physically into the space that she's holding. I think that there was always a slight flirtation between those two characters, even when they were mad at each other. It wasn't something that was ever explored on the show, but Chelsea and I would sort of joke around about it a lot. I always played her in a way that made sense. You know, it's sort of deeply down in there, just in case they ever wanted to explore it. And I'm really lucky that they did.

Writers are really smart people, and I think they saw what I was laying down and they started picking up the pieces of the track. They decided that they wanted to build something like a real track that way, and I'm really lucky that I was also invited into the space to collaborate with them on those storylines and collaborate on the direction that that was gonna go.

SMW: I love hearing about that. I went back and rewatched some of the episodes, including one where yours and Chelsea Peretti's characters say, "Yeah, in another lifetime we would have been a great couple." I'm so happy to hear the story behind that, too. When you were approached with "Hey, I think this is the direction Rosa is gonna go in," what was your immediate reaction? What did you feel?

SB: I was so excited. I was driving my car on the way to the mall to do some stupid errand. I was in the parking structure, and I saw [*Brooklyn Nine-Nine* showrunner] Dan Goor on my caller ID. So I picked it up because, you know, your boss calls, you got to pick it up. Dan asked me, and I'm parking my car, and I just sort of sat in my little Honda Civic and thought, I can't believe this is happening. He said, "We really want to take it in this direction. Do you feel comfortable exploring this with us? If you don't, then absolutely, we'll just like leave it alone. We can do lots of other stuff. But if you want to, next season, this is what we're thinking and we'd love to invite you into the writers' room to just discuss your personal

experience, anything you feel comfortable sharing with us."
And I was losing my shit sitting in the parking garage at the
Americana, in my little Honda, thinking, I can't believe this
is really happening. I can't believe I'm going to be able to
maybe say some things that might make it onto TV about the
experience of being a Latina coming out as bisexual to her
friends and family. It was like, "What? What, I'm gonna get
to do that?"

And then being in the writers' room I got to share some
personal stuff with them, and some things that I really felt
were important to put into the script. For example, the word
"bisexual." We say it so many times in that episode. There was
no "Now I'm dating women." Granted, that is some people's
experience. But for Rosa, the experience was very similar to
mine. Which is: I'm bi. That's who I am. I can date lots of different kinds of people, and that's how I describe myself. Also,
the sort of outright rejection by her family [in season 5, episode 10, "Game Night"], the "That's not a real thing. It's not a
real sexuality. Well, you can still date men, so it's okay." Those
were experiences that were personal to me. And so to have
them in the show felt really, really specific.

**SMW: I would love to back up a little bit and then come back to your
experience of actually having that storyline out in the world. When
did you come out to yourself?**

SB: I think I knew something was different when I was really
young. Say, eight, nine, maybe even younger. But I don't think
I like really grasped what it was until I went to college.

**SMW: So you're in college, and going into the entertainment indus-
try, and you have a pretty good idea of what's going on for you. I
would love to hear if you imagined that there would be a possibility**

for you to play queer characters, and if you were paying attention to the landscape in the twenty years between Ellen and Rosa?

SB: Well, you know, that's a really interesting question. I have a very specific trajectory, which is that I started in theater. Theater has always been a much more accepting place of LGBTQIA people, just in general. You know, theater is one of the places that was safe to be queer, gay, trans, like it was a safe space to be those things for a lot of people. So, you know, in a way I didn't think that a television and film career would be possible for me, because the history of queerness in Hollywood has been so hidden. So maybe that's why I gravitated toward theater, but maybe it was because I loved it and felt accepted there. From the time that I was in high school, I felt like those were my people.

Theater is sometimes many steps ahead. Sometimes it's a few steps behind. But the first experience that I had watching a play that was about queer people was *Stop Kiss* in college, and I just was like, "Oh, okay, here in this space, I'll be able to play lots of things, lots of kinds of people. Some of them will be queer, and some of them won't." There were lots of different kinds of scenes that we would do, and there were lots of opportunities to be queer in these spaces. Granted, some of the exploration of queer characters, especially lesbian characters, and characters who are outside of the sexual norm, can be dark. I did a lot of studying Tennessee Williams's work in college, and sometimes that world gets really dark and painful because his experience as a gay man sometimes was dark and painful. But there was just much more opportunity to be surrounded by it. I thought my career was just going to be theater, I really did.

Once I started working in theater, I realized that I was being drawn toward exploring film and television. I didn't know what that was going to be like, I didn't know if there was a place for me there, but I decided that I would move to LA and try it out for a little while. If it didn't work, no harm, no foul. And that's when I got really lucky and booked a pilot right away and booked some guest stars and then just started building things from there.

SMW: I don't know if it would have the same sort of cultural moment in which everybody is talking about it, but do you remember the first queer Latine character that you saw on television, if any?

SB: No.

SMW: None?

SB: It was me. And I don't say that to toot my own horn, but I just don't. There probably were; I haven't done my due diligence in studying it. I would be shocked if I was the very first ever; I don't think that that's the case. But in terms of the kinds of stuff that I watch and consume as a viewer, nothing had crossed my path in a way that felt significant to me. That's not to say it's significant to the culture or significant to anyone else, but for the kinds of things that I was wanting to watch or even had time to watch, it was me.

SMW: There were queer Latine characters before Rosa Diaz; not very many, that's for sure. But if they weren't even within your awareness, how did that milestone settle in when you were asked to take Rosa's character in this direction? Did it feel like it was a responsibility?

SB: No, it didn't feel like a responsibility. It felt exciting. It felt thrilling. Like, "Surprise!" You know, it felt like a gift or an invitation to a party or something that I was going to be able to give to people. I didn't feel like, "Now we're gonna do this really important big thing." I knew that it was important. And I knew it was big. But it didn't feel heavy with responsibility. It felt full with possibility.

SMW: What a beautiful gift! In 2016, a year before Rosa's storyline premiered, you came out on Twitter. Of course, as queer people we're coming out all the time, and sometimes are out for many, many years before people larger than our immediate circle know it. But it is quite a bit different to do so in a very public spotlight. You came out by posting an Aubrey Plaza interview in which she comes out, and I was wondering what changed for you that this was the time for you to come out on Twitter, and effectively to a much wider circle?

SB: You know, I don't think I thought it through. Like you said, I had been out to my immediate circle, and I think at the time, I was a bit naive about the reach of social media and Twitter and how things can take off. I just saw that interview and thought, "Oh, yeah, same. Yes, I'm so glad somebody said it that way, just exactly how I feel." I just tweeted it off the cuff. And then in my phone, I've got some texts from people who were like, "Whoa, that's so cool, Steph! I didn't know you were, like, out to share that!" I was like, "What? What do you mean?" The reaction just surprised me.

I think the reason it had a little bit of a ripple effect was because people saw the track that I mentioned I was laying down for Rosa. They could see it while watching the show; they could feel it. Audiences are really smart. They pick up on lots of little clues all the time. That's what we're doing when we're watching TV, we're picking up on clues. Little detectives. And I think people felt really validated by my coming out because they thought, "Yes, I was right. Rosa's queer, too! Rosa's bi; I knew it!" You know? But I honestly didn't think it through! Twitter was still so new to me. I was just like, "Yeah. You know, how many people could possibly be looking at my Twitter? Not that many. You know, it's probably just, like, my friends."

SMW: So you're out, far more publicly than perhaps you had antici-pated. Before the first coming-out episode aired, did you have any sort of anticipation around the episode specifically? Were you wait-ing to hear reactions? What was going through your mind?

SB: Specifically, I was thinking about my parents, because some of the language in the episode is reflective of my fears around what my parents were going to say to me or what they had said to me already about queerness, about gay people, about the LGBTQIA community. Specifically, I was nervous that my parents wouldn't like it and that they would reject me because of it. At the time, my parents would often call me after the episodes and tell me how funny it was or how great the episode was or whatever, and I waited for a call that did not come after that. I could give a fucking shit about what the audience thought at that point. Before the episode aired it was like, "I hope people think it's funny. I hope they're all moved by it." And then after the episode aired, and my par-ents didn't call me, I just hyperfixated on it. And they didn't call, they didn't call, they didn't call, and I got nervous to call them.

Eventually what happened was that we didn't really talk about it. We didn't ever have a discussion about it. And then I believe it was the next year that the whole *B99* cast went to Comic-Con, and there was an interview where I was asked about that episode specifically and asked about their reaction to it. I mentioned my parents and said something like, "I don't know if they liked it, they still haven't talked to me about it." And I think my dad must have had some kind of Google Alert on, you know, like parents do. He messaged me, and he actually used language from the episode. He basically paraphrased the episode, where Danny Trejo's character, my dad in the episode, says, "We love you no matter what, no matter who you are, no matter what. And we're proud of you, and we love you." My dad took that language and paraphrased it and made it his own in a message. He couldn't call me and say it to me, but he gave me that gift, gave me the best he could give me.

On a more bird's-eye-view level, I thought, well, if the language that was used in the episode around a dad trying to come to grips with his queer kid's queerness in a way that's loving and accepting of something he didn't expect . . . if that language in a television sitcom episode can be used by a parent of a person who is queer, to try to be loving and accepting of something they didn't expect . . . then I did it. I did something really special and cool. If my dad could do that, then maybe other dads are doing that, and trying to do that, watching this sitcom with their kid who's queer, who's maybe just come out to them. Maybe they don't know how to relate, and they don't really know what to say, because it's not what they expected. But we've given them some kind of model to use. I think that that's the thing that art can do. And that TV especially can do. It can allow us to visit these stories that are unlike ours, or maybe very much like ours, and perhaps give us more versions of the story.

SMW: Did coming out, both as a public figure and then as a character as well, deepen your understanding of your own identity and queerness?

SB: In some ways, it was a great experience. It was just like, "Whee!" I've had really special things happen to me. I've had friends I've known for over twenty years come out to me as bi because they saw something in my joy and freedom that they felt inside themselves, and they wanted it out into the world. That feels like such a gift. There have been all these little pockets of gift moments, from being at pride parades, and wearing the bi flag, and screaming when I see another bi also waving the flag. There's just this true joy in being fully who you are. There's also a lot of pain, sometimes, because there are lots of people who don't want anything to do with anything outside of heterosexuality, you know, for whatever reason they've got. It's usually multiple reasons, all woven into this fabric of bigotry and fear. They're underneath that blanket and they're not coming out. That can be really painful. Especially when, like so many of us, it can be unavoidable. Sometimes they're people in our families, sometimes they're people whom we've known forever, who suddenly don't want us to be ourselves. I sometimes wonder if I hadn't ever said anything, would those people just accept and love me? It's an awful feeling because it almost feels like a self-betrayal. Like, why would you ever even want to be accepted or loved by those people? What would that give you?

Maybe it's this naive idea that like, gosh, wouldn't it be great if everybody just liked each other? And we all got along, and everyone just looked out for each other and wanted the best for each other? That's not the real world, obviously. Specifically for me, some of my husband's family is incredibly loving and accepting, some are more reticent to get to know me as a person, and some truly don't want anything to do with me. That's their prerogative, but it is painful, because I never in a million years would have imagined that the person I married's family just wouldn't get along. Because I love

family. I love many members of his family. I extend love to all
of his family. But I know that that isn't necessarily given in
return because of who I am, because I'm open and out about
who I am and what I believe. That includes what I believe
politically, what I think about lots of parts of myself, what I
think about immigration, women's rights, and queerness.

So, sometimes it's beautiful. And then you flip it on the
other side, and it's really dark.

**SMW: There are a lot of actors who are in your position or in a posi-
tion that you've been in over the past five years, in which they're
considering whether or not to come out publicly. That can be something so incredible for audiences, but it's also transforming something very personal into something very public. From your own
experience, is there any advice that you would give to other actors
who are in that position? Or if you wouldn't give it to anyone else, is
there something that you would say to yourself, when you were starting on this kind of public foray?**

SB: I don't have advice, because in the grand scheme of what
my life is going to be, the last five years are such a tiny little
nothing moment. I think it's an individual choice. The hard
thing about our art form, specifically—and I'm talking
about acting—is that part of our job is to slide into these
characters and create something where there were just
words on a page and an idea in someone's mind. We help
take that off the page and bring it to life, so much life that
people get connected to the characters that we create and
feel that they're real. They trust that the story is real, so
much so that they get joy out of something that we do or feel
emotionally connected in a way that moves them to tears
sometimes. And it's making believe; playing pretend so
hard that people feel like it's real.

The challenge that comes with that sometimes is the feeling of well, if a character is X, then they have to be X in real life, and I don't always know that that's the right fit. Sometimes it's exactly right. Sometimes there's maybe a fluidity in there that needs to happen for a character to be matched with the actor who's going to play them in a way that feels the best for the pretend that they're trying to make. This is a very strange answer. But depending on the actor, they'll know. They'll know whether or not it's the right time. I think the thing that happens sometimes is that there are a lot of people who help you get hired as an actor. There are agents, there are managers, sometimes there are PR people, sometimes there are a lot of voices in the mix, and the more and more you can tune into your own intuition, the stronger you're going to be as an actor and as a person, because your intuition will tell you whether or not it's right for you to be out. I don't know that it's always the right decision for people, and I think the timing is what is the most important for most people. From the time that I was eighteen to where I am now, I could never have imagined how much times have changed, and they will change more. So I don't really have advice other than growing your intuition. It's not always right, but it's usually a pretty good compass.

Chapter 6

GAYS IN "REAL" LIFE

In researching this book, many generous, queer interviewees have shared the same sentiment: that queer and queer-coded characters gave them purchase to feel a little less alone in a seemingly heterosexual world. However, as much as it might have seemed like queer characters were the closest one could get to finding a reflection the slightest bit like their own, fictional gays weren't the only queer presences on the small screen. Since the 1950s, real queer people have been risking their livelihoods and sometimes their lives to come out or be out on television, sometimes for education, sometimes for entertainment, and, more recently, for purposes of pure chaos. Nonfiction television (as much as any edited medium can be deemed truthful) began as one of the most hostile defining spaces of the abnormalities of homosexuality, but over the decades it has morphed into a defining cultural artifact.

As sober news and talk shows of the fifties and sixties were joined by a new form of intimate, observational storytelling that turned the camera back on real families that might as well have been the viewers at home, queerness revealed itself as part of the fabric, and not solely the fringes, of American society. In the seventies, experimental television documentaries revealed that the changing American family wasn't nearly as white bread as sponsors would have previously had its viewers believe. In the eighties, shock and tabloid talk dominated, with hosts bringing queer people out from behind the ferns and into the spotlight in a more aggressively colorful version of previous decades' 20 Questions for Queers. In the nineties, a lowered barrier to entry allowed queer people to create their own local cable access programs, while in the early 2000s, the demand for sensationalist and wall-to-wall programming encouraged exploits and sexual experimentation that would titillate. In the 2010s, anyone could be a star—presumably that included queer people, too. Now, whole reality empires are built on the commercial viability of drag queens, and dating shows have finally realized that they get a lot more interesting when their contestants go both ways. Though the entertainment value of gays on a screen near you can often tip into exploitation just as much as it would well-intentioned education, there's no doubt that real live queers have made their mark on what many consider to be the lowest, most addictive form of populist entertainment.

The First Real Live Gays

As much as *RuPaul's Drag Race* (2009–) seems like a ubiquitous, world-swallowing television entity, it took many decades before real queer people were celebrated for serving Charisma, Uniqueness, Nerve, and Talent on national TV. Instead, the very notion of real homosexuals would enter the public forum and historical television record as an angry blip during a giant, raging stain on national history. In April 1954, ABC and the then dominant DuMont Television Network began airing the monthslong Army-McCarthy hearings. Over eighty million Americans tuned in to the court proceedings between legal counsel for the United States Army and Senator Joseph McCarthy, whose notorious hunt for communists in the US government was finally being challenged now that it was pointed at the Armed Forces.

The hearings were considered a turning point in bringing McCarthy's "demagogic bullying spree"* to an end—but not before McCarthy could lay claim to one of the first times the word "homosexuality" was spoken on national television. McCarthy is best known for stoking a climate of violent xenophobia around communism, pithily remembered as the

---

* As historian Jelani Cobb so eloquently puts it in the PBS *American Experience* episode "McCarthy."

Red Scare, but his aim for supposed Soviet infiltrators at all levels of American life widened to include homosexuals, too. According to McCarthy, not every communist was a homosexual, but every homosexual was either a communist or would fall prey to communist blackmail because of their homosexuality.[1] As the first episode of AppleTV+'s wide-ranging, thoroughly researched look at queer political activism and representation on television, *Visible: Out on Television* (2020), emphasizes, McCarthy's supporters took to that notion easily.

Years before these hearings, the US government had already begun firing suspected gay and lesbian federal workers, and in the 1940s, states enacted laws (on top of long-existent "sodomy" laws) that specifically targeted gay men, labeling them as mentally ill and encouraging their arrests.[2] Under McCarthy's purview and repeated vitriol, homosexuality became officially linked with traitorship to the state. The purging of said federal employees is now known as the Lavender Scare. Though not as all-encompassing as the Red Scare, it was estimated to have affected tens of thousands: those who were fired and those who didn't even attempt to apply to jobs because of the threat of institutional disbarment if they were to be found out. Even as McCarthy was ousted in the court of public opinion, many real queer people mostly remained "vague specters" in the public eye, shadowed, diagnosed, and quietly expelled from polite society if they were found out.[3]

Despite this attempt to purge homosexuals and other undesirables from public life, queer talk show and news participants weren't having it. They did their best to communicate through a shroud of collective anonymity, especially as organizers began to target media as their most effective strategy of material gains. Investigative and discussion-based news shows like *Confidential File* (1953–1959), *The Open Mind* (1956–), and *Showcase* centered homosexuality as the topic of the week, occasionally giving real gay and lesbian people microphones so that they might confirm or combat psychological diagnoses of their "conditions" from so-called experts. As scholar and former CNN reporter Edward Alwood notes in his study of lesbian and gay subjects and journalists, *Straight News: Gays, Lesbians, and the News Media,* many were often interviewed in shadow or blocked behind potted plants and other props, leaving presumedly heterosexual experts to have the final word and studio light.[4]

Through sometimes sympathetic but often diagnostic and shame-fueled exposés, some, like Dale Olson on *Confidential File,* calculated the risk of being outed against the reward of advancing the Mattachine Society's agenda to make life the slightest bit easier for other gay men.*[5] On the promisingly named "Homosexuals and the Problems They Present" episode of *Confidential File,* Olson, introduced under the alias Curtis White, firmly declares that he would not want to be "cured" of his homosexuality if given the chance. When asked why he's agreed to do the segment, though it may (and did) cost him his job, Olson gives an answer that summarizes much of the publicly voiced driving sentiment today regarding queer people appearing as themselves or writing their own voices into media representation: "I think that this way I can be a little useful to someone besides myself."[6]

Though there were volunteers who were similarly willing to represent for the Daughters of Bilitis, the United States' first formal lesbian organization, lesbians had a much more difficult time breaking through censors, producers, and panels of heterosexual psychologists until 1962. The DOB's Los Angeles convention presented an opportunity to advertise to press, resulting in talk show host Paul Coates interviewing its LA chapter president, "Terry."† Terry's appearance not only served to finally let a

---

*   The Mattachine Society was one of the first notable pro-assimilationist, anti-discrimination gay groups in the United States, whose members came together to support one another's well-being in a hostile environment and, as noted by one of many dry and communist-hunting FBI surveillance briefs, discard anything "subversive" in favor of "discussing their own problems of adjustment to the world around them."

†   One such notable discussion of lesbianism never made it to television: host and "unorthodox" writer Fannie Hurst's *Showcase* series on WABD-TV was allowed to conduct its usual psychologist-driven episode on male homosexuality in 1958, but station managers pulled its lesbian episode the very next day.

lesbian speak for herself on national television but also provided a hefty boost in the awareness of the DOB, which reported an increase in membership with each subsequent television appearance by its members.[7]

Early appearances by real trans people also took longer to make it to the small screen, despite Christine Jorgensen being one of the most written-about people by American newspapers in 1953, generating millions of words of both scorn and awe.[8] Jorgensen was one of the first who had very little choice in the revelation of their identities on such a wide scale, but thanks to newsreels and newspapers capturing her eloquence and studio star-like emulation of aloof, upper-class elegance, she grabbed ahold of her fifteen minutes under the microscope and extended it as long as it could possibly go. Celebrity and entertainer were among the only financially viable avenues Jorgensen could realistically pursue after her very public outing in December 1952, and though she herself was not given much television airtime until the late fifties and sixties, her name and transition were cited, mostly through innuendo, all over the airwaves.

While Jorgensen did eventually make it out of newsreels and onto television talk shows, first locally in 1956 and then nationally in 1959, she wasn't a fixture until the late sixties, long after she had been inoculated against Hollywood's fascination and the turbulence of print and broadcast media's approval of her womanhood waxing and sharply waning. The time for receiving such accolades as "Woman of the Year" and appearing on Broadway and Los Angeles stages had passed, and what remained was a naked fascination and provocation for the woman who had once publicly requested a quiet life. Around the time of her memoir's publication, Jorgensen appeared on programs that poked and prodded at her either as the walking embodiment of previous decades' punch lines or as a founding entry in the *Diagnostic and Statistical Manual of Mental Disorders.*

One of Jorgensen's most notable interviews of the late sixties was in 1967, when she appeared on proto–shock jock Joe Pyne's often explosive talk show, squaring off with a man who was known for his conservatism, anti-communism, anti-feminism, and most of all his delight in shouting

down audience members and guests alike.[9] As expected, Pyne arrived to
the interview with questions designed to be taken aback by Jorgensen's
very existence, but Jorgensen evaded Pyne's planned outrage. After the
camera captures her reacting to her introduction in close-up, raising an
eyebrow at Pyne's description of her as "sexually disturbed," she pro-
ceeds to candidly and assuredly correct Pyne on his presumptions, giving Pyne and the audience a lesson on, among other things, Magnus
Hirschfeld, the misconception that cross-dressing was exclusive to
homosexual men, and the frank optimism that tens of thousands of
trans people like herself existed in the United States.

Viewing Pyne's program today in the wake of his offspring Rush
Limbaugh or Joe Rogan, one might expect a much larger offensive front
from the usually contrarian host, but Pyne was something of a mildly
ignorant conversationalist in comparison to some of Jorgensen's other
interviews, including a 1968 interview with now legendary talk show
host Dick Cavett. Cavett and Pyne were only two of many voices on
television who were disarmed when faced with the prospect of interviewing queer and trans people, especially those who were face-out.
Even as news and talk programs understood that enough queer people
existed to interview them alongside psychologists, physicians, and
anthropologists, they treated their interviewees, especially gay men,
as helpless zoo animals and often balked or redoubled their efforts to
undermine when their subjects did have the wherewithal to answer
invasive questions intelligently. After absorbing and spewing so much
propagandistic vitriol, it was almost as if journalists scarcely had the
room to capably do their jobs when in the presence of a real live homosexual. The paragon of this approach can be seen in the 1967 episode of
the television documentary series *CBS Reports*, "The Homosexuals," an
hour-long investigative report hosted by eventual *60 Minutes* host Mike
Wallace.

Wallace opens the episode with a blunt statement—according to a
poll conducted by CBS, "Most Americans are repelled by the mere notion
of homosexuality." Over the course of the episode, Wallace and CBS

work to affirm that majority opinion. Though a better proportion of gay men to experts are included in "The Homosexuals" than in many of the panels of the fifties, and there's an understanding that the general public has at least heard the word "homosexual," progress mostly stalls there. After it was filmed, the episode's airing was delayed by years, changed producers' hands, and was reedited to more heavily feature the interviews that saw homosexuality as a moral failing and sickness.[10] Gay interviewees who are shown from the shadows, only their mouths visible to speak nervously on their immaturity and illness, are shamed for their shiftiness. Interviews with well-spoken, out gay men who have no issue with their identities and share that they have been accepted by their families are shortened and edited to imply their lack of shame is itself shameful and tenuous.

Unscripted approaches to gay and trans people would swim in the shallow waters of confusion, discomfort, and disapproval until the 1970s. This didactic outside-looking-in approach remains popular with certain news and talk programs even now, but a new, far more immersive and artistically contemporary style was about to thoroughly shake things up, expanding the options for voices of authority to come not just from the "impartial" outside interviewer but from taking the audience into lived experiences of the interviewee.

Homosexuality Enters the *American* Home

In January 1973, one Santa Barbara family's divorce would change the face of unscripted television forever. Incidentally, it would also introduce over ten million viewers to an out young adult whose rebelliousness, humor, and magnetism catapulted him to unplanned television stardom. *An American Family*, creator Craig Gilbert and filmmakers Alan Raymond and Susan Raymond's twelve-part PBS documentary series, was an unlikely smash with audiences who tuned in over three months to watch the members of the Loud family simply live their lives. It just so happened that their lives were the opposite of what much of American television had depicted as normal, and the Raymonds employed cinema verité, a style of French documentary filmmaking pioneered in the sixties, to get audiences as close to experiential viewing as they possibly could.

An American Family had a monumental influence on many aspects of contemporary television, but for our purposes, its two distinct claims to fame were introducing Lance Loud to the world and creating the reality TV we see today. Though *Candid Camera* and *The Match Game* existed before it, there had never been a lifestyle genre or ice-cold immersion into the drama of everyday life. Without *An American Family*, who knows how anyone would keep up with the Kardashians.

Lance was a long-haired, bright, occasional blue lipstick–sporting, self-aware drifter and revelation who, in his own words, "more out of laziness than activism," made no secret of his homosexuality, "a 'feat' considered brave at the time."[11] As viewers tuned in to watch Lance's parents' marriage implode, they also got their first taste of reality TV stardom in the making. Out of the entire family, Lance seemed the most comfortable with the crew, and was subsequently performative, often aware and inviting to the camera as he delivered musings on depression, youth in revolt, and love.

In one such instance, Lance delivers a self-deprecating and generational zinger while explaining to his mother, Pat, why he's not interested in the go-getting she wants for him. Pat expresses her fear and frustration that Lance's lack of ambition and cheerful nihilism will leave him floundering were she or Lance's father unavailable to bail him out. To that, Lance responds dryly, "Well, you know, as I said, sooner or later it's gonna end. And if that's what happens, then it's gonna be sooner, honey."[12]

Pat's consternation is turned into a flip, entertaining dialogue that exemplifies the mild, myopically high-stakes personal drama that reality programs would bank on for years to come. It's also one of the many examples of Lance's interactions with parents who don't completely understand him, not only for his queerness but also for the chasm left in the wake of crumbling 1950s and '60s middle-class white American family values.

On the surface, it could feel wildly serendipitous that the first American reality program also happened to feature a young, flamboyant gay man. Some critics of the program's very conceit spoke of the Louds' separation and Lance's identity skeptically, accusing the Raymonds of manipulating the family's image to such a point that both the impending divorce and Lance's homosexuality were only put on for ratings.[*] But as much as cutting three hundred hours of footage down to twelve episodes of conflict was by definition manipulating their image (and Gilbert's edit did not paint the family members in the most flattering light), the combined breakthrough of television form and content was neither a stunt nor a fluke: they went hand in hand. Fewer families were the white-bread Brady Bunch than network sponsors would have liked to admit; turning cameras on a visually normative family and letting them break down shined a harsh light on the perfect image of a stoic patriarch, a soft matriarch, and carbon-copy children.

As scholar Michael Lovelock blisteringly puts it in his chapter on the blanket of compulsory heterosexuality broken by the advent of reality TV, broadcast television up until that point was almost entirely scheduled and programmed around the idea, not the reality, of the majority of American society conforming to a nuclear family structure. He writes:

> The family audience of traditional, broadcast television has . . .
> always been an ideological projection, a cultural construct which
> brings into being a discursive ideal of what the "normal" television

---

[*]   As now openly gay actor Thomas Dekker, who played Lance in the fictional 2011 *An American Family* HBO reinterpretation *Cinema Verite*, pointed out in an Associated Press interview, reality television hadn't yet become so blatant in its melodramatic manipulations. As an openly gay young man in a time that queerness was far from the most accepted social norm, Lance was subject to even more of the scrutiny and disbelief of audiences who couldn't understand why a family would let a camera crew into their home.

viewer is, even as this semi-fantastical norm fails to cohere with the
lived reality of those before the TV screen.[13]

Even with editorial manipulation, by keeping an outside narrative
voice almost silent and encouraging its subjects to exist on camera as
themselves, *An American Family* moved queer and straight people alike
closer to the realism that previous programs purposely avoided. In
short, showing a real queer person in a real (and really screwed up)
family had the potential to blow up the entire family unit as a concept—
and as a market. Upon watching the program in 1973, the *New York
Times*'s critic Anne Roiphe was so unsettled by the Louds' ordinariness
that she notes they were "enough like me and mine to create havoc in my
head." Their possible similarities evoked panic—how could any family
Roiphe might call familiar also contain a bad apple like Lance, whose
"flamboyant, leechlike homosexuality" and disrespect of traditional
gender roles was nonchalantly displayed throughout the series?[14]

It was no accident that *An American Family*'s experimentation came
through PBS rather than one of the big three commercial networks.
Following the establishment of the Public Broadcasting Act in 1967,
PBS's broadcast network debuted in 1970, swallowing National
Educational Television (NET), which had once aimed to be an aggressive educational competitor to the big three and was now served a
directive to rededicate its portion of the airwaves to content that
reflected and elevated its national audience. PBS was to be "for the
enlightenment of all the people," and at first it wasn't held accountable
to the same interests.[15] Where ABC's, CBS's, and NBC's sponsors may
have balked at the integration of a young gay man into a microcosmic
depiction of real America, PBS's initial federal funding actively encouraged experimentation, newness, and programming that fostered a sense
of public ownership. *An American Family* interrogated the white heterosexual, patriarchal idealism that the big three were selling simply by
reflecting a real American family in various states of the unideal. The

Louds could be your family, too.[16] Lance could be your brother—or maybe (God and the *New York Times* forbid) even you.

Unfortunately, as ground shaking as *An American Family* was, a combination of outrage toward its filmmakers, an increasing awareness of the power of television by the Religious Right, and the conservative switch from the Johnson administration to the Nixon administration (you may recall their almost hilariously offended reaction to *All in the Family*'s gay story arcs as mentioned in Chapter 2) wrapped caution tape all around PBS's deconstructive family programming. Reality television as we know it wouldn't take off for another two decades, and certainly not with the same lack of emotionally instructional voiceover that allowed Lance, and the other *American* family members, to speak for themselves. Instead, Lance and other out queer and trans people would continue to find their way into the family hearth through an ever-popular and increasingly combative medium: daytime talk shows.

Talk, Talk, Talk

In May 1970, Daughters of Billitis's Barbara Gittings and the Mattachine Society's Lilli Vincenz became the first out lesbians to appear on a nationally syndicated talk show, and, as luck would have it, it was the godfather of contemporary daytime talk. Gittings recalls the audience of *The Phil Donahue Show* (1967–1995) as a group of "hostile housewives," a demographic that would become Donahue's to lose.[17] The next year, syndicated talk show *The David Susskind Show* (1958–1987), formerly titled *Open End*, invited a panel of lesbian activists including Gittings, Vincenz, and the National Organization for Women's Barbara Love to try their hands at breaking down stereotypes about women who slept with and loved women, debating the host the whole way. That fighting, at louder and louder volumes, would soon characterize the daytime talk show. Though they became rife with appearances by queer people, syndicated talk began to move away from guests with a clear, dedicated mission to improving lesbian and gay visibility and toward booking guests who would provide them with spontaneity, charisma, and mag-netic, spectacular mess.

In 1973, after being introduced and much maligned in critical reac-tions to *An American Family*, Lance Loud secured his reality TV star-dom by appearing on Dick Cavett's talk show alongside the rest of the family. The same skeptical host who couldn't handle Christine Jorgensen was amused by and lightly condescending toward Lance, spending far more time addressing him than any other Loud child. In an open suit jacket, Hawaiian shirt, and bright pink socks, Lance more than held his own, as comfortable and entertaining in the guest chair as he had been in front of the Raymonds' lens. Now, he had the added benefit of know-ing how audiences had received him and was able to answer his critics fairly unedited. Full of quips and that same energetic nihilism he'd shown on PBS, Lance was a curiosity basically unafraid of the televised era. Audiences won out over media critics, and a true reality personality was born.

With his talk show appearances, Lance Loud opened up an avenue for out queer people to appear on television in a less formally investiga-tive or baldly activism-motivated capacity than shows like *Confidential File*, *CBS Reports*, or even those activists before him on *The Phil Donahue Show*. While openly closeted celebrities like Paul Lynde and never-closeted television staples like Charles Nelson Reilly had long dished innuendo through game shows like *Hollywood Squares* (1965–1980) and *Match Game*, daytime talk shows became a forum that sought out the citizen homosexual.[18] That's not to say it was an easy, fair plat-form. Drastic as daytime talk shows' shifts in tone were, like their predecessors of the fifties and sixties, many talk shows of the late seven-ties and eighties positioned a queer person as the antithesis to normal guys and gals watching at home.

Impassioned gay activists and humble veterans would join the ranks of Christine Jorgensen and Lance Loud on television throughout the decades, but they did not remain the majority real queer presence on television for long, especially as the talk show circus we're well familiar with today developed. The growing "women's market" was secured by *The Phil Donahue Show*, with *Donahue* (as it was later known) leading the way in audience participation, combining the personal and political into one controversial package and furnishing spotlights for real people to tell and yell their most polarizing stories to a fickle in-studio crowd. From *Donahue*'s forehead sprang forth the daytime tabloid talk show as we recognize it: confessional, confrontational, regrettable, and (the producers hoped) unforgettable. In the eighties, Phil Donahue would find himself joined by forever one-upping hosts and producers chasing that spontaneous thrill that could be found only in putting real Americans on television to duke it out with their friends, neighbors, spouses, children, and strangers, or to tearfully open their hearts to reconciliation and revival of the human spirit. *Oprah*, *Sally Jessy Raphael*, *Geraldo*, *Ricki Lake*, and many more would follow, each with their special brand of connection to oddity, primal humanity, and that addictive sense of watching an imminent emotional or social car crash.

As scholar and daytime talk show's biggest fan/nemesis Joshua Gamson notes in the fantastically thorough and entertaining tome *Freaks Talk Back: Tabloid Talk Shows and Sexual Nonconformity*, there's no question that exploitation is baked into the DNA of daytime talk. Queer people, especially those who bucked gender norms or otherwise engaged with taboos, were welcomed alongside the rest of what polite televisual society deemed utterly undesirable. Poor, uneducated, divorced, Black, brown, kinky, criminalized, disabled, and mentally ill guests were invited to share their deepest shame and be gawked at, a more verbose version of a freak show of old. Talk shows were a bastion of cruelty and indecency purely for inviting these guests, and "goodness, normality, and stability . . . are all threatened by the drivel, exploitation, and monstrosities of daytime TV talk shows."[19] At least, that's what talk show detractors peddled when faced with the prospect of a habitual spotlight on the dregs of society.

While early narrative depictions of gay men and women associated deviant sexuality with literal crime by casting them as manipulative homicidal maniacs, the queer people who appeared as guests on talk shows had the advantage of writing their own dialogue, even if hosts' introductions meant to position their identities as shocking. Many talk show detractors played right into this shock and disgust, ignoring the speech of the person onscreen and instead lumping queer, non-white, and working-class talk show participants, no matter the content of their story, with accused murderers, rapists, assaulters, and, of course, the cardinally shamed sex worker. And they weren't just dangerous or weird or tacky. The moment they voluntarily stepped into the spotlight, if only for fifteen minutes, they were branded as losers.

But talk shows weren't necessarily objectionable to socially conservative critics, both in media and politics, because of the way they treated their guests. It was more the normalization of the obscene, the perverse, and the bizarre that posed a threat. Sure, audiences might suffer psychic damage and nosebleeds by looking down on vulnerable guests in front of them, participating in a gleeful, superior voyeurism, but they also become "desensitized" and inured to the weirdos. And that, emphasized by critics such as President Ronald Reagan's secretary of education William Bennett, was the true danger: with talk shows, the barometer of morality gets spun totally off balance, especially if you're a young and impressionable viewer.[*20]

You probably recognize this type of hot air; across the decades, it's the same logic used to protest the portrayal of queer and trans people on television at all, especially in hours or programs that are accessible to children. More recently, it's the rhetoric used to criminalize the existence of trans people anywhere around children in public life. According to right-wingers and to concerned centrists, television was just the start: by allowing the freaks out of the shadows and under the harshly

---

*   "Neoconservative" secretary of education William Bennett was so disgusted by the content of talk shows, he launched a campaign to wipe daytime television clean of "cultural rot," turning up the heat on advertisers to drop their spots with the shows that encouraged those gut-spilling emotional money shots *or* that issued invitations to homosexuals and transsexuals.

judgmental, expository eye of a talk show audience, American values were under attack. This protest of daytime talk can be fallible at the same time that it is unquestionable that talk show hosts and producers shamelessly manipulated their guests at a time when such shows became one of the most dependable forums to find not only queer people but also people who fit producers' canny and often cruel visions of those who had long been without a public voice. After all, talk shows were the ultimate combination of show and business. Sometimes, that ruthless combination wasn't just offensive or exploitative—it was deadly.*

Nonetheless, with *Donahue*'s offspring dominating cable television throughout the 1980s and an explosion of cheaply made, syndicated talk shows reaching almost thirty individual programs in the 1990s, the type of queer people that associations like the Mattachine Society and Daughters of Bilitis would urge networks to erase from their scripts held onto a microphone. Reading the laundry list of LGBTQIA2S+-related guests that Gamson documents as having appeared in the few years before writing his book has a sort of incantational quality. It's as if all the queers, having been locked out of their own authorship for so long, were summoned to one place that would continue to hold a fraught space for them to live out an impossible fantasy: broadcasting a message to America.[21]

As exploitative as talk shows still are, as Gamson underlines, they deserve credit for opening up a mass-seen form of "potential agency" for queer people that was lacking from factual and fictional television before it. When we brush off even the most outrageously, sneeringly voyeuristic talk programs as unimportant for their bad taste and social tragedy, we miss the not-insignificant autonomy of real queer people in them.

---

*   One of the more publicized cases of direct tabloid talk show tragedy was that of Scott Amedure, a young gay man who was murdered by his neighbor Jonathan Schmitz after confessing his crush on the 1995 "Same-Sex Secret Crushes" episode of *The Jenny Jones Show* that was never aired. Amedure's family sued *The Jenny Jones Show*, Telepictures, and Warner Bros. for their involvement.

Bi Local, by Queers, for Queers

Daytime talk shows were certainly some of the most popular forums for real queer people to be introduced to the presumably heterosexual world, but on a smaller scale, queer people were harnessing the power of local cable access to broadcast within their own communities. As early as 1977, *The Emerald City* began airing twice a week out of Manhattan's Channel J, combining long-form interviews; community news; a dedicated cabaret segment that hosted comedy, musical, and drag acts; and man-on-the-street interviews to call itself "the world's first television show for gay men and women."[22] *Emerald City* co-founders Eugene B. Stavis, Frank O'Dowd, and Steven Bie banked on the newly available power of leased cable to purchase airtime and independently sold advertising space by marketing the concept of "narrowcasting," which, at the time, considered almost any demographic—from "Jewish or Roman Catholic interests, to movie buffs, to Irish-American consciousness-raising or South American folk arts," to French speakers—as niche.[23]

While their program lasted only until 1978, they managed to stuff their short run full of some of the most culturally significant names in seventies gay history. Director John Waters, actress Divine, performer Wayland Flowers and his puppet Madame, artist David Hockney, playwright Larry Kramer, singer Selma Hazouri, female impressionist Lynne Carter, and more appeared as guests, with legendary gay porn filmmaker Wakefield Poole and trailblazing gay media historian Vito Russo contributing as moderators and hosts—a lineup that would have any queer history nerd today drooling. While the creators first acknowledged they didn't want the program to be *too* specialized so as to ostracize a heterosexual audience, it was without a doubt primarily for and about their own community—and it did eventually travel to San Francisco and Los Angeles markets as well. As Bie reflected in 2018, "It was really pretty glamorous, pretty exciting to have this level of people and just a lot of people who were pretty big in their careers and not minding just saying matter of fact that they were gay."[24]

The very same year *The Emerald City* pronounced itself to be mired in a gay social context rather than a sexual context, another leased cable access show was reveling in the joy of all things sex. *The Robin Byrd Show*, formerly named *Hot Legs*, began airing in 1977 and took every delight in pushing the limits of who and what could be seen on television. Hosted by porn performer and bisexual local legend Robin Byrd, who at that point was best known for her appearance in seminal porn *Debbie Does Dallas* (1978), the show was unlike any other, and it was so iconic that it was eventually parodied by *Saturday Night Live* (1975–) in 1997. Byrd interviewed fellow adult film performers, strippers, sex workers, and queer guests of all stripes, often including stripteases alongside conversations about labor, health, safer sex, and sexuality. Subjects that would have been treated with shock and shame on daytime talk shows were instead a part of casual conversation and flirtatious banter. It was certainly titillating, but that was mostly because of the tits.*25

Following *The Emerald City*'s and *The Robin Byrd Show*'s leads, local queer cable access shows popped up throughout the 1980s and '90s, celebrating, protesting, documenting, and connecting queer people to one another over the limited airwaves. Vito Russo took up hosting duties with *Our Time* in 1983, welcoming the likes of Tennessee Williams, Harvey Fierstein, Quentin Crisp, Rita Mae Brown, and Lily Tomlin to his short-lived show. The Gay Cable Network began its broadcast with male erotica in 1982 and eventually shifted to New York–based gay news programming for a whopping nineteen years. The astounding *Dyke TV*, founded by Ana Maria Simo, Linda Chapman, and Mary Patierno, broadcast from 1993 to 2005, using majority volunteer staff to produce 355 episodes that would eventually air in upward of sixty US cities, spreading the gospel of dyke luminaries like Sarah Schulman, Cheryl Dunye, Ellen Cantor, Carmelita Tropicana, Carolee Schneemann, Dorothy

---

*   Not everyone was happy with the level of "explicit content"—both in conversation and physical presentation—that *The Robin Byrd Show* celebrated, and Byrd was embroiled in legal battles with Manhattan Cable, Time Warner Cable, and the Federal Communications Commission for years as she staved off attempts to "scramble" her show and make it inaccessible to the public.

Allison, Guinevere Turner, and the Lesbian Avengers, among hundreds of others.

Not all gay cable was exported from New York either. Out of the Twin Cities in Minnesota, experienced journalist Brad Theissen hosted *GAZE-TV*, later named *Green And Yellow (GAY) TV*, which began primarily as an AIDS education program in 1986 and transformed throughout its nine-year run to include political reporting, arts and culture coverage (with film coverage provided for a time by *Rainbow Age of Television* favorite Jenni Olson), and coverage of Minnesota's rising police brutality. In Springfield, Missouri, Cruz Devon led the short-lived but engaging *This Gay Life* from 1994 to 1995. In Santa Monica and the greater Los Angeles area, Nicholas Snow gave his best *Larry King Live* with *Tinseltown's Queer!* from 1993 to 2000 and currently continues to produce news segments for his YouTube channel.

With very little money, and little acknowledgment from other media sources, local queer cable also became service journalism for its constituents, thoroughly covering topics that national news touched only with a ten-foot pole. Nowhere did that divide become more apparent than in the chasm between commercial news media and *In the Life*, the gay cable access show that turned into a nationally broadcast lifeline for queer people seeking information, coverage, and collective outrage about the HIV/AIDS epidemic.

In the Life: National News, by Queers, for Queers

Like its predecessors, *In the Life* is an indisputably extraordinary program and, thanks to its preservation, a well of archival information. Initially broadcast on PBS affiliate WNYC-TV in 1992, it became the first nationally broadcast show of its kind, with a preliminary format similar to its local predecessors, which included stand-up comedy, music, sketches, and an overall daytime talk show aesthetic. By 1992, the format itself was not innovative, nor was the idea of a show based around a particular demographic, but *ITL* was the first nationally broadcast program to provide news, entertainment, and a communal rapport specifically dedicated to the United States' lesbian and gay, and later LGBTQIA2S+, communities. Over its twenty-year run, it evolved into a newsmagazine format that focused on both local and national domestic investigations and became a staple of accurate and sensitive journalism before it aired its final episode in December 2012. While it was initially broadcasted to a paltry twenty domestic television markets, by its end it had grown to two hundred markets that were able to watch queer news and entertainment through a specifically queer lens.[26]

Although it began as a sort of mishmash variety hour, *ITL*'s focus soon transitioned to its newsmagazine format, highlighting the queer news of the world, as well as the local, which every other form of mainstream news either addressed curtly or skipped entirely. By 1994, *ITL*'s audience had expanded to 1.5 million households by Nielsen measurements. It was a feat unimagined by its creators and PBS, who had initially tried to remove it from its first scheduled lineup for fear of alienating its viewership.[27] Over the years, *ITL*'s coverage was most heavily dominated by profiles and spotlights of queer artists, advocates, political and religious leaders, athletes, musicians, and organizers of nonprofits that brought queer rights to the forefront. *ITL* did its own activist work outside these individual profiles, with consistent segmental updates on the HIV/AIDS crisis, coverage of queer youth homelessness, in-depth investigations of the murders of trans people, deportation of queer immigrants, and the ongoing legal battles for same-sex marriage and adoption.

Even on a shoestring budget, with no federal funding (including no funding from PBS), *ITL* persisted by relying on private donations and some underwriting from various advertisers, although most advertisers that the *ITL* board approached were worried about isolating their base if they were to be associated with "homosexual" programming.[28] The ethos that brought *An American Family* to PBS in 1971 had been ravaged by ongoing conservative culture wars and administration cycles, meaning that producers initially needed to argue with PBS to distribute the show to more than just New York City markets. Despite these major blockades, producers of *ITL* invested in direct advertisement to its audience and were able to continue creating monthly episodes even without revenue from syndication or international distribution.

According to producer John Scagliotti, the show's subscribers came from all backgrounds, including heterosexual partnerships and individuals who believed in the relevance of *ITL*.[29] *ITL* was the only national news outlet to give an intentional voice to the continuing AIDS crisis, after most mainstream media outlets (except for—wait for it—the daytime talk show) relegated it to the back page or dealt with activists only if they threw themselves in front of cameras, and it was one of the forerunners in covering the federal and statewide fights for and against same-sex marriage. Some of the most recognized (and accoladed) pieces from *ITL* focused on the continuing crisis in a way that broke stigmas of "criminalization" and undermined myths about the transmission of the virus, as well as keeping its audience informed and aware of methods to prevent transmission, care for oneself after transmission, and how to seek out resources necessary to survive and thrive through a diagnosis.[30]

To put it plainly, visibility, as well as information on queer issues that could not be easily accessed elsewhere, were worth the overwhelming cost of production and the hellish, continuous fight for the right to distribute on public television. When *ITL* announced its halt in production and distribution, the board was careful to release a statement acknowledging the importance of its run and the promise that the board would find a way to "provide access to this material so that it will continue to be used to advance equality."[31] In 2015, the UCLA Film & Television Archive announced that it would become the channel to that access, working with *ITL* in order to create an online portal that would eventually house all twenty-one seasons and make them completely free and viewable to the public.[32]

Although *ITL* will never create another episode, its value remains in its archival access. There is always room for the content it provided and will continue to host in perpetuity, but the changing landscape of broadcast television, and the infinite self-created content encouraged by digital media, ensures that *ITL* will never come back on the airwaves in a new form.

I Want My (Ho)M(osexuali)T(y)V

Among the queers who grabbed their chance at public access was one Andy Warhol. In 1979, Warhol launched *Fashion*, his first fashion world interview show on Manhattan Cable TV, by buying airtime alongside the rest of his New York cohort. Cable access was just a launching pad for Warhol, who went through several evolutions and names of his show before developing *Andy Warhol's Fifteen Minutes* in 1985 for a hip, burgeoning channel that was mostly aimed at teenagers, young adults, and newfound devotees of the music video.

Warhol's celebrity-filled program wasn't the only aesthetically queer media on MTV, which had launched in 1981, just in time for glam rock to shake its glorious tresses all over national television. In 1991, animation showcase *Liquid Television* (1991–1994) hosted short films that would launch venerated animators' careers and included shorts from a trans filmmaking duo by the name of the Art School Girls of Doom. But the network's real claim to queer fame would emerge in 1992, with its launch of the allegedly *An American Family*–inspired social experiment series, *The Real World*. A poppy, colorful, friendly young show, down to its funky instrumental soundtrack and aerial city interstitials, *The Real World* threw young adults from disparate backgrounds together in a house to see what coexistence total strangers (often with diametrically opposite personalities) could create. It was an instantly classic formula, but the show didn't reach permanent pop culture status until its second season, *The Real World: San Francisco*, and its introduction of Pedro Zamora.

An introspectively soft-eyed and soft-spoken young Cuban-born man, Zamora was an HIV/AIDS educator who decided to audition as a cast member when he realized television's potential reach was unfathomably greater than his individual speaking engagements. In that, Zamora succeeded beyond measure, as viewers tuned in week after week to watch the escalation of tensions between himself and two of his castmates in particular—one a homophobic and misogynistic but charming miscreant, one an ambitious Young Republican. Even as his health failed, Zamora continued to serve as both an introduction for many to the realities of living with HIV and the possibilities of gay relationships and a cynical lesson to reality television producers everywhere. Even at the cost of their own health and well-being, placing queer people in conversation with the "rest" of America made for high-stakes, cheaply produced, and sometimes world-altering television. It may not have been exploitative in the same way that talk shows were, dedicated to showing a young gay person in a positive light as it was, but the stress of filming contributed to Zamora's early passing at twenty-two, mere hours after *The Real World*'s finale aired. The new era of presenting queer people to the world via reality TV was born.

Start Your Engines

While future seasons of *The Real World* would continue to cast young queer and trans people to tell their stories to teens around the nation, not all of MTV's, and sister channel VH1's, attempts to harness the power of queerness would be accoladed by the White House for their sensitivity and humanity. As the 2000s approached, so, too, did a willingness to reappraise queerness, not just as educational material but as pure ratings shock and awe, especially when it came to dating and competition series. Shows like British import *There's Something About Miriam* (UK, 2003; US, 2005 and 2007) and *A Shot at Love with Tila Tequila* (2007–2008) harnessed trans and bisexual identities for their potential to deceive and titillate (and the latter awoke many a latent bisexual, even through confused fear and shame). A far cry from the openness of *The Real World*, as soon as it could be put at odds with expectations of heterosexuality and gender conformity for laughs, gags, and fetishization, these were reminders that queerness could always be transformed back into a dirty little televised secret.

Throughout the 2000s, the emergence of the reality competition, beginning with *Big Brother* (2000–) and *Survivor* (2000–), both on CBS, started synthesizing approaches toward real live queer people on television to present a sort of "best of all ratings" scenario. Utilizing the concept of *The Real World* to plop ordinary Americans into an unfamiliar scenario and simply see how they might cope, the shows combined surveillance, mind games, and *1984-* and *Lord of the Flies*-esque scenarios, respectively, to inadvertently experiment with the ways queerness might exist in a new society. That's probably not what they would tell you (although I personally think "Outwit, Outgay, Outlast" would have been an excellent *Survivor* tagline), but even their earliest seasons featured players who weighed the value of the closet as a tool for triumph.

Unlike later technical skill–based (and popularity-based) reality competition programs like *American Idol* (2002–), *America's Next Top Model* (2003–2018), *So You Think You Can Dance* (2005–), and *America's Got Talent* (2006–), the gays of *Big Brother* and *Survivor* were in a totally contained social experiment, without the immediate pressure of a designated judge, or the judgment of wider America, to dictate the ways they disclosed their identity. In the isolation of the wilderness or under the scope of a thousand closed-circuit cameras, the only people they had to impress in order to survive were their fellow contestants. And, as critic, filmmaker, and reality TV enthusiast Juan Barquin points out, once removed from the assumptions of regularly operating society, queerness was not automatically a weakness.

In the case of Richard Hatch, winner of *Survivor: Borneo* (2000), verified queer television villain, and the first contestant to look at *Survivor* as a psychological (as well as physical) game, Barquin points to the weaponizing of Hatch's comfort with his own nudity and sexuality to ward off the camera and isolate contestants of all genders, Hatch's nonreaction to the more bigoted slurs thrown his way, and his alliance with former Navy SEAL Rudy Boesch as tipping points for how the game could be won. Still on the air today as one of CBS's biggest ratings giants, *Survivor* remains rich in queer contestants, with its part-survival, part-talk show format as a breeding ground for unpredictable betrayal, bigotry, and sometimes both. In one memorable case, gay contestant Jeff Varner outed fan favorite Zeke Smith as a trans man in a last-ditch, 2000-and-late bid to prove his untrustworthiness in *Survivor: Game Changers* (2017), and the show became a national stage for not only villainous gameplay but also for a conversation around trans identity.

Other reality competitions hosted queer contestants—it would have been nigh impossible to cast *Top Chef* or *Project Runway* (2004–) without queer talents—but it wasn't until networks bravely discovered that the only thing more entertaining than one queer person in a room, fighting for their life, are several, preferably squabbling with one another, that what we know today as certified gay reality TV was born.

May the Best Straight Guy Win

Bravo's original *Queer Eye for the Straight Guy* (2003–2007) was a surprise reality hit when it first aired, capitalizing on stereotype, outstanding charisma, and heterosexual fascination with the concept of the preternatural talent gay men have to be able to tell a man what a woman wants. Copycats sprung up in its initial wake, including VH1's *TRANSform Me* (2010), a short-lived makeover show starring Laverne Cox, Jamie Clayton, and Nina Poon, which took the conceit that metaphorically, the concept of desiring transition could apply to any person—and trans women have the skills to make that holistic transition a reality. Nothing on the small screen, however, quite took the concept of queer talent to the masses like *RuPaul's Drag Race*.

A mix of *Project Runway* meets *America's Next Top Model* meets *The Carol Burnett Show* (1967–1978), this fifteen-season, four-spin-off, and fourteen internationally spawned dupes (and counting) reality program has burgeoned into an empire, cementing drag queen and gay rights advocate RuPaul Charles's status as a pop culture icon among younger generations. *Drag Race* now has yearly bicoastal conventions, ravenous fans, a prime-time slot, and Emmys for Outstanding Reality Television Program (Unscripted) and Outstanding Host for a Reality or Competition Program. And all this from a little show whose first season could barely be viewed through the sepia-tinted, Vaseline-covered filters of what seemed like Logo TV's shoddiest cameras.

As *Drag Race*'s star has climbed—and along with it a top prize of $250,000—it has become a beacon not only for queer viewers but for a more widespread mainstream audience for whom it is the only example, or the most authentic, original example, of drag. As such, its views on who can engage in drag, what drag looks like, and what drag's message is are often taken as gospel, which have only recently become friendlier to trans women, trans men, and nonbinary performers. Above all else, it's entertaining as hell, making revered stars, and notorious reality TV antagonists, out of its parade of endlessly creative personalities, who have internationally and domestically toured their own shows to sold-out crowds, booked roles on Broadway, become the faces of ad campaigns for major brands and political campaigns alike, popped up in cameos and roles across narrative television, and hosted their own talk shows. Other drag competitions have also successfully launched, in partial response to RuPaul's restrictive views of drag paragons, with the most engaging being *The Boulet Brothers' Dragula* (2016–), a cutting, home-grown search for the drag creature (including drag kings) who embodies the Boulet Brothers' key tenets of "Horror, Glamour, and Filth."

Sasha Colby, longtime, long-admired drag performer and winner of *RPDR* season 15, boils down the show's enduring appeal to one simple component: shade. She explains, "It's taking competition like *Survivor* and cattiness like *The Real Housewives* and putting glitter on it. That's why we are so successful. Because it's shady! And nobody can give shade like queer people."[33] It's a far cry from newscasters having to cut around an intelligent response from a gay man in order to downplay his acceptance of himself—now one of the most courted representations of a real queer person is a bejeweled, Teflon-like resolve to be the funniest, smartest, most cutting, and most beautiful in the room.

The Future of Queer Reality

Even within the last fifteen years, we've seen a mainstream nonfiction television landscape that seems like it could be a funhouse mirror of our first appearances in each nonfiction genre. Some of the most trusted voices of a certain center-left political leaning audience are openly gay newscasters, including Anderson Cooper, Rachel Maddow, and, for a time, Don Lemon. One of our most cuttingly vicious late-night talk show hosts is flamboyantly gay producer, instigator, and general menace Andy Cohen. Ellen—yes, that Ellen—hosted a daytime talk show for nigh on twenty years and was beloved by moms everywhere. In addition to hosting and dotting said talk shows, queer people have had full series welcoming people to poke around in their lives (*I Am Jazz* [2015–], *I Am Cait* [2015–2016]) and invitations to explore the lives of others (*Gaycation* [2016]).

Dating franchises are beginning to catch on to queer potential beyond an artificial "gotcha." In 2019, MTV dating competition *Are You the One?* (2014–) dedicated its eighth season to "sexually fluid" individuals, upping the stakes and difficulty of a secret soulmate match game so any competitor had the potential to match with absolutely any other. It was a brilliant idea, producing some of the most thrillingly horny, unflattering, and organically queer fuckery seen on any dating show . . . and then the subsequent season reverted right back to heterosexual couples. For a time, too, queer talent found another excellent showcase outside *Drag Race*, with *Legendary* (2020–2022), the explosive voguing competition series straight out of New York's ballroom scene. The show had everything. Enthralling talents, respectful rivalries, periodically disrespectful judges, top-notch technical direction, and a performance budget that actually seemed to provide the contestants with what they were worth provided a euphoric queer experience that should have lasted far longer than its three seasons.

On the other hand, reality TV still doesn't seem to know how to successfully sell communal queerness beyond *Drag Race* or the instructional queer-as-fairy-godmothers found in *We're Here* (2020–) or the rebooted *Queer Eye* (2018–). Depicting the "real life" and desires of queers from the outside looking in remains a puzzle—especially when attempting to rep-licate a "straight" formula. Queer lifestyles in a vacuum are so passé that they've produced some of the most boring and obviously manufactured seasons of reality television in recent history (see *The Real L Word* [2010–2012], *Tampa Baes* [2021], *The Real Friends of WeHo* [2023]).

Contemporary reality television is in a bind when it comes to packag-ing queerness. If it's sold as a digestible formula and not an intrinsic facet of life that could surprise and engage audiences on anything from *An American Family* to *The Bachelor* (2002–) to *The Real Housewives* (2006–), then there's no wonder it falls flat. If queerness is sanitized, sanctioned, and scripted as its own drama in a medium that thrives on unpredictability, you can forget the lightning in a bottle. Throughout it all, there's a truth that viewers will never know exactly how many real people, drifting through any of our favorite varnished and melodramat-ically elevated versions of reality, are queer in a way that just isn't read-able by a prying camera. If we're to truly equate these peeks into the lives of others with real life, it's safe to say that the number, throughout the history of the genre, is much, much higher than any of us could real-istically tally. Considering the decades of microscopic inspection, judg-ment, shame, and exploitation queer people have been subjected to while trying to live their lives, that may just be the aspect of queer reality television that doesn't need any meddling.

Queer & A: Melissa King

Credits: *Top Chef: Boston, Top Chef: All-Stars, Tasting Wild*

From 2006 to the present, one of the most consistent habitats for a queer woman on reality television has been in the kitchen. Namely, the *Top Chef* kitchen, wielding a knife sharp enough to slice and dice their way to $100,000. Bravo's cooking competition stalwart, in which profes-sional chefs are put through grueling challenges to out-gourmet one another under the judgment of the American culinary scene's most esteemed restauranteurs, has also been a staple of queer contestantship.

Across seasons, there have been competing lesbian couples, conscientious objectors to bachelor/bachelorette catering on the grounds of gay marriage still being illegal, mass gay weddings officiated by host Padma Lakshmi, enough queer chefs to form a Team Rainbow, and at least one lesbian contestant on almost every season. And in 2023, former winner and out lesbian Kristen Kish was announced as Lakshmi's successor.

Chef Melissa King, who first competed on *Top Chef: Boston* in 2014 and returned to win *Top Chef: All-Stars*, acknowledges that *Top Chef* was neck and neck with *The L Word* for the places she could find any sort of queer representation—especially those who looked even the slightest bit like her. King hopped on a call with me to discuss growing up as a tomboy, how incredible it feels to be surrounded by queer chefs, and how *Top Chef* capturing their journey from newbie to self-assured All-Star to competition judge has changed their life. This is an edited excerpt of our conversation.

SHAYNA MACI WARNER: Do you remember the first queer character or person you saw on TV?

MELISSA KING: When I was really young, definitely Ellen. I would say high school to college was when I discovered *The L Word* on Showtime. Rosie O'Donnell, I remember when she came out and it was such a big, big deal. I'm born in '83; I'm trying to think further back. I suppose those were the women characters I noticed.

I don't think I fully connected the dots yet, because I didn't come out until I was twenty-one or so, a little bit later. But I do remember seeing Rosie O'Donnell in *A League of Their Own*, as kind of more masc-leaning. I just remember thinking, "She's so cool." I myself grew up like a quote-unquote "tomboy" around that time. I was always playing in the dirt and quite sporty. Even like Sporty Spice! I was like,

"Is Sporty Spice gay? I hope Sporty Spice is queer." There really wasn't much now that I'm thinking about this.

SMW: A few other people I've interviewed couldn't tell me the first queer person they remember seeing on TV, but they did remember, along the lines of a coded character, that sort of tomboy presence.

MK: Exactly. That's what I saw more of, and I remember feeling connected to those characters and people. There weren't many people I knew who were a representation of that. When I grew up, I would resist and fight my mother to death to not wear a dress. She would try to get me a dress and I would fight to wear pants or overalls, shorts. And then seeing characters a little later dressing in a more masc-centric-or-leaning identity, I think I felt more connected to that. Like, oh, a woman can wear pants and it's not a big deal. It's not the end of the world, which was the way that my family might have been making me feel at the time.

SMW: When you were older and watching *The L Word*, did you see characters that you connected to in that way?

MK: *The L Word* was interesting. I look at that show, and I don't even know if there's a specific character that I even really connect with. There are bits and pieces of each person, but there wasn't one singular person that felt like, "Oh, this is me." Shane [McCutcheon] is more masc-leaning in the outward appearance of their clothing and style. But the other characters . . . I think looking back on it now, I remember more problematic parts of the show. But when I watched it at the time, I was amazed that this show even existed. It was displaying a subset of the community, but there was nothing else out there. *Top Chef* was the other show that I do remember seeing where I saw a queer character, or a person who came out on the show, or was very openly proud of who they were. I remember watching the early seasons of *Top Chef* before I was even on it, where I noticed a couple people who were on there and open.

I remember seeing Tiffani Faison [from season 1] being fairly open and out on the show, and just proud. I remember her being very open and honest about her life. And Sandee [Birdsong, from season 3], who had a mohawk. Even though I myself didn't have a mohawk, I was excited to see other people be so expressive in their identity. That person's doing their thing and are quite unapologetic about showing the world who they are. Over the years, you start seeing *Top Chef* cast quite an array of talents, beyond the kitchen, and a quite diverse group of people. And it was kind of what drew me into it, wanting to go on my first season.

SMW: When you decided to go on the show, was that something in your mind, that maybe you were going to be one of these stories?

MK: It's interesting, yes and no. My first season wasn't as clear. My first season, I was sort of pressured by friends and family members to try out for the show. I was painfully shy and was like, I don't know if I want to do something like this. But I did it more as a personal challenge, to challenge myself creatively as a chef, and as a life experience. But being a former fan of the show, watching it previously and recognizing that it did have quite a diverse array of people, I remember there was no hesitation on that front for me to want to apply. I didn't actually realize how exposed my life would become after the show aired on television. When you're in it, you're in a bubble, and I was fully in the mindset of just competing and doing my best and wanting to focus on my career of being a chef and showcase my skill sets from that part of me. At no point was I thinking about how that would affect viewers.

After the show aired, I started receiving so many messages on social media, e-mails, and in real life, if I ran into someone who was a *Top Chef* fan. They would express it to me in person and say, "We're so proud to see someone like you on the show, and to see another queer Asian woman, fighting for their dream." I think that's where it started to click. After it aired was when I realized the impact of *Top Chef* on a personal scale for the community of people that are watching, and really how important that representation is.

So when it came to *All-Stars*, that became a more clear decision of going back the second time. I was like, "You know what, I'm not just going back to cook and try to win the title, I'm going back because there is such a huge community of people cheering me on to go and try to win." I recognized the value of how continuing to put my story out there and put myself out there can impact people's lives. That's kind of what ended up happening in real life. But going back to the question, the initial, like, thought of going on the show, it wasn't based around my identity at all, it was more like cook and see if I can win this show. Pretty simple, pretty straightforward.

SMW: When you were on the show in that bubble, in your first go-round, was there any sort of thought about your own level of being out in your personal life and how that would be affected when the show did air?

MK: Sure! So to give you context, I was already out to my mom, my stepfather, my sister, and the people I was close to within my family. But my father, my biological father, I had not come out to until maybe like a year before I went on *Top Chef.* He's the last person I ended up coming out to. At that point, my immediate family all knew, and then I decided to go on the show and I remember consciously thinking, after we had filmed it, "Oh my God, Grandma's gonna find out, and aunts and uncles and it's all going to be out there in the world once these episodes air." And even when I was in competition, there are moments when you do those confessionals and you talk to the camera—it's almost like a therapy session and you just start talking and disclosing a lot of information about your personal life. There are moments when I would catch myself and be like, "Oh, this might go on TV." But then there are also moments when you forget, and you just kind of keep rambling. You don't know what the editors are going to pick and choose for the show. So I remember thinking, "I'm just gonna be myself, I'm gonna really just put it all out there. I'm not going to hide the fact that I have a girlfriend."

My girlfriend at the time had written little love notes and passed those off to me. I was very open with reading them and just going through my normal life while I was in the bubble. Of course, they happen to catch little glimpses of that on camera. But when I was in it, I didn't know what they were going to show. I think I was a bit naive, and I was thinking, "They're just gonna focus on the food, it's a cooking competition!" until I watched it. I started seeing more of the depth of the development of each person and really, truly diving into more of our identities.

SMW: Fast-forwarding through your time on *Top Chef*, you've competed twice and are now a judge. Do you ever think about or notice how many queer chefs are your peers and judges?

MK: It's funny because even as a competitor, that comes up in conversation among each other. I remember in the *All-Star* season, it was me, Gregory Gourdet, Karen [Akunowicz],

Lisa [Fernandes] . . . I remember, we scanned the room in our cast house. And we're like, this is awesome. We're high-fiving each other, feeling the sense of pride for how many of us, more than a third of the group, was queer. When you look at earlier seasons, it might have just been one person out of sixteen chefs. And now you see four or five of us at that season that were openly queer. So yeah, there were head nods and approval and pride to be selected and competing among each other. But I think there was a bit of recognition when we scan the room that things are changing, and the show is support-ing that change in the media. And so it was exciting.

Judging, same thing. You know, it's me, Kristen [Kish], Gregory . . . at least from the generation I grew up, I didn't see much of that on television. I have a tremendous amount of pride when I'm in a room of queer people who are tal-ented and being supported through the media. It was pretty cool. And it wasn't even just the queer community, it was the Asian American community, the Black community. We started seeing that diversity was important to *Top Chef* and the casting, and that they really wanted to show their support giving everyone an equal opportunity. So it was really excit-ing to go in and see how it's changed since the first season.

SMW: Is there anything on your first season, *All-Stars*, or your guest judge appearances that you want to be remembered for in "A History of *Top Chef*"?

MK: Wow. I have a couple of proud moments, but one of my proudest moments was winning *All-Stars*. And it wasn't just winning, it was the food I was presenting. It was really impor-tant to me. On my first season, I'm a bit young, in my career and in my confidence as a chef. You can tell through the food that it's not fully speaking. By the time I get to *All-Stars*, before I started competing I had a very clear sense of the type of chef I wanted to be, and what type of chef I wanted to present to the world. So I went in being very unapologetic. I'm making Chinese food, using Asian flavors, and you either like it or you don't. And I tried not to second-guess myself. I felt like a very different competitor from my first season to that season. I really went in with full confidence, showing the judges my identity through food. I feel really proud that I did that. I kind of came out in many ways on my first season. And the second season, you see someone who has just fully embraced who they are, and their identity, and is just running with it. I'm really, really proud of the decisions that I made on the show and the outcomes of it all.

SMW: One of the pretty exciting pieces that the editors chose to share was your reconnecting with your biological father. I was wondering how that felt for you to be able to share that and watch it back?

MK: *Top Chef* really changed my relationship with my dad for the better. It's weird for me to credit a TV show with doing that. But that was the reality. It did break down a lot of barriers between me and my dad, and it exposed so much all at once on the first season. It really forced us to sit down and have a deep conversation in real life with each other. And it brought us a lot closer. So I'm the closest I've ever been to my dad in these years of my life. And I look back, and oftentimes I thank *Top Chef* for that. It's crazy that a TV show can influence someone's life that much, but for me it did—on a personal level, with my relationship with my family, but also with myself, with my own confidence and figuring out my life, it really brought me out of my shell and helped me to find the person that I am today. *Top Chef* really did a lot for me.

SMW: I know it was many years ago at this point, but do you remember any moments, whether on your first season or right after the season, where it clicked for you: "Oh, I am more confident in this aspect of myself" or, "Oh, this has really changed for me"?

MK: You actually see it happen in real life, when you watch season [12]. Season [12] I'm a bit of an underdog and it's truly because I'm not fully confident in taking a big risk. I'm playing a bit safe, and you can see there's hesitation in the decisions that I make. And then they bring my mom on the show. That episode really unlocked a lot in me, it kind of got me to realize, "Don't overthink it. Just enjoy this moment with your mom." [That episode was] honestly one of my favorite moments of *Top Chef* because I was able to kind of let the show and competition part of it disappear and focus more on just having a good time with my mom. I think it really translates into how I perform in the rest of season 12.

And then in *All-Stars*, it's the same type of confidence getting continually pulled through the season. It was such a crazy journey. I look back and watch it and I can actually see baby me. I look really shy and nervous, timid. It's a completely different person when I watch it. But the person that you see on *All-Stars* . . . it's always the same person, but it just like unlocked somewhere in between. Yeah, it's quite beautiful.

SMW: That's amazing. It's very strange to have someone quoting something you said back to you, but as an audience member, I think the line that really peaked was the *All-Stars* season when you do get to [the Final Four in] Italy, and that first Quickfire, and you talk about possibly winning $10,000 and going on a vacation and having a cute girl on the back of a scooter.

MK: I didn't realize that! It just came out of my mouth! A lot of the time I'm not conscious of what they're gonna take or not take of the things that I say because you're filmed all the time and you start to forget that there's even a camera there, or you forget that the stuff may end up on TV some-day. So I don't know, it just came out of my mouth. I love that they kept that line in there. Yeah, it is this arc that I think *Top Chef* did a great job at continuing to follow. Because it truly was happening in real life to me, building the confidence and feeling stronger every day, through that competition.

Queer & A: Sasha Colby
Credits: *RuPaul's Drag Race* Season 15 Winner

Sasha Colby is your favorite drag queen's favorite drag queen. Sasha Colby is a Goddess. Sasha Colby is straight-up God. Sasha Colby has about a dozen different catchphrases and fawning nicknames, because after years of steadily working as a drag performer, winning Miss Continental, and garnering the respect and admiration of her fellow performers, Colby competed on and won the fifteenth season of the ulti-mate queer reality TV behemoth *RuPaul's Drag Race*, sweeping week after week as the first Native Hawaiian competitor and the latest in a series of high-placing trans contestants and winners.

I first met Sasha when working on fellow winner Sasha Velour's short-lived but gorgeous Quibi documentary series *NightGowns*, and her magnetism was clearly itching to burst off the screen even in those brief ten-minute "quick bites." Now, Sasha's star has been launched interna-tionally, and the sky is truly the limit.

Right after Sasha's win, we spoke about her own relationship to real-ity TV growing up, her emotions at seeing her community succeed, and how she stays grounded during an era of conflicting visibility.

This is an edited excerpt of our conversation.

SHAYNA MACI WARNER: What was your relationship to television growing up?

SASHA COLBY: Oh, television raised me, like most kids. I'm born in the eighties, like '84, so it was the eighties/nineties, baby. So a lot of sitcoms.

I think for anybody growing up with the MTV era it was *Daytona Beach Spring Break*, *Singled Out with Jenny McCarthy*. I remember Ananda Lewis and Serena Altschul, they were just the coolest girls in the nineties and 2000s. Then there were things like *Family Matters* and *Step by Step*, and [ABC's TGIF lineup], that I just loved. Usually because I put myself in one of the girls' roles who had a boyfriend. I was already putting myself into these gender roles. You know, Disney princesses, *Mickey Mouse Club*, *Sailor Moon*, let's get into it. We're talking about coded queer.

SMW: Please! Was that the first queer-coded character you recognized?

SC: When I was growing up, I would wake up at, like, five in the morning, because on this one Japanese station in Hawai'i, there would be *Bananas in Pyjamas*, which was a children's show. *That* was the first queer-coded show [I watched] when I was a kid. And then right after that was *VR Troopers* and then *Sailor Moon*, so I would watch those three things while getting ready for school, and then would go to school and play Sailor Moon with my friends on the the jungle gym, and I was always Sailor Venus. We all had our characters. Those two were really big ones in the beginning, and *X-Men*. I was really obsessed with the comics, and the animated series made me fall in love with someone like Rogue, who was giving me lesbian vibes for sure. Like she has very strong energy.

Then there was this powerful idea of mutants, and it's so funny that the congressman [Florida Republican state rep Webster Barnaby] was just calling us mutants. The idea of mutants and being an outcast, but that actually being your superpower, was so appealing to me. So I would lose myself. I think that's where I got into being a trivia fact nerd. I just wanted to know everything about Storm. My first drag name before Sasha was actually N'dari, and that's Storm's mother's name. It was the high-chiefstress, princess thing, goddess. So yeah, I was coded heavily.

SMW: When you were watching these, did you recognize that you were thinking about these characters as queer, or was it just this feeling of connection?

SC: It was a feeling of connection—it definitely wasn't queer, but I feel like it was pushing my trans narrative in my head. And I never noticed until later, when I was talking with my nieces, maybe like five or six years ago, who I grew up with. Three nieces who are a little older than me actually, because I'm from a big family, the youngest of seven. So I had nieces and nephews who were older. And of course, there were three nephews and three nieces—I was definitely with the nieces. I never realized they allowed me to live this trans girl experience by playing with them. We would play dress up, always as girls. We would play house, so we would have boyfriends. And I remember all of us had boyfriends named Chad, Chad, and Brad. So funny to me. They allowed me to live this girl dream, and I remember even playing with Barbies. And my parents were like, "Get that out of your hand. Here's a Hot Wheel."

SMW: Moving on from this subtextual or coded queerness, which is everywhere, and people interpret it in so many different ways, do you

remember the first explicitly queer or trans character or person that you saw on TV?

SC: [*To Wong Foo, Thanks for Everything! Julie Newmar*] was probably the most openly out, like, just unapologetic, queer person I can recall. I don't know if that happened before or after, but there was this other movie that I love to watch to this day. It's called *Woman on Top* with Penelope Cruz. There's a drag queen character named Monica, and she is definitely living the experience of a trans woman in Brazil, which was so wild to me, and I thought, "Oh." I felt connected, yet, like, "Can anybody see that I'm loving this?"

SMW: Did you keep those close to your chest? Like, "I hope nobody else is actually seeing this"?

SC: Yes, or like, I hope no one's seeing me live so hard. Luckily, I could have it for myself while my whole family would be watching or it would be on the TV. It was definitely some education. *To Wong Foo* does definitely show trans people, but they're not being acted by trans people or queer people in general, so it was interesting to see how Hollywood still had to be cishet male oriented, you know? "I'm just playing a part." No queers were harmed in the filming of this.

SMW: You talked about being raised on MTV, and there have been so many gay characters, gay people, queer people, trans people, even on reality TV.

SC: I now remember, Pedro [Zamora] was probably the first. Me and my best friend Preston were talking about this. That was the first queer person he remembers seeing, and seeing him go through the AIDS epidemic, seeing everything happen, was very scary. It was like, "Oh, wow, that will be our inevitable fate if I choose to embrace this queerness." And it was a story that needed to be told; it definitely needs to be told still, but we were definitely still in this place. Like when we talk about *Boys Don't Cry*, where we were still in a place of letting people understand and be empathetic to us. So we were very trauma oriented. We were very about the pain just so people would be shocked into understanding. And that's about, what, three decades now, so I think it's time to get joyous again.

SMW: Do you have any kind of more recent examples of queer and trans narratives that are really joyous onscreen?

SC: When I first saw Candis Cayne on *Dirty, Sexy Money*. It was on ABC right after *Ugly Betty*. And that was just so wild to me. That's the first time I'm like, "Oh, that's a trans woman on TV." She was able to even have a love interest in a very big Hollywood star [Billy Baldwin]. That was wild in the early 2000s. So that really to me stuck out and said, "Okay, they're pulling out our seat at this table." They're allowing us to have a seat.

SMW: Can you recall a time, and this may be never, when television narratives started to reflect what your life looks like, actually, instead of one isolated person or character?

SC: I think in high school discovering my transness there was *Will & Grace*. It was really powerful to see funny gay people and quips. Although looking back now at it, there were a lot of trans-centered jokes. Now that there's a reboot, and those things are much more enlightened, I guess, the jokes are. But in that moment, it was just "Give us anything, give us something." I'm down to even hear self-deprecating jokes, or like, in-house jokes of each other. But it definitely felt like, "Oh, there's some gay people in that writing room." Maybe not trans queers, but there were some gays, cis gays.

SMW: Was there a show that made you feel like there were any trans people in the writing room?

SC: The first one I noticed was *Transparent*. That felt fully, like, family going through this moment. I really enjoyed the acting of the children on there. And of course Trace Lysette, and a personal idol of mine, Alexandra Billings, seeing them in this relaxed way was just really nice. And to see how the children of people who are late to transition deal with things. It was really, really interesting, and it seemed accurate.

SMW: Do you remember if that had an impact on you at all? Or if it was just kind of like, "This is interesting. This is new"?

SC: It was nice. It was nice to see. I think the thing that had an impact on me the most in the most recent years would be *Veneno*. I think that out of anything I've seen created on TV, that is the most accurate depiction of what the trans experience is like. It seemed like it could have been in Hawai'i. And all those girls were girls we grew up with. It was true, it was honest. It was everything. Every trans story is that. We could have a million amazing shows if they just let us tell our stories.

SMW: You've been in community with trans artists and performers way before there was a public spotlight or a show like *Transparent*. What's it been like to watch your peers and people you've recognized as being so talented actually be introduced to a larger audience?

SC: It's beautiful. It gives me hope. Because I love acting, and I love telling stories. I think at the end of the day, my drag is about storytelling, and I think that is innate to my Indigenous queer background. Hawaiians tell stories. We didn't have a written language until much later, so we passed our stories on through word of mouth. When you had to remember all these stories, and you made music to it, and then you had songs about it, and you made dances about it, hula, that's how we kept our history. I think that's something that I use with drag. I convey a story through my drag. And the next level of storytelling for me is to act and to tell other stories and to tell my stories. So when I see someone like Trace Lysette at the Cannes Film Festival starring in a movie, it feels so beautiful. I'm getting emotional, because it's just so wild to see trans talent. And maybe just even being in a world where we can just not say "trans" in front of it. Seeing talent, seeing great stories being told. It's really beautiful. That shit is so crazy.

SMW: I could talk about TV all day, in any capacity, and these answers have been really enlightening, so thank you for that. I would love to move to *Drag Race*. When did you realize that *Drag Race* was going to have an impact on drag?

SC: After the first few years, and as you've seen a lot of the events, celebrities in drag, like the Rajas, and the Sharon [Needles]s, and the Bianca [Del Rio]s. But I think it was probably around I feel like the Bianca era. And then it just picked up such momentum with people like Bob the Drag Queen and Violet [Chachki] and Sasha Velour, who were all like these New York queens. The comedy, the burlesque, and this beautiful art. This beautiful artist Sasha. I think that's when I knew that we were not just a mirror to pop culture.

Now we were making pop culture. We weren't just referencing what we saw. Artists are referencing us. We are looked at as sources of inspiration for videos for fashion, for movies, and we all share the same designers as most of the big pop stars.

Also, watching the whole network of drag being formed. Comedy, artists, crafters, musicians, sewers, people who rhinestone, all these specialty artists, wigmakers, all now have a job all year long for as long as you want it because there's so much drag to be done. I think it's really beautiful that we managed to make our own, I guess, economic bubble to really source each other. I love the idea of supporting queer businesses and it's great to have that interaction. That's when I realized, "Wow, this is something big."

It's really nice, the whole pipeline of this drag on mainstream. And now there's things like, you know, *Dragula*. And, you know, even Manila [Luzon's] drag show in the Philippines. It's just allowing so much more space for drag and so much more commerce for drag.

SMW: You've spoken about seeing more trans queens come on the competition, especially in recent years, and how that was kind of like an indicator to you that this was your time. And I would love to know how it feels now to be a part of that recent slate of trans winners.

SC: Oh, man, I just am so happy. I think about it all the time lately. I'm like, "Wow, I get to make history." Queer history! To be able to be of influence to kids who feel alone and for me personally, just to be able to feel validated in this art that I've loved so much for so many years. And to be not even validated, but celebrated, it's more than I could ask for. The love and support have been amazing.

SMW: You assume this really valuable role on this season, which, of course, was as a really respected and formidable competitor and winner, but also as an educator for Native Hawaiian, queer, and trans history. Did you go into this competition thinking that was going to be really important for you to represent and speak about?

SC: Yes, absolutely. Vulnerability was really the key word for me. I noticed that when I won [Miss] Continental, it was the moment when I was vulnerable about my drug addiction that I had dealt with before that allowed me to finally win, and then be of use to so many people who are dealing with drug addiction, ten years ago. So I realized coming on here, having this platform, I want to show every part of me, every part that made me, and a lot of it is my Hawaiian culture, a lot of it is my transness. Even though my transness was never brought up in the show or during competition from anyone. It was always my experience, and that I did good drag, and I was a good competitor. But I would be remiss if I didn't talk about how much drag and being trans is intertwined in many, many places. I would be of disservice if I wasn't the first Native Hawaiian to talk about it. I mean, there has never been another Native Hawaiian to ever make it on the show, let alone have RuPaul say the word "Māhū." That's amazing.

I'm a nerd, so when I was doing interviews, they could tell that I would get excited about fun facts about Hawai'i or any sort of history. So when we would be doing our makeup and in those workroom areas, [the producers] would be really nice, but they would be like, "Talk about Hawai'i and Hawai'i drag" or "Talk about Continental." To see it edited in the show how it was makes me feel proud, especially in these times with Hawai'i losing so much of its identity to gentrification. At the last census, we are now completely displaced. There are more Native Hawaiians living in Las Vegas than in

Hawai'i. The Hawaiian state. So I think it's very important, because we've been losing our culture, we would fight to hold on to our language, and our methods and our teachings. And I think one of the last frontiers is to understand that this hate against trans people and queer people is not Indigenous. It was taught, it was another form of colonialism. I think it's really important to break that and and have Hawaiians be proud of every Hawaiian. Have these Indigenous people be allies to the queer people in their own ethnic community. It is very important. So I felt the need to celebrate it. To give voice.

SMW: When you won you spoke directly to it, but obviously, we're at a really wildly reactionary time. It's always been there, but it's pretty extreme at the moment for anti-queer, anti-trans, and anti-drag political sentiment. And you've already very gracefully spoken to that, but I was wondering, how do you keep yourself grounded and hopeful as this is happening?

SC: Well, with all this happening, and I don't think I'm alone in this, I felt pulled back to when [I was] being bullied as a kid for being queer and having to shrink up, and feeling very alone, feeling very scared and unsafe maneuvering in my own body and throughout this world. That all came back. Which was really wild to process, especially at this moment, where I'm being praised for being unapologetically queer.

You know what it feels like when this all happened? Like they took our voice, and we're not even allowed to even say what is true. They're just gonna lie and throw all this kind of rhetoric that is just making people scared. And it's definitely a part of control. It's controlling our bodies, it's controlling our minds. It's people who don't love themselves, people who are really afraid that they might like all of this, and they probably do, you know? It evokes such a strong emotion in certain people. You can't hate something unless you actually love it. Or like you actually secretly have passion for it. It's not the hate of a person. It's the hate of what that person makes you feel. And if you're getting a tickle in your pants, because I'm trying to live my truths, don't come at me. Go and address that tickle in your pants.

So now, feeling unsafe and feeling unheard; it's like growing pains. You have to get through this pain of eliminating that childhood trauma for yourself. So you can stand up louder and stronger and remember how clear and resilient you are. I'm trying to work on that and definitely talking and having this platform helps, but I can't help but think about everyone else who doesn't, you know? So when I talk, I speak hopefully to and for these people who are hearing and listening to me, and maybe they feel a little more comforted that in whatever little way, I am trying to do my part, and my work and my drag are a protest. And for lack of better words, kiss my beautiful ass.

Chapter 7

FOR THE VERY SECOND TIME: REBOOTS AND REVISIONS

Though many original LGBTQIA2S+ shows and characters premiered and disappeared in the space left by some of the first and most recognizable queer shows on air, in recent years the reboot machine decided it was high time to churn through a few queer properties. Among the most recognizable are *Tales of the City*, *The L Word*, *Will & Grace*, and *Queer as Folk*, all unearthed from their (apparently shallow) graves, reinvented to suit the modern times and what their creators and executives see as more "modern" identities and sensibilities. Previously only tacitly queer shows (and even subtextually or minimally queer films) have roared back with new out-and-proud characters. Whether attempting to reinvent themselves by way of trans inclusion or committing to remaining exactly as radical as they were when they first aired, an age-old question emerged: Who asked for this?

The original runs of *Tales of the City*, *Will & Grace*, and *The L Word* may not have the same critical reception across their series, but they are all regarded as enormously impactful on both the media landscape and American social attitudes for their spotlighting of gay and lesbian characters as the major players in their own narratives. When their reboots were announced within three years of one another, they were anticipated with a mix of excitement and trepidation. How successfully could an old framework reflect what its builders consider to be a new and unexplored age? Were they taking up valuable real estate that could go to original queer programming? And in one of the most frequently

posed questions from LGBTQIA2S+ publications and mainstream outlets, would the shows fix what they had originally fouled regarding trans
casting and representation?

Will & Grace was proud to be gay, but the original featured no trans
characters and some in-style transphobia—for the reboot, would characters of other identities be played for a joke, or would they be in on the
joke? For *Tales* and *The L Word*, which included trans characters (some
played by cisgender actors, some by misgendered nonbinary actors in
their original series), there was little doubt that trans characters would
be somehow included or even featured, especially in the face of a growing push for inclusion and increased awareness by audiences and advertisers alike. More questions centered around *how* trans characters
would be revisited or created anew—would they be given equal weight
to their gay and lesbian counterparts? Would they be saved from the
common pitfalls of series past? And perhaps most urgently, would they
be played by trans actors?

A Trans Casting Timeline

Among the first wave of resounding successes in new queer and trans
representation in American television were *Transparent* and *Orange Is
the New Black*. Massive attention went to their methods of distribution
and the artistic agency afforded by new original content arms of Amazon
Prime Video and Netflix, respectively. They were also applauded for the
inclusion of trans members among their casts and characters. However,
where *Orange Is the New Black* employed then widely unrecognized
trans actress Laverne Cox in her Emmy-nominated role of Sophia
Burset, *Transparent*'s transitioning matriarch, Maura Pfefferman, was
played by well-known cisgender actor Jeffrey Tambor. The critical successes of both shows, as well as the unexpected popular success and creative control ceded by both studios to their showrunners, contributed
largely to the oft-cited "Trans Tipping Point" bequeathed largely upon
the shoulders of Laverne Cox and Caitlyn Jenner by *Time* magazine
journalist Katy Steinmetz.[1]

In late 2017, three years after Cox's cover of *Time* and Jenner's cover of *Vanity Fair*, Jeffrey Tambor was accused by colleague Trace Lysette and former personal assistant Van Barnes of inappropriate sexual conduct.[2] Both Lysette and Barnes are trans, and their reports, which were backed by other trans members of the cast and crew, including primetime guest spot veteran Alexandra Billings, led to nonbinary showrunner Joey Soloway intending to fire Tambor before his preemptive resignation.[3] Eventually, the major shift in both cast and atmosphere surrounding *Transparent* culminated in Amazon Prime Video cutting *Transparent*'s final season to a single special episode, and it reignited a conversation that had been stifled by the series' success: Why was a cisgender actor being praised for taking on a trans role, and what did that imply for real trans people?

A digital campaign, which featured *Transparent* alums Billings, Lysette, and Ian Harvie, and actors D'Lo, Rain Valdez, Elliot Fletcher, Alexandra Grey, and Jazzmun, and was helmed by writer and actress Jen Richards, had aimed to answer this question a few months prior to the allegations against Tambor. Richards broke down the equivalency argument written by many scholars and journalists: with the absence of real trans people in trans roles, there exists a direct comparison of trans identities to pure fiction. As Richards has repeated in various articles and actor roundtables, when cisgender male actors such as Eddie Redmayne, Jared Leto, Matt Bomer, and Jeffrey Tambor appeared on the red carpet without their wigs and makeup to promote their trans-centric films and shows, a portion of authenticity in a trans identity was automatically dismissed. Richards claims that this reinforces the widely held idea "that trans women are really men in good hair and makeup, that trans men either don't exist or are just butch women in a suit and fake mustache."[4] With the casting of cis men, the idea persists: trans people (especially trans women) could take off their hair and makeup, and underneath they're still men.

In a time when trans-exclusionary radical feminist (TERF) ideologies are increasingly threatening the lives and human rights of trans people, worries of trans women just being men bent on invading women's spaces and bodies are lent a falsely rational face by casting cis male actors. Tambor's having asserted his own privilege to harm two of the actual trans members of the community he (and *Transparent*) purported to fight for led to an opening for Richards's campaign to be even more widely circulated and deeply felt. Richards's solution was obvious: shows could and should hire trans actors to represent themselves. It was into this complex landscape that *Tales of the City*, *The L Word*, and *Will & Grace* announced their revivals, preparing themselves, in varying degrees, for audiences no longer as starved for breadcrumbs of trans representation and instead demanding satisfactory treatments for themselves, their characters, and the actors who stood in for their communities.

Tales of the City

Tales of the City could easily have its own chapter for its sheer amount of material, influence over serialized storytelling, and the utter fear it struck into the hearts of hapless PBS viewers like you (or so its conservative censors would have you believe). When its original television series premiered in 1993 (UK) and 1994 (US), it already had an established presence in literary form. Author Armistead Maupin, whose satirizing and highly melodramatic serial first appeared in installments in the "Style" column of the *San Francisco Chronicle* in 1976, created a landscape filled to the brim with adventure for his straight, cis woman protagonist, Midwestern-runaway-turned-San-Francisco-journalist and undeniable free spirit Mary Ann Singleton. Mary Ann would step off a bus from Ohio and be transformed by her encounters with gay, eventually HIV-positive romantic Michael "Mouse" Tolliver, Peter Pan–syndrome womanizer Brian Hawkins, and mysterious, wise trans landlord and patron saint of San Francisco potheads, Anna Madrigal, along with Madrigal's collection of strays. Following in the style of serialized Victorian domestic novels, Mary Ann's intrigue with the city served as a portal both to San Franciscan readers of the *Chronicle* and to millions of outsiders whose purchases of *Tales* in volume form bought them a virtual ticket to a rainbow city.

Before the PBS series had hit the air, Maupin's portraits of the city and its queer inhabitants had charmed and intrigued enough demographically disparate readers to lend some valence to academic Robyn Warhol's theory that the soap was a Trojan horse that questioned "heterocentric norms for 'intimacy,' 'family,' 'privacy,' and 'sex.'" In short, it had the potential makings of a cultural revolution. The television series itself, which became PBS's most-watched series up to that point, would further boost this claim. That PBS eventually caved in to federal threats of funding removal for homosexual themes and drug use only emphasizes how seriously the US government took that potential toppling by television.[5]

The first season of *Tales*, which was set in the 1970s, when Maupin had first started the series, did not shy away from the heightened, deliciously gossipy melodrama of the novel series. Pedophile ring–leading private eyes, white models faking Black identity for the industry, smarmy bisexual businessmen cheating on their equally cheating wives, and the most high-stakes male go-go competition set to slow motion in PBS history all swirled around the key mystery of Anna Madrigal's true origin. Alongside Laura Linney's effervescent Mary Ann, one of the most notable names in the original miniseries was Olympia Dukakis, who gracefully inhabited the role of Anna Madrigal—Maupin's anagram for "A Man and a Girl." At the time, Dukakis was praised for her choice to play a trans woman—a move that in the nineties was polemically thought of as a mix of ultimate bravery and potential career suicide, much like the since-revised opinions around Jeffrey Tambor's decision to play a trans woman.[6]

The camp of *Tales* made no realist exceptions for sensitivity with a trans storyline at the time, stretching Anna's identity out to the utmost of high-wire tension. For example, portentous violin warns Anna's lover (played by Donald Moffat) of her true nature, as Mary Ann also discovers incriminating letters that could give hints to the terribly costly truth.

And at the time, what was most emphasized in a trans identity was loss—Anna's loss of her family, her past, and her safety in love being played for overblown tragedy—more than any other emotion or consideration of a trans existence. Anna is never villainized in the original series, and in fact she seems to be far more comfortable in her older identity than most of the tenants of her building on Barbary Lane.

When openly gay screenwriter Lauren Morelli, perhaps best known at that point for her public coming out and writing on the *Orange Is the New Black* team, was tapped as showrunner for the 2019 Netflix modern continuation of the series, press attention immediately focused on what a modern update might mean for the politics of the series and especially Anna's character. What would happen to Dukakis? Was it still appropriate to have a cis actress play a trans character, especially when *Tales* had the chance to both continue the original stories and create entirely new, more inclusive representations as the foremost LGBTQIA2S+ show it was claiming to be?

It wouldn't have been so unthought of for Dukakis to be recast—several key characters, including Brian, Mouse, and dyke-fluid nomad Mona Ramsey (originally portrayed by Chloe Webb) had been swapping actors over the course of Showtime's eventual sequels, *More Tales of the City* (1998) and *Further Tales of the City* (2001). When it was revealed that Dukakis would stay on as Anna, *Vanity Fair* immediately ran an authoritative headline: "How *Tales of the City* Avoided a Trans Casting Controversy."[7] In this article, executive producer and original *Tales* producer Alan Poul provides a preemptive defense of Dukakis, stating, "'Having Olympia was critical to making the show again . . . Olympia is clearly grandfathered in and paid her dues . . .' and cited Dukakis's 'very bold' decision to play a trans character in the 1990s, a time when there was little trans representation in media."[8] In the same article, Morelli's empathy to the "starvation for representation" from a younger queer audience is cited, as well as the casting of nonbinary actor Garcia as Jake Rodriguez and trans highlights of Morelli's writers' room and directing slate—writer Thomas Page McBee and directors Silas Howard and Sydney Freeland, familiar names to an independent trans filmmaking scene.

Another familiar name was featured in the *Vanity Fair* article and listed among the cast and crew: Jen Richards was cast as a young Anna Madrigal for a 1960s flashback episode. Directed by Poul and written by Morelli, "Days of Small Surrenders" features a crew of trans actresses, including Daniela Vega of *A Fantastic Woman* (2017) fame, Eve Lindley, and Keilly McQuail, caught up in the Compton Cafeteria Riots. Modeled after much of the historical information found in Susan Stryker's documentary, *Screaming Queens: The Riot at Compton's Cafeteria* (2005), the riot, as well as the institution of Compton's itself, is referred to as "Stonewall before Stonewall" in an earnest attempt to educate younger viewers. Richards and Vega are especially compelling, and as a standalone, the episode is one of the best of the series. Unfortunately, it still suffers from awkward pacing in an effort to condense all of San Francisco trans history into one episode and an inability to transfer *Tales*'s original camp and melodrama to a capitalization of the sobriety of trans history and representation.

Throughout the ten-episode revival, the tension between Morelli's inclusion-driven catering to modern (read: younger) queer audiences and Poul's devotion to an original fan base and spirit never quite reaches a fluid or cohesive compromise.

In a dinner scene demonstrable of what the series imagines as one of the most pervasive arguments between generations (episode 4, "The Price of Oil"), Mouse's boyfriend, Ben (Charlie Barnett), is chastised by a group of older, white, cis gay men for daring to correct their use of the word "tranny." The argument is unable to come to any sort of reconciliation—where Ben asks for sensitivity and consideration in calling people what they would prefer to be called, the other dinner guests take this as a show of ungratefulness and ignorance of ancestral history, telling Ben that his affront clearly demonstrates how easy he, a twenty-eight-year-old Black gay man, has it. After being told that he "probably doesn't like the word 'faggot,' either," the generational divide comes to an oft-repeated leveraging of accusations around language and privilege.

Eventually, Ben and Mouse decide that their generational frustration with each other is based on unresolved personal insecurities that need to be discussed between themselves, not in front of a dinner party. The realistically uncomfortable conversations that could stem from a gay white man exploding at a gay Black man for his apparent lack of cultural-historical context while omitting the work of the identities inconvenient to his self-aggrandizement and earned passion are laid to an uneasy rest.

Much of this uneasiness is reflected in the confused tone of the series. It continues the original *Tales*'s focus on relationship drama (much of hyped trans character Jake's characterization comes from a portrait of his difficulty staying monogamous and discovering changes in attraction during his transition) and a blackmail plot against Anna that is a direct facsimile of the original series, but all the hyper silliness of the original installments are replaced by a self-seriousness that seals characters in competing boxes based on their identity markers. Trans characters are only concerned with transition and misdeeds of their clueless cisgender friends and heterosexual families, millennials with the stagnant attitudes of their elders, monogamists with the unfaithfulness of polyamorists, and working-class dyke bartenders with old-money bisexual mansion dwellers. Each episode ends with a still of an updated version of the gay pride or trans pride flag, as if to semiotically stamp: we are the LGBTQIA2S+ show, and our community—our *entire* community—approves this message.

On an ensemble show such as *Tales*, something like a stamp of approval without taking a real stance serves to protect the show from community criticism—the show is doing the work of moving community forward by virtue of inclusion, so any hard-line stances against it or requests for different types of characters have the option of being dismissed as either retrograde and against the LGBTQIA2S+ agenda or asking for too much when the show has already done everything it could.

The L Word

The L Word is a puzzle. Simultaneously a product of its time and miles ahead of any show that had ever dared to depict an ounce of lesbian sexuality onscreen, it's been an object of devotion, ridicule, anger, community building, and intense discussion since the first moment it aired. There's no question that it was a milestone. As Angela Robinson recalls, she couldn't believe that Showtime was going to put a series about lesbians on the air—and she was about to join the writers' room.

"Before I got the job," Robinson says, "I remember [Guinevere] Turner called me and said, 'They're making a *Queer as Folk* but for lesbians.' I thought she was kidding. I didn't believe that there was going to be a television show about lesbians. They'll never get that through—they'll never give us the money."[9]

Jamie Babbit, who directed two episodes of the original series, shares the sentiment: "*The L Word* was always revolutionary. We had never had lesbian sex on TV, written, directed, and acted with real lesbians. We got to define ourselves and have it be by women, about women, for women."[10]

When Ilene Chaiken, showrunner of the original series, began formulating her pitch, her goal wasn't to show a group of lesbians who were representative of all queer women. In the 2019 documentary *Queering the Script*, Chaiken relates that she only ever set out to show the world her own community—that of "hip," beautiful lesbians in Los Angeles.[11] One could easily read Chaiken's statement for what *The L Word* starts out as: a soapy drama of a group of rich, thin, femme lesbians whose exploits of "Talking, laughing, loving, breathing/Fighting, fucking, crying, drinking" often vocally disrespects the few butches, trans women, or bisexuals who exist in Los Angeles, if they acknowledge them at all.[12]

Rose Troche, who wrote, directed, and eventually co-executive produced on the series, gave some insight that not all the casting decisions, especially with regard to excluding butch women from much of the series, were something Chaiken held sole blame for:[13]

> When we were casting *The L Word*, it was like [to the network], "I'll
> trade you two femme-y girls for this one butchy girl. Can I have
> that?" They were like, "I don't see it, I don't see how that person's
> gonna play it," and you think, oh my god, are you kidding me? It's
> called *The L Word*. There was resistance to having anybody who
> seemed authentically queer and to anyone authentically butchy.
> They got pushed to the margins.

Despite Chaiken's insistence that she had no initial resolutions to
think bigger than the specificity of her own community, *The L Word*'s
2004–2009 edition did respond to many an impassioned forum com-
plaint and within its initial run attempted to tackle issues of race and
class, to occasionally mortifying results (including Iranian American
actress Sarah Shahi playing Mexican American Carmen de la Pica
Morales, and Indian American actress Janina Gavankar portraying
emphatically accented Latina lothario Papi). From its many narrative
blunders, however, none is remembered with as much collective disappointment as Max Sweeney's (Daniel Sea) fake bearded, one-note,
pregnant-for-shock-value female-to-male transition storyline. From
this portrayal, and one other "lesbian-identified male" trans character,
writer Grace Lavery has named Chaiken as choosing to "spend time in a
universe where all trans people belong to some species of trans man, and
all transness is a more or less tortured negotiation with desirable masculinity," in order to concretely separate the desirability and power
inherent within lesbianism from the unthinkability and angst-ridden
torture of a transmasculine identity.[14]

As with *Tales*, *The L Word*'s reboot announcement prompted a flurry
of attention from interested media outlets asking for the chance at a
"second revolution," this time, in relation to trans representation.[15] New
showrunner Marja-Lewis Ryan was expected to rewrite and right history—a track she pursued as soon as her position was announced. In her
first interview with the *Hollywood Reporter*, Ryan declared to fans that
she was "one of [us]" and was "aware of all the things the original series

got right (depicting the daily lives and loves of lesbians)—and what it got wrong (casting a cis actress to play a trans character). And she is ready to do right by the LGBTQ community and devoted viewers as well."[16] Throughout the press tour, Ryan took care to emphasize that her pitch was to make Los Angeles more representative of the *real* Los Angeles— that was, "a little browner and a little less cis," and the network was apparently now at a place to be on her side.[17] At the same time, however, she clarified that she wasn't interested in talking politics at the expense of story—a concept that *Tales* all but steamrolled.

Ryan did keep her promise of "more than one trans character," putting out an open casting call for two trans men—one specifically Asian and the other of "any ethnicity, many years into his transition"—who would eventually come to be played by newcomer Leo Sheng and Brian Michael Smith (*Queen Sugar, 9-1-1: Lone Star*), respectively.[18] Every interview with the two men, as well as any press junket involving the creative team associated with the reboot, was aware of the precariousness with which *Generation Q* rested upon its foremother's shoulders. *The L Word* was not in any way gone from queer women's public memory, and although many fans publicized their excitement with lesbians finally having a place on their televisions again, headlines boiled many of the "sins" of Chaiken and rested most of the success of the reboot onto improved representation for trans men.[19] *Bitch Media* contributor Mey Rude pointed out that even with the casting of two trans actors in significant roles, *The L Word: Generation Q* did not seem to have the same interest in featuring trans women on a show about women who love women.[20]

In *Generation Q*'s first season, intergenerational conflict, trans dating, polyamory, and racist institutional and political structures were all introduced as major themes in a mission-driven script. This zeal to correct the political clumsiness of its past, while admirable, weighed its return season down, with new characters who paled in comparison to their original, fully backstoried counterparts and dialogue that could ring symbolic and hollow. Season 2 seemed more aware of the missing magic of the original series' easiest-going charm and unselfconscious pleasures of soapy, improbable plot and stepped up its game by falling back into its old story patterns. New cast members, now characters rather than symbols of past stumbles, started to find their groove; focus on interpersonal conflict and sparkling sensuality returned; and hints of what made it such a sensation in the first place started to shine through.

In May 2021, a few months before *The L Word: Generation Q* would air its second-season opener, a small miracle began unfolding. *Autostraddle* published a long-form interview with Daniel Sea, the actor behind the pilloried Max Sweeney. In the interview, which Drew Gregory conducted over at least a year of conversations, Sea finally reemerged to correct the record. At the time of filming *The L Word*, they didn't identify as a cisgender person and had even used the term "gender expansive" to describe themselves, but the press they were speaking with at the time didn't understand the concept, and Showtime didn't help. As they recounted to Gregory:[21]

> I think there was a unique difficulty being what we now call nonbinary. Gender expansive works better for me and that was what I tried to describe when I was interviewed by *TV Guide* in 2006. They asked how I identified and I said I live on a spectrum of gender. I wanted to leave room for the person from a small town who might use the word lesbian because that's all they know. I just felt like it was a lot on one character because the show didn't have any butch representation and a lot of people identified Max that way. But then he was supposed to portray this transmasculine experience. I wanted to leave room for people to project whatever they needed in order to see themself reflected. But nobody knew what I was talking about when I tried to explain my relation to the spectrum, the expansiveness, of gender.

Sea then explains, in no uncertain terms, that the inability of trades and outlets like *TV Guide* to comprehend that spectrum led to the

widespread airbrushing of Sea's thoughtful political discussion of gender into a confirmation that he was a cisgender woman, from the time of
The L Word's initial run to its reboot. To correct the record, Sea identi-
fies as transgender and nonbinary.

The entire interview is a revelation and insight into not only the original series but also an industry environment that would make it impossible for a gender-expansive performer to thrive—or even to let others
know that they exist. It also began a series of conversations within Sea's
community, prompting filmmaker Jenni Olson to connect with them
and offer a bridge between Sea and showrunner Ryan, who eventually
approached him with a desire· to bring Max back to WeHo—well, Silver
Lake at that point. Lo and behold, on season ʒ of *Generation Q*, Max
(and Sea) reappeared, in stark contrast to his depressed, defeated past
characterization. He was now a calm, engaged parent, a loved and loving partner, and a mentor figure to Micah, the next generation's trans
masc presence.

Max's one-episode return is both an indictment of what the original
L Word wasn't equipped to handle and an exaltation of its most successful quality: deeply connecting queer audiences with one another and
their onscreen representations, no matter their love or exasperation.
Speaking to earlier seasons of the original, Rose Troche reminisced, "I
think one of the most special things about being queer is the families
that we make, and I feel like *The L Word* showed a glimpse of that
sweetness—especially in the beginnings of it—and that little safety net
that we create for each other."[22] With Max's return, it felt like he, and
Sea, were finally experiencing that warmth.

Will & Grace

Originally rebooted as a Hillary Clinton campaign ad, NBC's full series
revival of *Will & Grace* held fast to its acclaimed "revolutionary" status
for its portrayal of positive, assimilatory gay characters in the nineties
and early 2000s.[23] Interviews with not only the show's creators but
also its stars focused on the original series' impact on making "gay" a

nonderogatory household word, and the same questions of trans inclusion to update a modern revival were pitched as follow-ups to the show's claim of its legacy. These interviews were peppered with even more mixed replies than *Tales* when it came to modern attitude and demographic targeting.

Star Debra Messing was completely onboard with the necessity of the revival, proclaiming, "When we started it was revolutionary to have two gay characters . . . We were 'LGB,' but we stopped at B. My hope is we can now finish the alphabet."[24] In the same interview, co-creators David Kohan and Max Mutchnick emphasized the "topicality" of their revival but steered away from explicitly promising trans representation under the prospect of sullying the "pee-on-your-couch" level of humor inherent to the show—an argument reminiscent of Poul's defense of preserving *Tales*'s original character for the sake of respect to its fan base. Kohan then reiterated that he didn't want to focus "too much on issues," for fear of dragging down the sitcom form.[25]

The same attitude largely remained in place throughout *Will & Grace*'s revival: *Will & Grace* has always been modern and relevant in the eyes of its creators, and it will continue to be relevant to the entire LGBTQIA2S+ community. Yes, even if it brings back a joke of an intersex character and does not develop a single trans character. Yes, even if it backtracks on supporting star Karen's (Megan Mullaly) sexual orientation, which, through a "reverse puppy episode," parodying Ellen's in her 1997 sitcom, had the previously bisexual Karen declaring (to guest star Samira Wiley) that she was actually completely uninterested in women. Even through this erasure of the "B" and inability to approach the "T" in the acronym, stars, creators, and some media outlets rested on *Will & Grace*'s historical impact in the nineties to declare its reboot as similarly revolutionary.

"Just saying the words 'husband' and 'gay' out loud is very powerful out in the world," actor Sean Hayes, who plays gay and now "gay-married" Jack, emphasized, when the *Hollywood Reporter* asked about the show continuing to pursue the depiction of "LGBTQ+ issues."[26] This was true during the series' original broadcast. But even as US state governments regress to attitudes held before the original run of *Will & Grace*, that doesn't mean queer television has to. Compared to the landscape of queer television that had come and gone in its wake, the sitcom had nothing new to add, quickly losing half its viewers in the eighteen-to-forty-nine demographic. As *Vanity Fair* critic Tara Ariano pointed out in 2020, there ultimately didn't seem to be a point to its short new cycle of life and death, though she hoped it might set an example and prevent more "unnecessary" revivals.[27] Unfortunately for Ariano, and us, that hasn't quite been the case.

Big-Screen Straights to Small-Screen Sequels

Several other queer television reboots of older television properties joined *Will & Grace*, *Tales*, and *The L Word* in their quest to satisfy original viewers' nostalgia while courting a younger market. *Queer as Folk* (2022) came back for a brief but intriguing reboot that quickly expanded the demographics of its main characters while swan diving off one of the original series' most devastating plot points before its quick cancellation. *Sex and the City* spawned a sequel, *And Just Like That . . .* (2021–), that introduced one cosmopolitan counterpoint of color for each of the original white ladies (minus an absent Kim Cattrall) and a nonbinary butch love interest whose (unintentional? So bad it's good? No, it's just bad.) parody of their community has earned the ire and obsession of many a queer viewer. Even long-running, notoriously homophobic series like *Law & Order: Special Victims Unit* and series that previously had little in the way of queer representation reinvented themselves with trans and bisexual additions.

Massive, zeitgeist-defining hits like *Star Trek*, *One Day at a Time* (1975–1984; 2017–2020), *Quantum Leap* (1989–1993; 2022–), *Charmed*, *Gossip Girl* (2007–2012; 2021–2023), *Perry Mason* (1957–1966; 2020–2023), and more all made their way back to television, with most opting to follow *Tales* and *The L Word: Generation Q* in their head-on confrontation of their original series' exclusions and missteps, though often by

way of subplot or side character. In one of the most interesting develop-
ments of the Rainbow Age of television, these weren't the only pieces of
media to arrive back on television with the determination to acknowledge that which had only been minutely explored, hinted at, or dismissed altogether. *High Fidelity* (2020) flipped its original script by
casting the effortlessly cool Zoë Kravitz to play a mercurial, bisexual
Rob. *Interview with the Vampire* (2022–) came to AMC+ with an aggressive sexuality, violence, and ambitious curtain ripping on period-era
racism that the film never approached. *A League of Their Own* (2022)
launched the beloved 1992 film's lesbian subtext into the stratosphere
with queer central, supporting, and guest roles, much to the delight of
sapphic audiences and deep ire of conservative audiences convinced
there was no crying or lesbianism in baseball. Beating all of them to the
plate, however, was a fascinating early attempt to transfer an iconic
work to an updated streaming gem.

In 2017, Spike Lee adapted his hugely influential (and inflammatory)
1986 comedy on modern Black women's sexual freedom *She's Gotta
Have It* into a series for Netflix. Like the film, the central character is
Nola Darling, an intellectual, liberated, pansexual young artist in New
York City whose most sacred space is her candlelit "loving bed." The two
promises that Lee made, while the series was still in development at
Showtime rather than Netflix, were that (1) women would be in the writers' room, and (2) his nonchalant treatment of its climactic rape scene,
which was so devastating it left many feeling betrayed by the film's
premise, would have no place in *She's Gotta Have It: The Series*. Another
notable change is that, rather than just speaking about her queerness,
twenty-first-century Nola (played by captivating and playful DeWanda
Wise) stumbles her way through an onscreen queer relationship.

Nola Darling is a "sex-positive, polyamorous pansexual" but dislikes
labels, as she confesses to her therapist in season 1, episode 4, "#LuvIzLuv
(SEXUALITY IS FLUID)," but, like the film, it's difficult to tell whether
we are supposed to take Nola's, or any character's, conception of herself
at face value. While her therapist is pleased to see that Nola is feeling a

little freer with her new fling, stunning, self-assured horticulturalist and lesbian mom Opal (Ilfenesh Hadera), most other people in Nola's life aren't so convinced that Nola is giving equal weight to her relationships with women. This includes Opal herself, who, despite being utterly enchanted by Nola, is suspicious of her dates with men, even if those dates are Nola acting as a beard for an old friend (Ato Blankson-Wood), whom she berates for not coming out to his old-school Trinidadian parents. He echoes Opal's skepticism from a different angle, reminding Nola that she has repeatedly referred to dating a woman as a break from men, and alleges that she's greedy for not being able to stick to "one thing for too long."[28]

Later in the episode, Opal calls Nola "bi curious" and "try-sexual," employing obviously hurtful stereotypes of sexual fluidity, but truthfully, Nola's attitude toward dating a woman is somewhat dismissive. She reduces her own pansexuality, by definition more about the person than the gender, to taking a pause from men, and her refusal to explain Opal's presence in her life as "anti-political." While characters challenge her on that, they do so by using biphobic language. Nobody here really seems to understand what pansexuality or polyamory is, unless it's in the context of stereotype, (i.e., not being able to choose and being a cheater).

As critic Princess Weekes writes on feminist news and culture site *The Mary Sue*, in the first season Nola's pansexuality is distinctly separated from the rest of her life, and the show doesn't seem to know how to engage her queerness unless Opal is onscreen.[29] Nola certainly doesn't have to have all the answers, but the show's treatment of her queerness is contentious within itself. Like so many other reboots seeking to engage contemporary audiences, characters use words that sound like they could be used by a real queer person defending themselves against various oppressions and phobias, but they end up replicating what they're supposedly investigating, turning all that slang and declarative language into rainbow word salad. Opal is an interesting, important lover in Nola's life, yet she's excluded from the show's poster, tagline, and main storylines.

The film's tagline declares *She's Gotta Have It* to be the "story of a woman and her three lovers." The show's tagline is the same. There's little room for Opal in that main three, and the show operates from that understanding. Pansexuality may be an additive flavoring, but the show's first season doesn't see it as something fully integrated into Nola's life. In keeping with the framework of the original, it's a story about one woman and three men—anyone else is shoehorned in. In the next episode, Nola decides to end her "man-cleanse," and while Opal occasionally reappears throughout the season, it's as a support system for Nola, not as a lover.

With a second season came a new poster image—this time omitting Nola's three main lovers and instead simply picturing her proud profile. It was a fitting change for a welcome pivot: the second and final season dropped almost all of its preoccupation with the bickering over Nola's sexual labels and rules for herself, instead choosing to focus on her journey as a young Black artist, navigating commercialism and gentrification while attempting to align her emerging identity with her community. This wasn't without its hyper topical, on-the-nose satire, or fallout from the prior season's melodrama, but it did give Nola the chance to live in her sexual identity rather than fight to claim its legitimacy.

She's Gotta Have It's decisive pivot to a Nola who was actively shaking off the structure of her former self demonstrates a common thread across almost every reboot in this chapter: the series start to succeed when they genuinely engage with their characters as complex people rather than arguments or callbacks toward their past or when they become their own story entirely. In perhaps the most successful example, *A League of Their Own* barreled out of the gate with entirely new characters, a new tone, and an ambitious, sprawling number of arcs, only really capitalizing on the name and setting of its godparent (and a few choice cameos) to tell an entirely new tale. *The L Word: Generation Q* had difficulty striking a balance between its beloved original characters and its new characters who sometimes struggled to compare to their fully formed, years-of-development and audience-invested counter-parts. *Will & Grace* and *Tales* took radically different approaches to following up their source material, but their entire series were still pred-icated on arguing with or trumpeting their pasts, not their present or future. It was almost as if each show was set up to fail from its inception just by virtue of having to argue with itself.

When a rebooted show breaks out of its frame entirely, we see the glimmer of something exciting and fresh, but even that rare triumph may not be enough. With few exceptions, a rebooted show is just not given adequate support or time it needs to develop its stride. *Generation Q, Tales, Will & Grace, Queer as Folk, High Fidelity, One Day at a Time, Perry Mason, Charmed, Grease: Rise of the Pink Ladies* (2023), *Gossip Girl*, and *She's Gotta Have It* have all been canceled, most within an aver-age of two seasons. In this environment, giving even the most promising of recycled IP a chance can sometimes feel like an exercise in futility. Reboots might measure up to, or break free of, the expectations set by their originals. They may genuinely court a queer audience with story rather than buzzwords and promises of inclusive casting for minor roles. But even the most highly anticipated and well-received of the projects in this chapter, *A League of Their Own*, had its four-episode second-season order revoked by Amazon Prime Video. The rise and fall of the queer reboot may just be a litmus test for the state of television as a whole; when studios can't commit to supporting a hint of creative innovation, the landscape will remain hollow, unstable, and, ultimately, pointless.

Queer & A: Jennifer Beals

Credits: *Flashdance, Devil in a Blue Dress, The L Word, The L Word: Generation Q,* **and many more**

It would be impossible to write a book about queer television without at least attempting to get an interview with honorary lesbian Jennifer Beals. When Beals first starred in *The L Word*'s original run, she hadn't considered that she might be stepping into the shoes and wide-collared power suit of an icon. Since 2004, Beals's name has become synonymous with Bette Porter, the take-no-shit art world maven and Official Femme Top of Los Angeles's greater metropolitan area, delighting queer audiences for years with her portrayal of an uncompromising, deeply emotional, deeply devoted (except when she's cheating) modern-day dyke. For *The L Word: Generation Q*, Beals stepped into an executive producer role. In 2023, she e-mailed with me about her own search for representation, what has and hasn't changed over the years, and the reason she felt *The L Word* needed to be back on the air.

SHAYNA MACI WARNER: Prior to *The L Word*, what was your own impression of LGBTQIA2S+ characters on television? Do you remember the first queer character (implied or explicit) that you ever saw on television?

JENNIFER BEALS: I don't remember the first queer character I saw on television. I don't think my radar was attuned to that search. I was looking for people who were like me. When we're engaged with those questions surrounding identity, we look everywhere for clues. I remember as a girl I had a small obsession with Spock. I had never heard the term "biracial." I knew that sometimes someone like me was referred to as mulatto, a combination between a donkey and a mule, which didn't exactly sound flattering. I looked to Spock to understand what being half of one thing and half of another meant as if there were two distinguishable sides to my very body. Spock was not a tremendous help, but it was better than being half donkey, half mule. Then I came across the trope of not only a mulatto but a *tragic* mulatto, which upped the negative association. Not even Langston Hughes, whom I admired, would give any quarter on that one. I certainly didn't feel tragic in any way shape or form. I felt beloved by my parents, respected by my peers at school. I realized when it was my turn to be on the screen, when I had an ounce of power, I would start to change the narrative.

That first came with *The L Word*. When Ilene first approached me about the project asking would I like to play Bette or Tina, I chose Bette and I asked if she could be biracial. I had never seen that on TV, or in a film that was anything other than negative. She said yes, and we were off. That was a gift I gave my younger self, and to anyone else who might need that mirror.

SMW: There's a long, documented tradition of actors being told their careers would end if they took on queer roles. Were there any risks you were weighing when you first signed on to play a lesbian character? If so, do you think actors would be warned of any of those same considerations today?

JB: I didn't think about it—not for a single second, nor did any of my reps say anything to me. It was a great, well-written part. It felt like a gift had been delivered to my doorstep with ribbon wrapped beautifully and a chorus of angels. The biggest reasons I did *The L Word* were (1) the pilot script was really good, (2) I felt Ilene Chaiken was an extraordinary creator and human being (see 1), and (3) it was my hope that somewhere out there some young woman who may never have seen herself represented would finally see some aspect of herself and know she was not alone. It is very challenging to discover who you are in a vacuum—not even a vacuum, actually, but within an environment which would rather vilify you or deny your existence. It takes monumental powers to draw in enough light on your own to dispel that kind of darkness.

SMW: The original run of *The L Word* saw so many incredible queer screenwriters and directors make their television debuts. Can you tell me a little bit about what it was like to work with this young and pretty radical crop of talents?

JB: It was amazing. We had an incredible group of established independent filmmakers who raised the bar week after week. Rose Troche, who directed several episodes, including the pilot, was incredibly inspiring.

SMW: How does it feel to work with so many budding directors and writers again for *Generation Q*?

JB: It's incredibly exciting to see how many new directors have come through our doors. It's a very different vibe on the *Gen Q* set. It feels like a really fun film camp. Don't get me wrong, the directors are still racing the clock, but they are being offered a seat at the table, a shot, and frankly we benefit from their talent and energy. They're the ones doing us a favor.

SMW: I've read that the reason *Generation Q* happened was due to you, Leisha Hailey, and Kate Moennig realizing that no real successor had quite taken *TLW*'s place, and there was still so much to explore in an evolving queer community. Can you tell me about that?

JB: In July 2013 my friend Jenna Menking, who at that time was running a social media company, said to me, "You all have been off the air for four years and people are still talking about the show." I had joined social media around that time at the urging of my publicist who was trying to drag me into the twenty-first century. I had noticed the conversation seemed to be very different than when we first started *The L*

Word. Frankly at the onset of the original *L Word* there was no social media as we know it today. What I knew of conversations was largely filtered through direct contact with fans, with Kate, Leisha, and Ilene. Now with contemporary social media we have a small portal, however incomplete in its scope. Looking through that portal at conversations it was clear an extraordinary group of people were starting to change the conversation around gender and sexuality. I became aware of a new generation who refused to be defined by anyone, who demanded [to define] themselves. That was incredibly inspiring to me. When I talked to Kate and Leisha, we talked about how we wished we could bring back the show to tell the stories of this new generation.

We were shocked nothing had taken *The L Word*'s place. It had after all run for six seasons, but no lesbian-centric narrative had taken its place. We were excited to explore these stories in ways we hoped would be both compelling and entertaining. We are all made better by hearing one another's stories and by telling our own. I reached out to Jenna who put together a presentation for Kate, Leisha, and Ilene. As imperfect as it may have been, *The L Word* had served a need for representation and community. That was on August 5, 2013. Jenna gave an amazing presentation. Ilene was interested in bringing the show back, but she was working on *Blackbox* and was soon after to be swept up in a little show called *Empire*. I went on my own and met with Gary Levine at Showtime. I talked about bringing the show back. He gave me a polite no.

After the presidential election of 2016, Ilene and I sat down for our own meeting. We knew this administration would be coming after the LGBTQ+ community and anyone else who they saw as Other. We talked in her office. Down the hall the *Empire* writers were despondent. It felt like every step forward toward equality was about to be erased. They weren't entirely wrong. But now was the time to light the campfire and start telling the stories that we needed and would need in the coming years. Ilene decided to pitch Gary the new version of *The L Word*. This time he said yes. Ilene invited Kate, Leisha, and me to be her partners as executive producers. In November 2017 we received an e-mail from Showtime PR that they would be announcing Marja-Lewis Ryan as our showrunner. It wasn't until February 1, 2019, that we received a green light from Showtime, but the boat was now officially in the water.

SMW: What have you been proudest of *Gen Q* for exploring that the original did not necessarily approach?

JB: The depiction of trans characters. One thing I'm so excited about [the third] season is we (finally) have a nonbinary character in the main cast. That is huge to me. When I first heard the term "nonbinary," that was the first time that I realized this younger generation was so forceful, so adamant about standing their ground that they had the power to radically shift culture. They had after all in a very short space of time changed our lexicon and forced people to rethink gender and sexuality.

SMW: Bette and Angie's [Bette and Tina's daughter] relationship is lovely in a television landscape that doesn't usually include that specific intergenerational, queer familial tie. Can you tell me a little bit about the casting process for Jordan Hull and if you have a hand in shaping the priorities for this particular storyline?

JB: We all saw Jordan Hull and fell in love with her depth and her honesty. Laurel [Holloman], Jordan, Marja, and I talked often and in depth about the nature of the relationship. The biggest moment over which I had any input was in episode 205, with Micah, Carrie, Tina, and Angie in Micah's office. I urged the writers to make that therapy scene as layered as possible. It reminded me a bit of scenes from the earlier iteration of the show when we talked about the complexity of race. When we started the show, I told the writers I was personally interested in exploring race and aging. Only because they asked . . . though frankly I probably would've offered it up anyway.

SMW: *Gen Q* is among a more recent smattering of rebooted properties—*Tales of the City, Will & Grace, Queer as Folk*—that makes up a good chunk of the specifically LGBTQIA2S+ shows on television. Have you watched any of these other shows? Why do you think the last five years have been the time these shows get the green light?

JB: I think the queer community has been very vocal about wanting to be represented and I think people outside the queer community are more aware that these aren't niche stories. They resonate with so many people. *The L Word* also spoke to the power of female friendships and female power and empowerment. Studios want audiences and they see the writing on the wall. The times they are a-changin'. So much has changed in the last few years. LGBTQ+ relationships are all over television. LGBTQ+ characters are no longer just there to be laughed at, or to be the gay best friend, or the person to be feared; they are much more fully realized. The storylines don't always focus on the pain of being Other, or of coming to terms with sexuality, which I think is a new idea. The relationships are not always front and center, but little by little the idea of love between two people being solely heteronormative has changed. It is becoming clearer and clearer that love is love and being such is filled with divinity.

SMW: Despite shows like *The L Word* and *Queer as Folk* being so successful, it still seems that queer shows, especially originals, struggle to be picked up, and most don't last beyond one or two seasons. Why do you think this is?

JB: I would say it's not just queer shows, it's shows period. It is really, really, really hard to make a television show; really, really hard to make a good television show; and really, really hard to make a show that finds its audience in this crowded space. Vocal fans who rally the community really matter. The fans of *The L Word* have been phenomenal in this regard. I have truly never seen anything like it.

Queer & A: Tanya Saracho
Credits: *Devious Maids, Looking, How to Get Away with Murder, Vida*

When asked for TV recommendations or a ranking of the best queer shows I've seen (a common enough occurrence that it's basically my party trick), *Vida* (2018–2020) always tops the list. The Starz series, which stars Mishel Prada and Melissa Barrera as two polar-opposite Mexican American sisters who return to East Los Angeles for their mother's funeral, only to discover they must contend with her grieving widow (portrayed with heartbreaking openness by nonbinary actor Ser Anzoategui), *Vida* is, to put it mildly, complex. It's also scorchingly sexy, wry, and an incredible example of what someone can do with a distinctive vision; an interest in both well-plotted story and engaging, searching characters; and excitement for the form.

Tanya Saracho is the queer Latina writer, producer, and powerhouse showrunner behind *Vida*'s three seasons. Originally a playwright,

Saracho brings an emotional gut-punch and visual imagination to queer television that was much needed—but with *Vida*, that only lasted two full, and one network-chopped, seasons. I spoke with Saracho about premature endings, the headwinds of the industry, and the investment queer makers put into their shows.

This is an edited excerpt of our conversation.

SHAYNA MACI WARNER: Can you remember the first queer character or person you recognized as queer on television—and this can be someone who was explicitly out, or someone who you just picked up a vibe from?

TANYA SARACHO: I'm sure that I saw queer characters or characters with perceived queerness before this, but the one that sort of did the most work for me was Sara Ramirez [as Callie Torres]. She was Latina. She was of size. And she was exploring her queerness. I remember it very well. I didn't watch [*Grey's Anatomy*] that much, but I watched it enough and that whole storyline with Callie's Latino dad, [played by] Hector Elizondo, stayed with me. After that, I noticed whatever was in the landscape, but I must have read queerness coded in other ways in film and television. I remember that those moments of that storyline. It was a big deal to meet [Ramirez] on Zoom during the pandemic, just to talk shop. I was just like admiring them because they're a Broadway star, you know, too. This was right before the *Sex and The City* reprise. Even talking to them, there was weight to the moment. I was like, "You were there. Which means I was there. You know, you existed. So it reaffirmed that I existed."

SMW: Do you remember if seeing that storyline changed something for you?

TS: The dad thing. I never came out. My dad disowned me ten, eleven years ago now. And I never did come out to my dad. He knows, he's talked to my entire other family. He's a very problematic guy, so that's why that Hector Elizondo scene . . . in those moments, I wished my dad was him! It was a lot of fantasizing. That's sort of what it did for me. "Oh, I wish my Latino dad would come around," you know? Also, seriously, seeing Callie in her underwear. I'm way bigger than her, but you didn't have that representation on television—size, and ethnicity, and sexuality.

Later on, a lot of masculine-of-center women and enby people came up to me because of Eddy [played by Ser Anzoategui] on *Vida*. And I can only imagine the alchemy of witnessing that, too: ethnicity, size, presentation, and the fact that they were like the heart of *Vida*, and not a joke. Sara Ramirez was representing a sexual being, which just does something that I think the dominant culture who often sees themselves represented and takes it for granted doesn't understand. It is a sort of alchemy, it is a chemical reaction that happens to you, and a validation that you can't explain to the dominant culture. It feeds a part of you that you didn't know needed feeding, and you're like, oh, the whole "we exist" narrative is real.

SMW: Since that first impactful experience that you can remember, have there been storylines or characters, between then and now, and even we can talk currently, that you've been really excited or creatively inspired by?

TS: I was crazy about *Gentleman Jack*, even when it came out. I was like, "Oh, what is this?!" Just the imagery and the period of it. It checks so many boxes for me because it had that "we were there." That we're here now is important, but we were there. And then it had me questioning like, how come we Latinas in this country don't have the "we were there." Where's our "we were there"? So it just stayed in my mind. And then when the second season came out, I still loved it. I kept tweeting the head of HBO about it. "Casey Bloys, this is the amazing!" and he's like, "Oh, I'm glad you're watching," or whatever. And then they canceled it!

It just did all these things creatively. I wanted in to the period, the "we were there" part of it. I needed to feed myself, for my own creative stuff like that, like "we were there." We've been there always. We've always loved each other, you know, that kind of thing. I wanted to explore where we've been too, and I'm always going to be myopic about us, about Latinidad. But also, as a fucking viewer, I just loved it. It was so lush. That one really did some shit to me. Two seasons, and you know, they only do six episodes, these Brits. They're like, "That's enough." No, it's not!

SMW: Speaking of that awful periodic trend that happens, where we get one season of an incredible queer show that we think can go on for five seasons, and maybe we get a second season if we're lucky . . . I know that, of course, you've had your own experience with that. Could we talk about the other shows that you think are gone too soon?

TS: I mean, every show is gone too soon. Obviously, *Gentleman Jack*, is the first one that came out, came to mind. I wrote on a show called *Looking* for two seasons. And a movie, you know, but it was a consolation prize. My last season [of *Vida*] was a consolation prize, too. They gave me six episodes. They could have said a movie, but thank God, they said six episodes. So yeah, that was such a tragedy to me, because I was like, "We have so much more story to tell!"

Right now, you do find narratives that include gay men, and I don't want to pit us against each other because it's not a binary. But you do find friendlier narratives that include gay men. I remember one of my agents, who I adore, who I told I wanted to take out this lesbian narrative. And he was like, "No one will buy that right now. People don't want lesbian." What do you mean? There's that Billy Eichner movie [*Bros*] that just came out! And he was like, "Yeah, gay men stuff is fine right now."

He was like, "I'm just telling you what the market is like." It's just like bars. We don't have enough, they don't want what we have. We have *The L Word: Generation Q*. Okay, that's enough, you get one. It's funny that he said that and it was like consensus. I hate it. But it's so real if you look at the land-scape of how they tolerate us. "You get one!" Just like bars! How come we don't have bars, we just have nights? We have nights!

And *A League of Their Own*! All the queers talking about it on Twitter! Will [Graham, *ALOTO* showrunner] has done everything they can. They tried to get Twitter support, to show how meaningful it is to us. Besides one of my beloveds, Roberta [Colindrez] being in it, I got so attached to all of it. Every queer woman I knew was in love with it. It doesn't matter, they take it away from us. It's a wound. It says you're not worth it, you don't matter.

And *Feel Good*, that was everything. That was [co-creator and star] Mae Martin leading with their addiction and their heart and I thought it was so well made, so succinct and beautiful. That's my vote for gone too soon.

SMW: Has what your agent relayed changed the way you write or pitch, or how you think about your projects?

TS: No. We're about to take out *Brujas*, which is basically like *Vida*. Some people are queer, some are not. In *Vida* it was not by design, it just happened, because the core relationship with the dead mother and Eddy was a queer relationship, and then Emma [played by Mishel Prada] happened to also be [queer], and then it just became a queer show. *Brujas* has that formula. It is queer because we are there, very prominently as leads, so I'm aware that it's an uphill battle. And that saying, "This is a queer brown show," is not a good sales pitch sometimes, which is crazy. Because in the summer reckoning of 2020, Hollywood was looking for us! It was like, "We want these otherized perspectives, we need to be inclusive!" and then that went straight away in 2021, and now we're here, where they're getting rid of all the otherized perspectives first, and serving, basically straight white men in middle America, because that's sort of the mandate. I mean, those are the mandates that HBO Max has put out, that Amazon has put out.

And then with the women, "We're gonna watch reality TV. That's what we like." Like, what? So I'm aware, but I don't let it affect me, I just know that I have to be prepared. But it sucks, because in this television landscape, I don't know if I have the kind of stuff that they're wanting to make. It's just a dark moment, because finance is running creative. At least before finance had a middleman—the creative executives—and then here was us. Now it's just direct. I guess they want to cater to the dominant culture in every way. All my show-runner friends are really scared, because most of them are of color. What are we gonna make? And then as a viewer, what are they gonna make me watch? What are we gonna watch? Superhero shit? We're gonna watch *Yellowstone*. Or *Jack Ryan*. Let's talk in two years, 'cause in two years, we'll know what they developed today, you know? So in 2025 will be like, *Jack Ryan V.* You know, *Jacqueline Ryan*. Let's hope we pass this hurdle of whatever is happening.

SMW: I've read in interviews and heard you emphasize, especially when *Vida* was first premiering, this relationship that you had with one of the execs at Starz, that was a major reason that *Vida* could happen. Could you talk to me a little bit about how that relationship formed, and throughout your run as showrunner, how your relationship to execs has changed?

TS: I do credit this relationship with getting *Vida* across the finish line. That's the part that's really hard, having a champion that you have cultural shorthand with, and creative shorthand with. And this woman, Marta Fernández, I mean, just look at her name. I've talked about this in other interviews, but, I had only been in Hollywood three years, and she handed me *Vida* without a babysitter, which is unheard of. If you look at other first-time showrunners, a lot of them have babysitters—that means like a co-showrunner. Especially for women of color, they don't let us steer the ship ourselves. But she was like, "Here's the ship," in everything. That means the decisions like, I want an all-Latina writers' room. It was after the first season of *Atlanta*. And I just kept saying, "*Atlanta* had an all-Black writers' room. Why can't we?" And I didn't have to convince her, she just had to do all the work, and convince the powers that be, and she did. And then first-time directors, and mostly Latinas getting to direct. And now these Latinas, oh my gosh, I can't even get them because they're working so hard, which is amazing, that *Vida* did that. My writers are all so fancy right now, I couldn't get them.

And I mean, look at what's happening to my actors, especially Melissa [Barrera]. It all just opened so many doors. But then what happened to the narrative? I thought after *Vida* more *Vida*s were coming—prestige stories told by and for Latinas about complicated subjects. I thought that that was going to happen, and it didn't. That's not progress. It was for individual careers. We care about the careers, but that's on the macro. Does it make the conversation move forward? Does it move the needle forward? There hasn't been the next thing and the next thing, and that's sad. I do think the dominant queer community has had those moments from like, Ellen coming out, to kisses on TV, shows on broadcast, all that stuff has happened, but not for brown queers. It stays still, suspended in air. We're still talking *Vida*, and it stayed there, the conversation of Latinidad and queerness. That's dangerous. It let us have this one moment.

Back to Marta, that was so beautiful. She had to leave halfway through season 3. All three bosses left, actually, and *Vida* was no more. Right now, I don't have a champion like that. I don't think we can the way it's set up. Like I said, finance and not creative is what's ruling all these decisions, and it's not the same system of decision-making. I know *Vida* could not be made today. Of course, I asked about my own career, "Was that it? Am I gonna have to work at Starbucks?" No, 'cause I want to make our stuff. Speak for us, you know, but the industry won't bear. I'm so sad that it's like, "Your lives do not matter." My agent is just translating and giving me the message. You don't have to tell me, I'm seeing what you're making. I'm seeing what you're buying. I'm seeing what you like, and take all the way to the finish line. There's even people who are lovely, and care, and want the work to go across, [but] the system is not set up for them to be able to be champions right now. There's a queer, Puerto Rican executive who's the head of my studio. He can only do as much as he can do, you know?

SMW: What do you tell people starting at the entry or mentee level, when you know what it looks like, and that there's a ceiling, even at your level?

TS: Well, the ceiling is real. But it also goes in cycles, even the little bit that I've spent here, only one decade. I've seen its ebbs and flows. So just hold on, and get all your skills. If you're a writer, a shit ton of samples, keep going. Don't just wait. I have to think that the pendulum will swing back. I don't lie about where we're at, right this second because I'm living it. But Gen Z, they're not going to be told no. They have to get into power and not change. Hopefully they won't change, like millennials changed. Millennials are just kind of like, "Well, okay. All right. We want houses. So we'll say yes to whatever." Poor millennials, they got a rough deal, but there's a complacency that I don't think Gen Z has. So I'm hoping that they come with all guns blazing, because I see them, already do in their spaces. And I'm hoping they come and don't let these motherfuckers shut us out.

They're at the starting point right now with little power. But they make enough noise about other things, like how they want a work environment to be, how they want to be talked to, how they want to be treated, how they will not be treated. You're demanding respect, we never demanded respect. Well, that's on us, we should have, but I hope that translates into a big fuck you to this establishment. That is sort of like denying narratives and denying personhoods by denying narratives, you know, and entire communities. So my hope is them. Young blood, the ones I'm going to be working for in only a few years. That's what I tell them, but also for them to understand they do have to change and break a lot of bones and reset. It's fucked, this industry, from go.

SMW: Rewinding a bit through your time in the industry, I would love to hear about the differences you found in moving from *Devious Maids* to *Looking*.

TS: Who was at the helm? That's what was it. They're both white, queer men, but Andrew [Haigh] came from film, and it was his first TV thing. I don't even think he'd ever even been in a TV writers' room, but he was running the room. He ran us, not like a traditional showrunner that I just had been in a room where levels mattered. Well, Andrew didn't know shit about it. Also, because he's British, and they don't even have writers' rooms over there, literally. He came with this cinematic cache, but not any TV experience, which was perfect to wash away all the sins of my first show that was just so problematic in so many ways. I was the diversity hire on [*Devious Maids*]. And I was told so the first day. I always felt my value, which was I cost the show nothing. For a few months, I was the only Latina in this "all Latina" show. I was also the writer with the least power, so it was just a horror.

So then we get to *Looking*. We were all calling it "The HBO Gay Show." And every day, we would like put up a board with offerings for a title, At first, it was *Looking* . . . because it's on Grindr. But the thing that was special about that show, personally, was that one of my dearest oldest friends, Raúl Castillo, was also on it. Joey Soloway was in that first season, too. And then they had to leave because *Transparent* got picked up so they were only in the room for like six weeks. Then I was the only girl. And it was just good. I don't know how else to say it.

I thought we came up with a beautiful first season of television that was just delicate and gentle, but it still spoke about mostly gay men. That didn't have much representation otherwise, even though I tried. I tried to get Roberta [Colindrez] on that. Roberta for everything! And then we shot it. I was there, which is very rare. Andrew let me be there, and I saw how he ran his set. Everyone was queer. Everyone in the room was queer, assistants were queer, and then most of the set was queer. I was like, "Oh, you can do this!" It was permission for later on. And then, second season, we were in San Francisco as the writers and Roberto Aguirre-Sacasa became showrunner. He's like the fanciest Latino showrunner we have in the industry. And he's my dear, dear friend, because of *Looking*. You get your concentric circles wherever you can, as queer Latinas. And he's now like a brother.

It was so beautiful. But I could tell that the reaction from season 1 from a lot of the community was really grinding on Andrew, because a lot of gay men were like, "We're more fun than this!" They wanted more scandalous, stereotypical versions of who we are. I thought *Looking* had everything. I mean, it was a little cross section of San Francisco that we were looking at, just three friends, but their orbits too, and one friend was forty. They wanted more *Queer as Folk* bombastic version of gayness, you know, and this was gentle and emotional, and it's about relationships. It was delicate and gentle and real and grounded. That's radical for us, because sometimes we're represented as bombastic and bigger than life or for comic relief. I obviously loved the show, I was really about it. I didn't work on the movie because it was just mostly Andrew doing the movie, but it was a beautiful experience. Watching him be a director on set, and how he handled it, was technical for me. He really respected his crew. For *Vida*, it really, really helped me with the crew. I've been in other shows since *Looking* that were not as respectful to the crew. That really affected how I dealt with my crew, and who I staffed and how I respected them.

I didn't have any other training, or have film training, and I didn't have TV filming training. Andrew has a lot of that—following him around and seeing how calm he was. Even though I knew he was freaking out, because I could see him taking the Tums and stuff. That was a good mentor, even though he didn't know he was mentoring me. But I just loved *Looking*. There is some *Looking* DNA on *Vida*. Andrew dealt with San Francisco as [the] fourth character, and I dealt with Boyle Heights or East LA as the fifth character. He taught me that without meaning to.

SMW: What would have been the storylines that you pitched Roberta? Do you remember?

TS: They needed a lesbian friend. Like, they just needed one. And in San Francisco! There should have been one, that's the only critique I have. But you know, I get it. The showrunner had a myopic point of view, meaning he was serving these three characters. I had a myopic point of view for *Vida*. I hate it now when executives give real estate notes, but, "We need real estate!" But it's a half hour. Three storylines to serve. You have to economize.

SMW: I think when people use the word "myopic" to describe whatever vision is usually there's a very negative association, but it's specificity.

TS: Yeah. Because you're defending your world and your characters as if they're real people. So you do become myopic. Like, I do not want to be away from these characters to do anything else. I resent when I have to go eat. I resent when I have to go make food, or get more coffee. I want to just be in this world. It's so funny because it becomes so real. The other day I woke up crying. It was like, I thought of this one thing for [current project]. It's not even that deep a moment, or that good of a beat, but I thought about it. It would make the lead character cry, so it made me cry, because I'm her right now. I was just bawling and I couldn't shake it. And I showed up to our writers' room for, like four days, I was like, "I can't stop crying!" And it was manic. Like, stop it. They're not real. These people are not real. But they're in my body right now. They are real. They're in my makeup. It's so funny.

For *Vida*, I have a little distance from it. When I used to talk about Eddy getting beat up, the stuff was very real. And those two sisters were so real to me, you know, and all four characters have a piece of me. But now, it's like the embers have cooled. And it's okay, it's okay.

SMW: I think it's gratifying to hear that. The characters were extremely real and meant a lot to your audiences. So it's fun to see that translate and just to hear how much you lived in it. And I'm glad you're not still living in it at this moment.

TS: The other day, I was doubting myself. I have not watched the pilot since we shot the first season. I watched the pilot, and I cried like an audience member. I forgot moments! I knew them so well when we were editing, and then at the end where Selena comes on and the two sisters are crying, I was like, "Oh! That's right! I forgot. Oh, that hit me." But it hit me like an audience member.

And I have to say something—I wasn't the only one who had this emotional investment in it, and skin in the game. Half of my writers were queer. All of us were Latinx. That matters. A lot of my directors were queer too. Especially season 2, when we shot a lot of the queer sex. My director of photography was queer. It matters how it's handled, because

it's not just the day you show up to shoot. It's all the conversations to create the content, to create the text, to create the
story, and then the production meetings to handle it cor-
rectly. It's so many moments that were done right, that no one
will ever see. Except you'll see at the end of season 2, a beautiful sex scene in the bathroom. And you see a character who
washes their hands because we fuck with our hands. The
three of us, the two actors and me, workshopped it. It's all
conversations, respectful conversations, all throughout to get
to that image, that edited image. It's so much, and that's the
part that people don't see. But it matters that there were
queers along the way to carry the flame in a way. Do it right.
So that I wanted to say. You can tell.

Conclusion

THE END OF THE RAINBOW

Let's get one thing gay: contemporary queer television is stuffed full of treasures. I have had to cut this manuscript down to the point that I'm anxious about how many personal favorites I've not been able to go long on. These include, but are in no way limited to, *P-Valley, Work in Progress, Betty, Harlem, Vida, The Other Two, The Lady and the Dale, Search Party, Yellowjackets, Los Espookys, Reservation Dogs, Special, Somebody Somewhere,* and *What We Do in the Shadows*—and that doesn't even take into account the breadth and depth of queer series outside the United States, which in many ways far outpace American television. Canadian gem *Sort Of* and Spanish masterpiece *Veneno,* for instance, are biting, explosive utter revelations that deserve their own chapters. If I ever have it in me to write another tome, I am only going to heap praises on this electrifying, brave, silly, gentle, off-the-wall queer work and not turn it into a worried screed about the politics of representation.

Similarly, there's no doubt that there have been massive strides in certain areas of queer television that this book only skirted. Nowhere has there been a more pronounced 180 than in attitudes toward children's entertainment. Where once queerness was deemed a mis-guided flight of fancy or an unthinkable danger for a young character or viewer to be in any proximity to, now children's shows feature queer neighbors, families, parents, friends, crushes, and even sweet, affirming young relationships. We're far past the stage where the most daring choice a young character can make is to be an ally.

However, the reason this book is what it is, and not a fluffy exhortation to watch my favorite queer TV with me (it is still that, kind of), is because, despite these strides, the future, and history, of queer television currently exists in a strange, circular limbo. There's certainly no shortage of stories or talented queer people to tell those stories. Once past the foundations of queer television, there are plenty of examples of innovators breaking rules to bring us moments of small-screen queer brilliance. You would be forgiven for yelling at me when I missed your favorite. But therein lies the dilemma—though the floodgates once seemed open not so long ago, we're now teetering on the brink of moments of queerness. Just a string of moments—seemingly gone as soon as they cross our screens.

The reboots of the previous chapter aren't the only queer series that are in a jostling, unpredictable mortal danger these days—and a show doesn't even have to be queer to be in trouble. The rate at which new series disappear is puzzling, and not a little frustrating, especially given the deluge of new programming that often comes and goes without a hint of a marketing budget. All manner of series with strong casts, unique premises, enthusiastic receptions, and something to say, seem as though they're here today, and despite the impression that people are indeed watching them and eager to engage in discussion around what they've just watched, gone tomorrow—not just canceled, but removed from streaming entirely.

As Julia MacCary reported in *Variety*, according to a 2023 survey, "A quarter of U.S. adults wait for streaming originals' finale before starting, citing fears over the show's potential cancellation with an unresolved ending."[1] It's a catch-22 stemming from streamers' games of cat and mouse with their audiences. How can an audience commit to a series if a streamer won't also commit to its completion, never mind its continuation? Why would a streamer continue to fund a series if they don't have evidence that anyone is watching, making social media impressions, and continuing to draw new subscribers to their platform?

It feels like a deep regression, as mind boggling as that concept is, this far into a history of queer representation on television. If we've come to the point of recognition where a hungry queer audience has proven themselves available and dedicated to sniffing out queer characters, and network brands depend on queer faces for a show of inclusion and new viewership, why on earth would we be moving backward? Now that we know shows are being made with queer people in mind, it seems like an insult that they just keep going up in flames.

One could look at the history of a mega success like *Star Trek* or *Firefly* (2002–2003) to know that networks don't always have the foresight to renew the series that end up being their biggest successes in syndication and rental. But there are a few complications to that past reassurance: with the way that streaming is currently purging their libraries, there's not an established precedent for their version of syndication or a hint as to where those works will be consistently available. The second complication is a concerning emergent pattern to the shows currently getting canceled. Many of them feature queer characters and queer and trans characters of color—casts and storylines that are historically associated with a niche, lesser audience.

On the surface, an answer could be a mitigation of risk. Greenlighting a queer show but not giving it the time or marketing budget it needs to establish an audience kills two birds with one stone for ultra-averse risk-takers. There is an equally cynical argument that streamers *aren't* homophobic; they're simply objective! They're just algorithm-driven corporations looking for "the next big thing," and when the thing they take a chance on doesn't turn a profit, it's getting axed. In some ways, this is an observant critique of late-stage capitalism hitting another sector of art so hard that the artistry of whatever's been whittled into "content" just collapses under the weight of investor expectations. However, it's not helpful to willfully strip a corporation (and the people that run it) of bias and accountability. As filmmaker Alex Schmider, who is also currently GLAAD's director of transgender representation, reminds us, data may be "fact based," but it can also be used for

storytelling. "If it is only being used to support the story that's dominant in a room," he says, and other patterns are going by the wayside,
then it matters not only what the data says but who's in the room to
interpret it.[2]

At the heart of this disappointment and frustration is the reason,
through the journey of writing this book, that I've come back around
to a solid "yes" on the question of whether queer representation on
television matters. There are real queer people being monumentally,
materially affected by a lack of support for queer series. Not only audiences, important as we may be. I'm talking about the queer people
behind these shows.

Queer writers, directors, performers, and editors face a total devalu-
ation of their labor when their work gets pulled from streaming platforms. Not only does it eliminate any meek residuals they might be
receiving, but it also makes it incredibly difficult for them to prove their
professional worth. Premature cancellations deprive us of the shows we
want to watch now, and perhaps more importantly, they make it that
much more difficult for an original queer show to break through in the
future, because a queer artist's CV and history is being personally
erased. If streaming continues to be allowed to devalue queer artists'
work at this rate, it may well signal the real end of the Rainbow Age of
Television.

But that's the thing: we don't have to allow that to happen. No one
rides harder for television than queer television fans. What might it look
like if we put our obsessive energy behind the queer people who don't get
paid enough to make the shows we love (and love to critique) so much?
What if we showed up, not just as viewers for the networks and streamers to count but as tangible support behind the queer people whose work
brings us joy? Moreover, what if we recognized that the elimination of
queer shows dovetails with an attempt to curb the worth of all television
workers who have something disruptive or original to say?

The interviewees in this book represent the tiniest fraction of tal-
ented, experienced, determined creatives dedicated to continuing the

existence of queer art. Many of them have ridden the waves of fickle industry decisions, barreled through closed doors, or held said doors open as soon as it was possible to usher others through. I encourage you to pay attention to them and the ways they continue to survive challenges to the worth of their work. Whether it's the conditions under which queer artists make the stories that spark the first light of recognition within us or the quality of queer storytelling itself, the crumbs are never all we deserve. And no matter how dire Hollywood's queer landscape may seem, regardless of whether the glittering, briefly prolific Rainbow Age of Television has actually come to its close, that doesn't change the fact that we, flesh and blood queer people, are never really alone.

Acknowledgments

Thank you to Jenni Olson for being my very first interview. Your dedication to kindness and to intergenerational queer strength is an incredible gift and guide.

Thank you to my agent, Robert Guinsler, for asking if I wanted to write a book! Thank you to my editors, Chelsea Cutchens and Sarah Robbins, for making sure I wrote a book.

Thank you to the critics, advocates, performers, and creators who generously gave me your precious time. Angela Robinson, Rose Troche, Jamie Babbit, Jennifer Beals, Jenni Olson, Ashley Ray-Harris, Princess Weekes, Juan Barquin, Cody Corrall, Stephanie Beatriz, Stephen Tropiano, Melissa King, Lilly Wachowski, Drew Gregory, Tanya Saracho, Jessica Sutton, Sasha Colby, and Alex Schmider, I tried to hide it when I was speaking with you, but it has been the greatest, geekiest privilege to be able to include your words in my work, and your work in my life.

Thank you to Steven Capsuto, Matt Baume, Stephen Tropiano, Susan Stryker, Joshua Gamson, and the entirety of *Autostraddle* and *LezWatch. TV* for all your work in documenting and thinking critically about queer media.

Thank you to Chris Straayer, Josslyn Luckett, and Alice Royer, whose classes sparked the ideas for some of these chapters. Thank you to everyone who helped with the monumental lift of transcribing audio from many hours of interviews: Elise Umetsu, Emma Gibbs, John e. Kilberg, Zoe Ziegfeld, Vigor Mortis, Raf Tawasil, Liana Kindler, and Molly Fusco.

Thank you to Lucy Jane Mukerjee for your dedication to queer storytellers.

Thank you to Alex Schmider for always, always opening doors.

Thank you to Donna Deitch for making *Desert Hearts.*

My deepest and sincerest thanks to the people who hold me and take me seriously when all I can do is talk about television and women. Nyx, Isabella, Bryce, Sal, Joaquín, Andy, Liana, Alexander, Mettie, Melina, Zoe, Eleanor, Cody. Thank you, I love you.

To my mom and dad, I love you around the world and back.

To Sarai, pretty cool that we're both the gay one, isn't it?

To my grandparents, no longer with us, I love you.

Notes

Introduction: On Owing Everything to (and Wanting More from) Queer TV

1. *Picket Fences*, season 1, episode 21, "Sugar and Spice," directed by Alan Myerson, written by David E. Kelley, aired April 29, 1993, on CBS.
2. Interview with Stephen Tropiano, July 14, 2022.
3. Interview with Jenni Olson, March 28, 2022.
4. Interview with Stephen Tropiano, July 14, 2022.
5. For more on visibility and "straight panic," read Ron Becker's *Gay TV and Straight America* (New Brunswick, NJ: Rutgers University Press, 2006).

Chapter 1: For the Very First Time

1. Karin Adir, *The Great Clowns of American Television* (Jefferson, NC: McFarland, 2001), 260.
2. Steven Capsuto, *Alternate Channels: Queer Images on 20th-Century TV* (New York: Steven Capsuto, Books and Translation Services, 2020), 71.
3. *Disclosure: Trans Lives on Screen*, directed by Sam Feder (Netflix, 2020).
4. *Medical Center*, season 5, episode 4, "Impasse," directed by Vincent Sherman, written by Frank Glicksman, Al C. Ward, and Barry Oringer, aired October 1, 1973, on CBS.
5. *Kate Loves a Mystery*, season 2, episode 7, "Feelings Can Be Murder," directed by Seymour Robbie, written by Mary Ann Kasica, Michael Scheff, and Richard Alan Simmons, aired December 6, 1979, on NBC.
6. Riese Bernard, "Lesbian and Non-Binary TV Characters Are All the Rage, Relatively," *Autostraddle*, February 21, 2022, https://www.autostraddle .com/lesbian-and-non-binary-tv-characters-at-all-time-high-wheres-our -check.
7. Ibid.
8. Joseph Longo, "How *Tales of the City* Avoided a Trans Casting Controversy," *Vanity Fair*, June 6, 2019, https://www.vanityfair.com/hollywood/2019/06 /tales-of-the-city-netflix-anna-madrigal-olympia-dukakis-jen-richards.
9. *St. Elsewhere*, season 1, episode 13, "Family History," directed by Kevin Hooks, written by Andrew Laskos, Joshua Brand, and John Falsey, aired February 8, 1983, on NBC.
10. *The Golden Girls*, season 3, episode 7, "Strange Bedfellows," directed by Terry Hughes, written by Susan Harris and Christopher Lloyd, aired November 7, 1987, on NBC.

Chapter 2: QIA2S+: Firsts and Far to Boldly Go

1. "Intersex Definitions," interACT, last updated February 19, 2021, https:// interactadvocates.org/intersex-definitions.
2. *Chicago Hope*, season 2, episode 20, "The Parent Rap," directed by Arvin Brown, written by Kevin Arkadie, Sara B. Charno, and Jennifer Levin, aired April 29, 1996, on CBS.
3. *Billions*, season 2, episode 2, "Dead Cat Bounce," directed by Anna Boden and Ryan Fleck, written by Wes Jones, aired February 26, 2017, on Showtime.
4. *Lloyd in Space*, season 3, episode 9, "Neither Boy nor Girl," directed by Howy Parkins, written by Eric Garcia and Richard Whitle, aired October 24, 2002, on Toon Disney.
5. Molly McArdle, "This Is How *Star Trek* Invented Fandom," *GQ*, September 21, 2016, https://www.gq.com/story/this-is-how-star-trek-invented-fandom.
6. *Star Trek: The Next Generation*, season 1, episode 2, "The Naked Now," directed by Paul Lynch, written by John D. F. Buck and D. C. Fontana, aired October 3, 1987, Syndicated.
7. *Star Trek: The Next Generation*, season 2, episode 4, "The Outrageous Okona," directed by Robert Becker, written by Burton Armus, aired December 10, 1988, Syndicated.
8. Rowan Ellis, "The Problem with Asexual Representation," December 18, 2021, YouTube video, 39:50, https://www.youtube.com/watch?app=desktop&v =P6v1J 7kQv_c&ab_channel=RowanEllis.
9. Ibid.
10. Thanks to the dedicated digitization efforts of the archivists at the University of Minnesota Jean-Nickolaus Tretter Collection in Gay, Lesbian, Bisexual and Transgender Studies, interviews with two-spirit people and other Indigenous queer people can be accessed in full at U of M's online GAZE-TV portal.
11. *American Gods*, season 2, episode 3, "Muninn," directed by Deborah Chow, written by Bryan Fuller and Michael Green, aired March 24, 2019, on Starz.
12. Ibid.
13. Nivea Serrao, "*Lovecraft Country* Showrunner Apologizes for Having 'Failed' Queer Indigenous Character," *SYFY*, October 14, 2020, https://www .syfy.com/syfy-wire/lovecraft-country-misha-green-failed-indigenous-two -spirit-representation.
14. Interview with Stephen Tropiano, July 14, 2022.
15. Interview with Lilly Wachowski, March 3, 2023.

Chapter 3: Just a Regular Jodie: Recurring, Regular, and Lead Queer Characters

1. Richard McGuinness, "Resurrection at Grant's Tomb," *The Village Voice*, August 24, 1972.
2. Wrap Staff, "50 Years Ago Today, 'The Corner Bar' Made History with TV's First Out Gay Character (Guest Blog), Yahoo!, June 21, 2022, https://www .yahoo.com/now/50-years-ago-today-corner-205404042.html.

3. John Jamison, "'All in the Family': Watergate Tapes Revealed Richard Nixon Vented Hate for Show," *Outsider*, April 8, 2021, https://www.outsider .com/entertainment/all-in-the-family-watergate-tapes-revealed-richard -nixon-vented-hate-for-show.

4. *All in the Family*, season 1, episode 5, "Judging Books by Covers," directed by John Rich, written by Burt Styler and Norman Lear, aired February 9, 1971, on CBS.

5. *All in the Family*, season 6, episode 4, "Archie the Hero," directed by Paul Bogart, written by Lou Derman and Bill Davenport, aired September 29, 1975, on CBS.

6. *All in the Family*, season 8, episode 13, "Edith's Crisis of Faith: Part I," directed by Paul Bogart, written by Bob Weiskopf, Bob Schiller, and Erik Tarloff, aired December 18, 1977, on CBS.

7. Tim Gray, "Norman Lear on Gay Characters, 'All in the Family,' and Big Scale Thinking," *Variety*, June 29, 2015, https://variety.com/2015/tv/news /norman-lear-gay-characters-all-in-the-family-1201529636.

8. Capsuto, *Alternate Channels*, 127.

9. Gerald Clarke, "Eve's Rib and Adam's Yawn," *Time*, April 25, 1977.

10. Jenna Busch, "Every Show and Movie That Has Been Quietly Removed from HBO Max So Far," */Film*, August 5, 2023, https://www.slashfilm.com /954649/every-show-and-movie-that-has-been-quietly-removed-from-hbo -max-so-far.

11. Larry Gross, "What Is Wrong with This Picture? Lesbian Women and Gay Men on Television," in *Queer Words, Queer Images: Communication and the Construction of Homosexuality*, edited by R. Jeffrey Ringer (New York: New York University Press, 1994), 143.

12. Capsuto, *Alternate Channels*, 157.

13. Lee Margulies, "'Hail to the Chief' Goes to a Quiet Death on ABC," *Los Angeles Times*, May 21, 1985.

14. Interview with Stephen Tropiano, July 14, 2022.

15. Lynette Rice, "How Soap Operas Pioneered the Depiction of LGBTQ Characters, *Entertainment Weekly*, June 11, 2021, https://ew.com/tv/daytime -dramas-lgbtq-characters.

16. *HeartBeat*, season 1, episode 6, "The Wedding," directed by Gene Reynolds, written by Sara Davidson and Dan Wakefield, aired April 21, 1988, on ABC.

17. Simon McCallum, "Festival Gem: South," British Film Institute, March 16, 2013, https://www2.bfi.org.uk/news-opinion/news-bfi/features/festival-gem -south.

18. FoundationINTERVIEWS, "Hal Holbrook on 'That Certain Summer'— TelevisionAcademy.com/Interviews," August 15, 2018, YouTube, 6:43, https:// www.youtube.com/watch?v=7_AKAkqeKys.

19. Capsuto, *Alternate Channels*, 89.

20. UCLA Film & Television Archive, "Visions: 'The War Widow' (10/28/1976)," Vimeo, 2:03:02, https://vimeo.com/582249451.

21. E. Alex Jung, "Laura Dern Doesn't Need Our Approval," *Vulture*, December 2, 2019, https://www.vulture.com/2019/12/laura-dern-vulture-honorary-degree .html.

22. Seth Abramovitch, "Joe Biden Cites 'Will & Grace' in Endorsement of Same-Sex Marriage (Video)," *Hollywood Reporter*, May 6, 2012, https://www.hol lywoodreporter.com/tv/tv-news/joe-biden-cites-will-grace-320724-0 -320724/.

23. Brett Lang, "Ellen DeGeneres Influenced Gay Rights Views More Than Any Other Celebrity (Study)," *Variety*, June 30, 2015, https://variety.com/2015/tv /news/ellen-degeneres-gay-rights-gay-marriage-1201531462/.

Chapter 4: The Rainbow Age Meets the Gray Area

1. GLAAD, "Transgender People," *GLAAD Media Reference Guide*, 11th edition, March 23, 2023, from https://www.glaad.org/reference/transgender.

2. Interview with Ashley Ray-Harris, August 3, 2022.

3. Ibid.

4. Adam Dunn, "The End of 'Oz,'" CNN, February 21, 2003, https://www.cnn .com/2003/SHOWBIZ/TV/02/21/oz.end/index.html.

5. Elon Green, "The Legacy of *Oz*: A Chat with Tom Fontana (and a Special Guest)," *The Toast*, August 11, 2015, https://the-toast.net/2015/08/11/the -legacy-of-oz-chat-with-tom-fontana.

6. Brian VanHooker, "An Oral History of 'Johnny Cakes,' Vito's Love Story on 'The Sopranos,'" *MEL*, December 18, 2020, https://melmagazine.com/en-us /story/oral-history-johnny-cakes-sopranos-vito-gay.

7. Lauren Huff, "'Oz,' 'The Wire' Creators Talk 'Homicide,' HBO Post-'Sopranos'— ATX Television Festival," *Deadline*, June 11, 2016, https://deadline.com/2016 /06/oz-the-wire-homicide-hbo-atx-tom-fontana-david-simon-1201771010.

8. Patrick Gomez, "EW's *Queer as Folk* Reunion: The Cast Gets Emotional about Their Groundbreaking Series," *Entertainment Weekly*, June 8, 2018, https://ew.com/tv/2018/06/08/queer-as-folk-reunion-ew-exclusive.

9. *Queer as Folk*, season 2, episode 3, "Hypocrisy: Don't Do It," directed by Michael DeCarlo, written by Karen Walton, Ron Cowen, and Daniel Lipman, aired January 20, 2002, on Showtime.

10. *Visible: Out on Television*, Season 1 Episode 5, "The New Guard," directed by Ryan White, aired February 14, 2020, on AppleTV+.

11. Interview with Angela Robinson, August 16, 2022.

12. Ibid.

13. Interview with Jenni Olson, March 28, 2022.

14. Interview with Princess Weekes, August 1, 2022.

15. *Mrs. Fletcher*, season 1, episode 4, "Parents' Weekend," directed by Carrie Brownstein, written by Eric Ledgin, aired November 17, 2019, on HBO.

16. *Better Things*, season 5, episode 4, "Ephemera," directed by Pamela Adlon, written by Pamela Adlon and Joe Hortua, aired March 14, 2022, on FX.

17. Ibid.

Chapter 5: Everybody Dies

1. Norman Lear, *Even This I Get to Experience* (New York: Penguin Books, 2014), 254.

2. Riese Bernhard, "All 230 Dead Lesbian and Bisexual Characters on TV, And How They Died," *Autostraddle*, February 27, 2023, https://www.auto straddle.com/ALL-65-DEAD-LESBIAN-AND-BISEXUAL-CHARACTE RS-ON-TV-AND-HOW-THEY-DIED-312315.

3. "Mom . . . I'm a Slayer: Coming Out in '90s Fantasy Television," screening and panel with Heather Hogan, Kristen Russo, and Shayna Maci Warner for NYU Cinema Studies, February 27, 2019.

4. *The Celluloid Closet*, directed by Rob Epstein and Jeffrey Friedman (Los Angeles: Sony Pictures Classics, 1995).

5. Edwina Bartlem, "Coming Out on a Hell Mouth," *Refractory* 2 (March 6, 2003).

6. Lila Shapiro, "Marti Noxon on *Sharp Objects*, Joss Whedon, and Going 'Toe-to-Toe' with Jean-Marc Vallée," *Vulture*, July 3, 2018, https://www.vulture .com/2018/07/marti-noxon-sharp-objects-buffy-feminist-legacy-dietland .html.

7. Interview with Drew Gregory, January 17, 2023.

8. Heather Hogan, "Autostraddle's Ultimate Infographic Guide to Dead Lesbian Characters on TV," *Autostraddle*, March 25, 2016, https://www .autostraddle.com/autostraddles-ultimate-infographic-guide-to-dead -lesbian-tv-characters-332920.

9. Maureen Ryan, "What TV Can Learn from 'The 100' Mess." *Variety*, March 14, 2016, https://variety.com/2016/tv/opinion/the-100-lexa-jason -rothenberg-1201729110.

10. Mike Wendling, "Fans Revolt after Gay TV Character Killed Off," BBC News, March 11, 2016, https://www.bbc.com/news/blogs-trending-35786382; Sarah Karlan, "How 'Lexa Deserved Better' Became a Rallying Cry for Positive LGBT Representation," BuzzFeed, September 21, 2017, https://www.buzzfeed .com/skarlan/for-the-love-of-clexa.

11. Damian Holbrook, "*The 100*'s Showrunner Explains Why [Spoiler] Had to Die," *TV Insider*, March 3, 2016, https://www.tvinsider.com/77170/the-100 -jason-rothenberg-explains-big-death.

12. Caroline Framke, "Why the Best Episode of *The 100*'s Third Season Has Also Thrown Its Fandom into Chaos," *Vox*, March 6, 2016, https://www.vox.com /2016/3/6/11169938/the-100-lexa-dies-clarke.

13. "About ClexaCon." ClexaCon, Dash Productions, 2017, https://clexacon.com /about/.

14. Dorothy Snarker, "'Wynonna Earp' Creator Emily Andras Talks WayHaught Survival," *AfterEllen*, June 2, 2016, http://www.afterellen.com/entertainment /490411-wynonna-earp-creator-emily-andras-talks-wayhaught-survival/2.

15. Dan Snierson, *"Brooklyn Nine-Nine* Star Stephanie Beatriz on Rosa's Revelation, What's Next," *Entertainment Weekly*, December 5, 2017, http:// www.ew.com/tv/2017/12/05/brooklyn-nine-nine-rosa-bisexual.

16. GLAAD, *Where We Are on TV: 2016*, https://www.glaad.org/whereweareontv16; GLAAD, *Where We Are on TV: 2022–2023*, March 16, 2023, https://glaad.org /publications/where-we-are-on-tv.

17. Interview with Drew Gregory, January 17, 2023.

Chapter 6: Gays in "Real" Life

1. Thomas Doherty, "Pixies: Homosexuality, Anti-Communism, and the Army–McCarthy Hearings," in *Television Histories: Shaping Collective Memory in the Media Age*, edited by Gary R. Edgerton and Peter C. Rollins (Lexington: The University Press of Kentucky, 2001), 197.

2. Judith Adkins, "'These People Are Frightened to Death': Congressional Investigations and the Lavender Scare," *Prologue Magazine* 48, no. 2 (Summer 2016), https://www.archives.gov/publications/prologue/2016 /summer/lavender.html.

3. Ibid.

4. Edward Alwood, *Straight News: Gays, Lesbians, and the News Media* (New York: Columbia University Press, 1997).

5. Federal Bureau of Investigation, "Freedom of Information/Privacy Acts Release, Subject: Mattachine Society," 1953, https://vault.fbi.gov/mattachine -society/mattachine-society-part-01-of-03/view.

6. *Confidential File*, season 2, episode 1, "Homosexuals and the Problem They Present," directed by Roger Barlow, written by Paul Coates, aired May 2, 1954, on KTTV-TV.

7. Capsuto, *Alternate Channels*, 500.

8. Susan Stryker, *Transgender History* (Berkeley, CA: Seal Press, 2008), 25.

9. Kevin Cook, "Joe Pyne Was America's First Shock Jock," *Smithsonian Magazine*, June 2017, https://www.smithsonianmag.com/history/joe-pyne -first-shock-jock-180963237.

10. Capsuto, *Alternate Channels*, 52–53.

11. Advocate.com Editors, "A Death in An American Family," *Advocate*, January 22, 2022, https://www.advocate.com/politics/commentary/2002/01 /22/lance-loud-death-american-family.

12. *An American Family*, season 1, episode 12, "Episode #1.12," written by Craig Gilbert, aired March 29, 1973, on PBS.

13. Michael Lovelock, *Reality TV and Queer Identities* (Cham, Switzerland: Palgrave Macmillan, 2019), 39.

14. Anne Roiphe, "An American Family," *New York Times*, February 18, 1973, https://www.nytimes.com/1973/02/18/archives/things-are-keen-but-could-be-keener-an-american-family-an-american.html.

15. Lovelock, *Reality TV and Queer Identities*, 41.

16. Roiphe, "An American Family."

17. Vern L. Bullough, ed., *Before Stonewall: Activists for Gay and Lesbian Rights in Historical Context* (Binghamton, NY: Harrington Park Press, 2002), 247.

18. Matt Baume, "Too Gay for Television? How Charles Nelson Reilly Proved NBC Wrong," September 18, 2022, YouTube video, 21:13, https://www.youtube.com/watch?v=jp9-hVEpLBA.

19. Joshua Gamson, *Freaks Talk Back: Tabloid Talk Shows and Sexual Nonconformity* (Chicago: University of Chicago Press, 2001), 13.

20. Holly Selby, "Screening Out 'Cultural Rot' in 'Gross' Taste: William Bennett Says TV's Tell-All Talk Shows Have Left Nothing for Americans, Especially Children, to Be Ashamed of Anymore," *Baltimore Sun*, October 27, 1995, https://www.baltimoresun.com/news/bs-xpm-1995-10-27-1995300002-story.html.

21. Gamson, *Freaks Talk Back*, 17.

22. John J. O'Connor, "TV: Cable Focuses on Homosexuals," *New York Times*, June 2, 1977, https://www.nytimes.com/1977/06/02/archives/tv-cable-focuses-on-homosexuals.html.

23. Ibid.

24. Mike Miksche, "The World's First Gay TV Program: 'The Emerald City,'" Logo TV, July 23, 2018, https://www.logotv.com/news/am8m6i/the-worlds-first-gay-tv-program-the-emerald-city.

25. Jesse McKinley, "Real and Live, but Maybe Not Nude," *New York Times*, November 29, 2012, https://www.nytimes.com/2012/11/30/theater/robin-byrd-onstage-live-but-not-nude.html.

26. Kelly Graml, "Groundbreaking Television Coverage of LGBT Milestones Now Online," UCLA Film & Television Archive, press release, June 30, 2015, https://newsroom.ucla.edu/releases/groundbreaking-television-coverage-of-lgbt-milestones-now-online.

27. Larry Closs, "I Want My Gay TV," in *The Columbia Reader on Lesbians and Gay Men in Media, Society, and Politics*, edited by Larry Gross and James D. Woods (New York: Columbia University Press, 1999), 466–73.

28. Dorothee Benz, "In the Life: PBS Keeps Its Distance from Gay Programming," FAIR, June 1, 1993, https://fair.org/extra/in-the-life.

29. Closs, "I Want My Gay TV," 466–73.

30. Stephen Tropiano, "The Time of Our Lives: *In the Life*—America's LGBT News Magazine," UCLA Film & Television Archive, https://www.cinema.ucla.edu/collections/inthelife/history/time-of-our-lives.

31. Camille Beredjick, "*In the Life* Will Air Last Show in December," *Advocate*, December 5, 2012, https://www.advocate.com/arts-entertainment/television /2012/09/05/life-media-will-air-last-show-december.

32. Graml, "Groundbreaking Television Coverage of LGBT Milestones Now Online."

33. Interview with Sasha Colby, April 19, 2023.

Chapter 7: For the Very Second Time: Reboots and Revisions

1. Katy Steinmetz, "The Transgender Tipping Point," *Time*, May 29, 2014, http://www.time.com/135480/transgender-tipping-point.

2. Dominic Patten and Nellie Andreeva, "Jeffrey Tambor Being Investigated by Amazon on Sexual Harassment Claims; Actor 'Adamantly' Denies Allegations," *Deadline*, November 9, 2017, http://www.deadline.com/2017 /11/jeffrey-tambor-sexual-harassment-claims-amazon-1202204220.

3. Dominic Patten, "Jeffrey Tambor Exits 'Transparent' After Sexual Harassment Allegations," *Deadline*, November 19, 2017, http://www.deadline.com/2017/11 /jeffrey-tambor-leaving-transparent-sexual-harassment-allegations - amazon-jill-soloway-1202211711.

4. Ellis Clopton, "What It Says When Cis Actors Are Cast in Trans Roles," *Variety*, August 7, 2018, http://www.variety.com/video/jen-richards-on-cis -actors-in-trans-roles.

5. Robyn R. Warhol, "Making 'Gay' and 'Lesbian' into Household Words: How Serial Form Works in Armistead Maupin's *Tales of the City*," *Contemporary Literature* 40, no. 3 (Autumn 1999): 378–402.

6. Joanna Walters, "Olympia Dukakis Hints at Screen Return for Armistead Maupin's Anna Madrigal," *Guardian*, December 7, 2013, http://www .theguardian.com/books/2013/dec/07/ olympia-dukakis-anna-madrigal-ar mistead-maupin.

7. Joseph Longo, "How *Tales of the City* Avoided a Trans Casting Controversy," *Vanity Fair*, June 6, 2019, http://www.vanityfair.com/hollywood/2019/06 /tales-of-the-city-netflix-anna-madrigal-olympia-dukakis-jen-richards.

8. Ibid.

9. Interview with Angela Robinson, August 16, 2022.

10. Interview with Jamie Babbit, August 17, 2022.

11. *Queering the Script*, directed by Gabrielle Zilkha (Undistributed, 2009).

12. "*The L Word* Theme Song (The Way That We Live)," Betty, APM, 2005.

13. Interview with Rose Troche, August 19, 2022.

14. Riese Bernhard, "*The L Word*'s Lisa the Lesbian-Identified Man: A Trans Symposium," *Autostraddle*, May 23, 2019, https://www.autostraddle.com /the-l-words-lisa-the-lesbian-identified-man-a-trans-symposium-459025.

15. Kam Burns, "TV's Second Chance for Trans Representation—the Right Way," *Wired*, February 11, 2019, http://www.wired.com/story/tv-trans-repre sentation.

16. Lesley Goldberg, "New 'L Word' Showrunner Reveals What to Expect from Showtime Sequel," *Hollywood Reporter*, February 19, 2019, http://www.hollywoodreporter.com/live-feed/l-word-showrunner-reveals-whatexpect-showtime-sequel-1187522.

17. Ibid.

18. Tracy E. Gilchrist, "*The L Word* Launches Trans Casting Call After Sins of the Past," *Advocate*, April 24, 2019, http://www.advocate.com/television/2019/4/24/l-word-launches-trans-casting-call-after-sins-past.

19. Ibid.

20. Mey Rude, "Missing the Mark: Where Are the Trans Women on 'The L Word' Reboot?," BitchMedia, August 1, 2019, https://web.archive.org/web/20230326221512/https://www.bitchmedia.org/article/the-L-word-reboot-trans women.

21. Drew Burnett Gregory, "Daniel Sea On 'The L Word,' Gender Identity, and Imagining Queer Liberation," *Autostraddle*, May 31, 2021, https://www.autostraddle.com/daniel-sea-interview.

22. Interview with Rose Troche, August 19, 2022.

23. Brooks Barnes, "'Will & Grace' Is Back. Will Its Portrait of Gay Life Hold Up?," *New York Times*, September 14, 2017, http://www.nytimes.com/2017/09/14/arts/television/will-grace-debra-messing-eric-mccormack.html.

24. Michael Schneider, "'Will & Grace': Beyond Its Gay Characters, Revival Will Tackle Transgender and Other LGBTQ Issues," *IndieWire*, August 3, 2017, http://www.indiewire.com/2017/08/will-grace-nbc-lgbtqissues-debra-messing-megan-mullaly-1201863480.

25. Ibid.

26. Jackie Strause, "'Will & Grace': All the Details About the Final Season," *Hollywood Reporter*, September 2, 2019, http://www.hollywoodreporter.com/live-feed/will-grace-all-final-season-details-far-1234947.

27. Tara Ariano, "*Will & Grace* Couldn't Stick the Landing—Again," *Vanity Fair*, April 23, 2020, https://www.vanityfair.com/hollywood/2020/04/will-and-grace-revival-series-finale-review.

28. *She's Gotta Have It*, season 1, episode 4, "#LuvIzLuv (SEXUALITY IS FLUID)," directed by Spike Lee, written by Elsa Davis, aired November 23, 2017, on Netflix.

29. Princess Weekes, "The Complex Queerness of Nola Darling in Netflix's *She's Gotta Have It*," The Mary Sue, November 30, 2017, https://www.themarysue.com/the-complex-queerness-of-nola-darling-in-netflixs-shes-gotta-have-it.

Conclusion: The End of the Rainbow

1. Julia MacCary, "Frequent TV Series Cancellations Altering Viewer Behavior, Survey Shows," *Variety*, March 16, 2023, https://variety.com/2023/tv/news/frequent-tv-series-cancellations-affect-viewership-1235553780.

2. Interview with Alex Schmider, April 13, 2023.

Index